Comprehensive Assurance & Systems Tool

An Integrated Practice Set

Frank A. Buckless
North Carolina State University

Laura R. Ingraham
San Jose State University

J. Gregory Jenkins
North Carolina State University

PEARSON
Prentice Hall
Upper Saddle River, New Jersey

Library of Congress Cataloging-in-Publication information is available.

Acquisitions Editor: Bill Larkin
Editor-in-Chief: Jeff Shelstad
Assistant Editor: Sam Goffinet
Editorial Assistant: Jane Avery
Marketing Manager: Beth Toland
Marketing Assistant: Patrick Danzuso
Managing Editor: John Roberts
Manufacturing Buyer: Michelle Klein
Production Manager: Arnold Vila
Cover Design Manager: Jayne Conte
Cover Photo: Andrew Ward/Life File/Photodisc/Getty Images, Inc.
Printer/Binder: Courier–Bookmart

Pearson Education LTD.
Pearson Education Singapore, Pte. Ltd
Pearson Education, Canada, Ltd
Pearson Education–Japan

Pearson Education Australia PTY, Limited
Pearson Education North Asia Ltd
Pearson Educación de Mexico, S.A. de C.V.
Pearson Education Malaysia, Pte. Ltd

PEARSON
Prentice Hall

10 9 8 7 6 5 4 3 2
ISBN 0-13-045186-X

Table of Contents

Preface

The **C**omprehensive **A**ssurance and **S**ystems **T**ool (CAST) provides an integrated learning opportunity that encompasses financial statement assurance and accounting information systems. CAST uniquely exposes students to these issues at The Winery at Chateau Americana, a hypothetical company that is based on an actual domestic winery. Unlike traditional projects and assignments that may offer little or no context, students develop a rich knowledge and understanding of Chateau Americana and its industry as they provide assurance on the company's financial statements and address a variety of challenging accounting information systems issues.

CAST is comprised of three self-contained, but complementary modules:

- The *Manual AIS module* requires students to complete real-world business documents, journalize and post a variety of transactions, and prepare a year-end worksheet. This module may be completed before or during the completion of either the Accounting Information Systems module or the Assurance module. However, students are not required to complete this module before the other modules.
- The *Accounting Information Systems module* is comprised of three components: spreadsheets, general ledger software, and databases. Although self-contained, this module's value is greatest when combined with the Manual AIS module.
- The *Assurance module* provides students hands-on experience with fundamental elements of financial statement assurance. This module is comprised of components related to the client acceptance decision, understanding the business environment, understanding and testing internal controls, assessing risks and materiality, conducting substantive tests, evaluating attorney's letters, performing analytical review procedures, and determining the appropriate audit opinion. These components build upon one another and should be completed in the order in which they are presented.

CAST can be implemented in either an undergraduate or graduate setting and is ideally suited for simultaneous integration across assurance and information systems courses. In addition, each of the modules can be completed either as an in-class or an out-of-class assignment. CAST affords students the opportunity to develop and strengthen their analytical thinking, written and oral communication, problem solving, and team building skills.

We believe your students will benefit from using CAST and we encourage you to contact us with questions or suggestions about how we can improve the materials.

Frank Buckless - North Carolina State University
Laura Ingraham - San Jose State University
Greg Jenkins - North Carolina State University

THE MANUAL ACCOUNTING INFORMATION SYSTEM: The Winery at Chateau Americana

LEARNING OBJECTIVES

After completing and discussing this module, you should be able to:

- Recognize and prepare common business documents
- Recognize and understand common control activities designed to capture, summarize, and report business activities
- Explain the objectives of maintaining an audit trail
- Recognize deficiencies in the design of common business documents
- Prepare journal entries, journals, and ledgers
- Understand the relationships among various documents, journals, and ledgers in the accounting cycle

BACKGROUND

In this module, you are required to prepare common source documents relating to the various accounting cycles, prepare journal entries, post entries to the general and subsidiary ledgers, prepare trial balances, and prepare a year-end worksheet and the financial statements. While working through this module, you will observe the data flows from their inception to their final reporting.

Due to constraints on students' and instructors' time and resources, the processes outlined in this module focus only on the wholesale segment, picking up after the wine has been manufactured and bottled in the winery and is ready to be sold to distributors.

Company History

Since its founding by Edward Summerfield in 1980, Chateau Americana (CA) has been a small, family-owned winery located in northern California. While CA is relatively new to the wine industry, it has already cultivated a reputation as one of America's finest wineries. The small, family-owned winery has an impressive vineyard whose 125 acres yields a variety of grapes including Cabernet Sauvignon, Cabernet Franc, Chardonnay and Riesling. CA planted its first grapevines in 1983 and began selling wine in 1988. These vineyards yield approximately 25% of the grapes (or about 800 tons) it requires for wine production. The remaining grapes are purchased from CA's suppliers. In the last several years, CA's wines have received accolades at several highly regarded wine competitions that have dramatically increased the demand for its wines. The company currently has annual sales of 385,000 cases.

OVERVIEW OF WINE PRODUCTION

Chateau Americana is a fully operational winery that produces red, white, and sparkling wines.

Red Wine Process

The process for making red wine begins by feeding the grapes into a destemmer/crusher machine. The crushed grapes, skin and seeds, called "must," is then piped into stainless steel fermentation tanks, each of which holds between 3,000 and 5,000 gallons. The must remains in the fermentation tanks at a temperature of 70-75° for a period of 8-21 days and is rotated 4 times a day to break up the skim containing the seeds which float to the surface. The fermentation tank is then emptied. Seventy percent of the juice comes out as "free run," much of which is later used for the more expensive wine labels. The solid remainder is then emptied into a presser that carefully extracts the remaining juice without breaking the seeds.

Red wine is typically aged in oak barrels. Aging of the wine depends upon the number of times the barrel has been used. If the barrel has never been used before, the aging process takes approximately six months. If it has been used once before, the aging process takes approximately 18 months. And if it has been used twice before, the aging process takes approximately 2 years.

White Wine Process

The process of making white wine begins by feeding the white grapes into a bladder press. Inside this machine, a bladder expands, pressing the white grapes between it and the outer shell. Only the juice is then piped into the fermentation tanks where it remains at a temperature of approximately 60° for approximately 30 days while the sugar in the grapes is converted to alcohol.

White wine is most often then aged in stainless steel tanks, although oak barrels may be used.

Bottling

The aged wine is bottled in an atmospherically controlled "clean" room where the air is filtered and exchanged every 60 seconds. Using an automated assembly line, bottles are sterilized, filled, corked, capped, and labeled at a rate of 50 per minute.

OPERATIONS

Organizational Structure and Personnel

CA presently employs 250 permanent employees. Its management team is widely respected in the industry. Because the winery is a family-owned business, the owners have invested considerable time and energies in hiring individuals whom they believe are competent and trustworthy.

Currently, members of the Summerfield family occupy most of the key management positions. Edward Summerfield is the family's patriarch and president of the company. He has received several entrepreneurship awards and is generally perceived as an astute business person. Edward's daughter, Taylor Summerfield, is vice president of marketing for the company. Prior to assuming this position, she had a successful career in sales and marketing. Taylor is well-educated and earned an MBA from an Ivy League school.

Edward's son-in-law, Jacques Dupuis, is vice-president of winery operations. He has an extensive background in viticulture (i.e., grape growing) and vinification (i.e., wine making). Rob Breeden, the company's CFO, is the sole individual to hold a key management position who is not a member of the Summerfield family. He has extensive financial experience and was previously employed in public accounting for nine years and served as controller and CFO for another California winery. Rob holds undergraduate and graduate degrees in accounting and is a CPA.

Chart of Accounts

Chateau Americana has developed a six-digit classification scheme for its Chart of Accounts. The Chart of Accounts is found behind the Year-End Procedures.

CASH SALES INVOICE

Chateau Americana, Inc.
3003 Vineyard Way
Huntington, CA 95394
(707) 368-8485
CA-NC-67

Invoice Number C2228
Invoice Date 12/3/03

Sold To:
Grapevine Selections
2864 Worth Street
Napa, CA 95748

Ship To:
Grapevine Selections
2864 Worth Street
Napa, CA 95748

Salesperson	Customer P.O. Number	Customer Number	ABC Number
RS	7563	0505	P45293X

Product	Description	Size	Quantity	Cost	Extended
W120019	Chenin Blanc	0.750	432	5.25	$ 2,268.00
R130056	Merlot	0.750	324	6.00	1,944.00
R130061	Cabernet Sauvignon	0.750	384	6.50	2,496.00
S140000	Sparkling Brut	0.750	228	11.00	2,508.00

Grand Total Bottles: 1,368
Total Cases: 114
Comments:

Grand Total Cost: $ 9,216.00

Date 12/3/03
Invoice Number C2228
Customer Number 0505

Distribution: Copy 1 — Accounting; Copy 2 – Shipping; Copy 3 – Customer; Copy 4 – Sales

Figure 1- Sample Invoice

Selling Prices and Costs

Chateau Americana maintains a list of wine costs and selling prices. Wine is sold by the case (12 bottles to a case). The list is found behind the Year-End Procedures.

Date 12/03/03 **Uniform Bill of Lading**

Ship From

Name: Chateau Americana, Inc.
Address: 3003 Vineyard Way
City/State/Zip: Huntington, CA 95394
SID No.: 122448

Bill of Lading Number: 136369

Carrier Name: *Pacific Freightliners*

Ship To

Name: Grapevine Selections
Address: 2864 Worth Street
City/State/Zip: Napa, CA 95748
CID No.: 542352

Trailer number: *ABC 3899*

Serial number(s): *313734449*

Special Instructions:

Freight Charge Terms: (Freight charges are prepaid unless marked otherwise)

Prepaid: ☐ Collect: ☒ 3rd Party: ☐

☐ **(check box):** Master bill of lading with attached underlying bills of lading.

Customer Order Information

Description of Items	Quantity	Weight	Pallet/Slip (circle one)		Additional Shipper Information
Wine	*114*	*3,876*	(Y)	N	
			Y	N	
			Y	N	
			Y	N	
Grand Total					

Where the rate is dependent on value, shippers are required to state specifically in writing the agreed or declared value of the property as follows: "The agreed or declared value of the property is specifically stated by the shipper to be not exceeding ____________ per ____________________.

COD Amount: $ 9,216.00

Free terms:

☐ Collect

☐ Prepaid

☒ Customer check acceptable

Note: Liability limitation for loss or damage in this shipment may be applicable. See 49 USC §14706(c)(1)(A) & (B)

Received, subject to individually determined rates or contracts that have been agreed upon in writing between the carrier and shipper, if applicable, otherwise to the rates, classifications and rules that have been established by the carrier and are available to the shipper, on request, and to all applicable state and federal regulations.

The carrier shall not make delivery of this shipment without payment of and all other lawful charges.

Shipper Signature *Jerry Richards*

Shipper Signature/Date

This is to certify that the above named materials are properly classified, packaged, marked and labeled, and are in proper condition for transportation according to the applicable regulations of the DOT.

Jerry Richards *12/03/03*

Trailer Loaded:

☐ By shipper

☒ By driver

Carrier Signature/Pickup Date

Carrier acknowledges receipt of packages and required placards. Carrier certifies emergency response information was made available and/or carrier has the DOT emergency response guidebook or equivalent documentation in the vehicle. **Property described above is received in good order, except as noted.**

Bruce Garrett *12/03/03*

Distribution: Copy 1 — Accounting; Copy 2 – Shipping; Copy 3 – Customer

Figure2 – Sample Bill of Lading

Processes

Sales. Chateau Americana sells its wine to most distributors on account and offers a few select distributors credit terms as detailed below. Sales to a small number of distributors are cash sales. When a purchase order is received from a distributor, a sales invoice (*Figure 1*) is generated and the requested items are pulled from finished goods inventory. Copies 1, 2 and 3 of the Invoice are sent to Shipping where the Bill of Lading (*Figure 2*) is prepared in triplicate. Copy 3 of the Bill of Lading and Copy 3 of the Invoice are sent to the Customer with the wine. Copy 2 of the Bill of Lading and Copy 2 of the Invoice are filed numerically by the Shipping department. Copy 1 of the Bill of Lading and Copy 1 of the Invoice are sent to Accounting where the Accounting Clerk updates the Sales Register. Copy 1 of the Bill of Lading and Copy 1 of the Invoice are then filed numerically.

The Sales Register is totaled monthly and then posted to the General Ledger.

Credit Memo

Chateau Americana, Inc.
3003 Vineyard Way
Huntington, CA 95394

Phone: (707)368-8485

Credit Memo : 2753	
Date: 1/8/03	**Salesperson:** CEZ
Customer Number: 2201	**Customer PO No:** 10654
Amount Net: $267.00	

Credit To: *Veritas Distributors Inc*

Comments:

Returned damaged cases of wine

Item # / Description	Quantity	Price: Unit Price	Price: Amount
R130061 / Cabernet Sauvignon	12	$6.50	$78.00
W120019 / Chenin Blanc	36	$5.25	$189.00

Customer Name: *Veritas Distributors Inc*

Credit: Amount:: $267.00

Chateau Americana, Inc.
3003 Vineyard Way
Huntington, CA 95394
Phone: (707)368-8485

Credit Date: 1/8/03
Credit Memo #: **2753**
Customer Number: 2201

Distribution: Copy 1 – Accounting; Copy 2 -- Customer

Figure 3 – Sample Credit Memo

Sales tax. Sales tax is not assessed on wholesale sales. Therefore, there is no sales tax applied to sales to distributors.

Credit Terms. Chateau Americana offers discounts for early payment to certain select distributors who have done business with CA for an extended period. The terms offered to these distributors are 3/15, net 30. Most other distributors are granted credit terms without early payment discounts.

Returns and Allowances. Credit memos (*Figure 3*) are issued for price corrections, overshipments, or when a shipment has been damaged in transit. Due to legal restrictions, wine cannot be returned to regular inventory. On the very rare occasions that wine is returned, it is put into special inventory for taxed wines.

Purchase Order

Bill to

Chateau Americana, Inc.
3003 Vineyard Way
Huntington, CA 95394

Phone:(707)368-8485
Supplier No.: P1892

PO #: 9682

Date: 3/20/03 **Date Required:** 3/28/03

Terms: Net 30
Shipped: Longhorn Shippers, Inc.
Buyer: Franz Bieler

Supplier
Crown Packaging, Inc.
1102 Commerce Street
Dallas. TX 75391

Phone: (214)555-1212

Ship To
Chateau Americana
3003 Vineyard Way
Huntington, CA 95394

Item #	Description	Size	Quantity	Unit Price	Amount
CAPCE12	Crème Caps Wine		2318	$ 0.110	$ 243.39
CAPGD12	Gold Caps Wine		2404	0.089	213.96
CAPGN12	Green Caps Wine		31173	0.095	2,961.44
CAPRD12	Red Caps Wine		7527	0.100	752.70

Total Amount	$ 4,171.48
Tax	
Total Invoice	$ 4,171.48

Message

Authorization

Name:	Michelle Radcliff
Date:	3/23/03
Title:	Purchasing Supervisor
Signature:	*Michelle Radcliff*

Distribution: Copy 1 — Supplier; Copy 2 – Accounting; Copy 3 – Receiving; Copy 4 – Purchasing

Figure 4 – Sample Purchase Order

Cash Receipts. The mail is received by the receptionist who opens it in the presence of another individual. At that time, all checks are restrictively endorsed by the receptionist. She also prepares and signs a cash receipts summary. The receptionist then prepares and takes a deposit slip, along with the checks, to the bank for deposit on a daily basis. The validated deposit slip received from the bank, remittance advices from the checks, and cash receipts summary are sent to accounting.

After receiving the validated deposit slip, remittance advices from the checks, and the cash receipts summary, the Accounting Clerk inputs the transactions, updates the cash receipts journal, and the accounts receivable subsidiary ledger if the cash received was from a credit customer. The validated deposit slip, cash receipts summary, and remittance advices are filed together chronologically. The cash receipts journal is totaled monthly and posted to the general ledger.

The Accounting Clerk prepares monthly customer statements in duplicate. Copy 2 is filed alphabetically in Accounting. Copy 1 is mailed to the customer.

Receiving Report

Date Received: *3/28/03*

Receiving Report #: **14891**

Received from	***Purchase Order #***
Crown Packaging, Inc.	*9682*

Freight carrier	***Received by***
Longhorn Shipers, Inc.	*BH*

Quantity	Item #	Size	Description
2318	*CAPCE12*		*Crème Caps Wine*
2404	*CAPGD12*		*Gold Caps Wine*
31173	*CAPGN12*		*Green Caps Wine*
7527	*CAPRD12*		*Red Caps Wine*

Condition:

Excellent

Distribution: Copy 1 — Accounting; Copy 2 – Purchasing; Copy 3 – Receiving

Figure 5 – Sample Receiving Report

Purchases. As raw materials are needed for production and bottling, a prenumbered purchase order is completed (*Figure 4*) in quadruplicate.

The purchase order must be approved and signed by a purchasing supervisor. Copy 1 of the purchase order is sent to the supplier. Copy 2 of the purchase order is sent to Accounting. Copy 3 of the purchase order is sent to Receiving. Copy 4 of the purchase order and the purchase requisition are held temporarily in Purchasing. As goods are received from suppliers, they are inspected, counted and compared to copy 3 of the purchase order. A prenumbered receiving report is prepared in triplicate (*Figure 5*). Copy 3 of the receiving report and copy 3 of the purchase order are filed numerically. Copy 2 of the receiving report is sent to Purchasing where it is matched with copy 4 of the purchase order and the purchase requisition and filed numerically.

Cash Disbursements. When invoices are received for items or services not requiring a receiving report or a purchase order, they are first routed to the appropriate department for approval (by the receptionist when she opens the mail). The approved invoice is then sent to Accounting.

When invoices for inventory are received from suppliers, the receptionist sends it directly to Accounting. These invoices are matched with copy 1 of the receiving report and copy 2 of the purchase order. They are then entered into the purchases journal. The purchases journal is totaled monthly and then posted to the general ledger.

Supplier invoices, copy 1 of the receiving report, and copy 2 of the purchase order are then filed in a temporary file by due date to insure that they will be paid on a timely basis and that any discounts offered will be taken. Supplier invoices not requiring receiving reports and/or purchase orders are also included in this temporary file. As the invoices come due, the accounting clerk pulls them from the temporary file and writes the checks. The accounting supervisor reviews the supporting documentation such as the check, invoice, copy 1 of the receiving report, and copy 2 of the purchase order for completeness, initials the invoices, and sends the documentation (commonly referred to as a voucher package) to the chief financial officer (CFO) for signature.

The CFO reviews the package for reasonableness, signs the checks, stamps the documents "Paid," and returns the package to Accounting. The checks are then mailed. The remaining documents are filed numerically.

The cash disbursements journal is totaled monthly and posted to the general ledger.

Inventory. Chateau Americana maintains a periodic inventory system for production inventory and perpetual inventory system for finished goods (bottled wines). The perpetual inventory records are updated based on the standard cost buildups for each bottled wine when inventory is moved from the bottling room to the warehouse. (Again, you are reminded that this module focuses only on the wholesale segment of the business and does not deal with production or selling of basic grape-stock).

A physical inventory is taken at the end of the year for production inventory and at the end of each quarter for finished goods inventory. Adjusting entries are made as necessary based on the physical inventory counts.

Payroll. Chateau Americana pays its employees on the 15th and the last day of each month. The department supervisors are responsible for approving and initialing the time cards for any hourly employees in their respective departments. The time cards are then sent to Accounting at the end of the payroll period. The accounting clerk calculates payroll for each employee using the current payroll information found in the employee payroll subsidiary ledgers. The accounting clerk enters the payroll into the payroll journal and posts to the employee payroll subsidiary ledgers. The time cards are then filed chronologically and alphabetically.

The accounting clerk prepares the payroll checks from the payroll checking account based upon the information from the payroll journal and enters the check number in the payroll journal. The accounting clerk also prepares a check drawn from the general checking account payable to the payroll checking account in the amount of the total payroll to cover the current period's payroll. The accounting supervisor reviews the payroll check and the check from the general checking account and initials the payroll journal before forwarding all the checks to the CFO for signature. The CFO reviews and signs the checks and returns them to Accounting. Accounting distributes the payroll checks to the employees and deposits the check for the payroll checking account in the bank.

For payroll purposes, you will be preparing the payroll for four employees: two members of middle management who are salaried employees (Anna Johnson and José Rodriguez) and two production workers who are hourly employees (Tom Bryan and Bob Hissom).

Anna Johnson is an Accounting Supervisor and has been with Chateau Americana for two years. José Rodriguez is a Shift Supervisor and has been with the company for 10 years. Both Bryan and Hissom are in the Operations Department. Bryan is a shift worker in the Wine Presses, and Hissom is a receiving clerk. Both have been with the company for several years. Hourly employees who work overtime hours receive 150% of their regular hourly pay per overtime hour worked.

The amount of federal income tax withheld for each employee is determined (a) by taking into account the employee's marital status and the number of withholding allowances claimed by the employee (both of which can be found in the employee payroll subsidiary ledgers) and (b) referring to the wage bracket tables on pages 35-55 of IRS Publication 15 (Rev. January 2003), Circular E. Assume there is no state or local tax withheld. FICA is taxed at 6.2% on the first $87,000 of gross wages and Medicare is taxed at 1.45% (there is no ceiling on Medicare). (**HINT:** You can find Publication 15 on the Internet. See www.irs.gov.)

Fixed Assets. Depreciation expense is calculated monthly. All assets are depreciated on the straight-line basis using the half-year convention in the year of purchase and the year of sale. A portion of the Fixed Asset subsidiary ledgers has been reproduced for you. Date of acquisition, estimated useful life, acquisition value, and accumulated depreciation for each asset are listed in the ledgers.

TRANSACTIONS

The books have been posted through December 15, 2003. The following selected transactions have been extracted from the period December 16 through December 31, 2003 and are to be completed in accordance with the policies and procedures explained above. Documents to be completed can be found in the Document Packet. For all required signatures on these documents sign your name. Supporting documentation for the transactions is provided behind the Year-End Procedures followed by all necessary journals and ledgers.

December	Transaction
16	Receive a purchase order from California Premium Beverage (page 16). Fill and ship the order. Complete Invoice No. 15535, Bill of Lading No. 136480 and record the sale in the journals and ledgers. W. A. Bierkstahler is the sales account representative. Relevant data: shipment weight - 12,532 lbs., trailer # - 122302, serial # - 999356278.
16	Order 18,000 lbs. white grapes at $1.05 per pound from Mendocino Vineyards. Complete Purchase Order No. 9682. Relevant data: date required - Dec. 22, shipper - Longhorn Shippers, Inc., buyer - Franz Bieler, supplier # - P0652.
16	Purchase a 2002 Ford truck for $26,750.00. The terms include a $4,750.00 down payment and a 3-year, 6% promissory note to Ford Credit for the remaining $22,000.00. Principal and interest on the note are due monthly beginning January 4, 2004. The company expects the truck to have a useful life of 5 years and no salvage value. Prepare Check No. 19257 payable to Potter Valley Ford for the down payment and record the transaction in the journals and ledgers.
17	Receive a phone complaint from Seaside Distributors about a case of Chenin Blanc that was damaged in shipment. The case was part of Invoice No. 15175, dated November 5, 2003, in the amount of $20,438.40. Seaside paid the invoice on November 19, 2003 and took advantage of the discount (terms 3/15, net 30). Prepare Credit Memo No. 2753 to write-off the damaged inventory that was not returned, and prepare Check No. 19286 to reimburse Seaside for the damaged goods. Record the transactions in the journals and ledgers. W. A. Bierkstahler is the sales account representative. Relevant data: customer PO # - MZ5713.
19	Receive $850 dividend income from investment in Seagate shares (page 17). Enter the receipt on Cash Receipts Summary No. 5712 and record the cash receipt in the journals and ledgers.
19	Receive payment in full from Pacific Distribution Co. on Invoice No. 15243 dated November 13, 2003, in the amount of $19,576.80 (page 18). Enter the receipt on Cash Receipts Summary No. 5712 and record the cash receipt in the journals and ledgers.

December	Transaction
19	Receive a purchase order (page 19) with payment (page 20) from Ukiah Distributors. Fill and ship the order. Complete Invoice No. C2489, enter the receipt on Cash Receipts Summary No. 5712, and record the sale in the journals and ledgers. W. A. Bierkstahler is the sales account representative. Relevant data: shipment weight - 7,650 lbs., trailer # - 279AJ1, serial # - 919515094. (Hint: The company records the journal entry for cost of goods sold and inventory for cash sales in the general journal.)
22	Receive 14,000 lbs. red grapes at $0.99 per pound from Mendocino Vineyards. Also received Invoice No. M7634 from Mendocino Vineyards with the shipment (page 21). Terms on the invoice are 2/10, net 30. Complete Receiving Report No. 17251 and record the inventory in the journals and ledgers using the gross method.
26	Receive utility bill from Pacific Gas and Electric in the amount of $18,887.62 (page 22). Prepare Check No. 19402 and record the payment in the journals and ledgers.
30	Receive Brokerage Advice from Edwards Jones for purchase of 500 shares of Microsoft at $49.20 per share plus $400 broker's commission (page 23). Prepare Check No. 19468 and record the purchase in the journals and ledgers.
31	Receive payment in full for the December 15 purchase from California Premium Beverage (page 24). Enter the cash receipt on Cash Receipts Summary No. 5718 and record the cash receipt in the journals and ledgers.
31	Prepare Check No. 19473 payable to Mendocino Vineyards for the shipment received on December 22 and record the payment in the journals and ledgers.
31	Prepare Payroll Checks (Nos. 7111-7114) for Anna Johnson, José Rodriguez, Tom Bryan, and Bob Hissom. Time cards for Tom and Bob are on pages 25-26. Prepare Check No. 19474 to transfer cash from the general cash account to the payroll account. Record the payroll transactions in the journals and ledgers.
31	Prepare Check No. 19475 to repay $50,000 of the principal on long-term debt to Bank of Huntington and record the payment in the journals and ledgers.

MONTH-END PROCEDURES

1. Calculate monthly accrued interest expense for the $22,000 installment note to Ford Credit (based on 365 days per year and interest starting to accrue on December 17, 2003). Make the appropriate adjusting entry. The payable is posted to Other Accrued Expenses Payable.

2. For your convenience, depreciation in the amount of $105,341.50 has been calculated on all assets for the month of December **except** for any current purchases of assets. Calculate the depreciation for the Ford Pickup purchased on December 16. Post the depreciation to the Fixed Asset Subsidiary Ledger and add the amount of depreciation expense to the rest of the December depreciation. Make the appropriate adjusting entry.

3. The office manager receives the bank statement on a monthly basis and reconciles it to the cash receipts and cash disbursements journals, identifying the necessary adjusting journal entries such as bank services charges, etc. (**Note:** The bank reconciliation has already been performed by the office manager and all necessary adjusting journal entries have been recorded in the journals and ledgers.)

YEAR-END PROCEDURES

1. Prepare the unadjusted trial balance using the electronic year-end worksheet provided to you on the CAST web site (your instructor will provide you with the URL for this web site).

2. Prepare the year-end adjusting journal entries:

   a. Calculate the allowance for bad debts using the net sales method. Experience indicates that 0.05% of net sales should be set aside for bad debts. Make the appropriate adjusting entry.

   b. The calculation of federal income tax expense is a year-end adjusting entry but it cannot be made until all other entries have been made and net income before taxes has been determined. Therefore, you must first complete the year-end worksheet and calculate net income before taxes. Then calculate federal income tax expense and post the adjusting entry to the worksheet. (**HINT:** Use rates in effect as of January 2003.)

3. Complete the remainder of the electronic year-end worksheet.

4. Prepare the financial statements including the income statement, the statement of retained earnings, balance sheet, and the statement of cash flows (using the indirect method).

5. Prepare and record the closing journal entries in the journal and general ledger.

6. Prepare the electronic post-closing trial balance worksheet.

The Winery at Chateau Americana
Chart of Accounts

Assets (100000)		
Cash (110000)		
	General Checking Account	111000
	Payroll Checking Account	112000
	Money Market Account	113000
	Savings Account	114000
	Petty Cash	119000
Accounts Receivable (120000)		
	Accounts Receivable	121000
	Allowance for Bad Debts	129000
Inventory (140000)		
	Inventory – Production	141000
	Inventory – Finished Goods	145000
Prepaid Expenses		150000
Land and Buildings		160000
Equipment		170000
Accumulated Depreciation		180000
Investments		191000
Liabilities (200000)		
Accounts Payable		210000
Accrued Expenses (220000)		
	Federal Income Tax Withheld	222100
	FICA Withheld	222200
	Medicare Withheld	222300
Payroll Taxes Payable (223000)		
	FICA Payable – Employer	223100
	Medicare Payable – Employer	223200
	Unemployment Taxes Payable	223300
Other Accrued Expenses		230000
	Federal Income Taxes Payable	235000
	Property Taxes Payable	236000
Mortgages Payable		240000
Other Long-Term Payables (260000)		
	Notes Payable	261000
Owners' Equity (300000)		
Common Stock		310000
Paid-in Capital in Excess of Par – Common		311000
Dividends – Common		312000
Retained Earnings		390000
Income (400000)		
	Sales	410000
	Sales Discounts	420000
	Sales Returns and Allowances	430000
	Gain/Loss – Marketable Securities	452000
	Dividend Income	491000
	Interest Income	492000

Cost of Goods Sold	510000
Expenses (600000 – 700000)	
Payroll Expense (600000)	
Wages and Salaries Expense	601000
Sales Commission Expense	601500
FICA Tax Expense	602100
Medicare Tax Expense	602200
FUTA Expense	602300
SUTA Expense	602400
Occupancy Expense (610000)	
Utilities Expense	611000
Irrigation & Waste Disposal Expense	611300
Landscaping Expense	612000
Marketing (620000)	
Advertising Expense	621000
Marketing Expense	623000
Festivals & Competitions Expense	624000
Communications Expense (630000)	
Telephone Expense	631000
Internet & Computer Expense	632000
Postage Expense	633000
Professional Services Expense (640000)	
Legal & Accounting Fees	641000
Other Consulting Fees	643000
Supplies Expense (650000)	
Office Supplies Expense	651000
Data Processing Expense	660000
Depreciation Expense	670000
Travel and Entertainment Expense	680000
Insurance Expense (690000)	
Other Insurance	691000
Medical Insurance	692000
Workmen's Compensation Insurance	693000
Other Employee Benefits Expense	699000
Dues and Subscriptions Expense	700000
Tax Expense (710000)	
Federal Income Tax Expense	711000
Property Tax Expense	712000
Maintenance Expense (720000)	
Repairs and Maintenance Expense	721000
Automobile Expense	731000
Lease Expense	740000
Other Operating Expense (790000)	
Bad Debt Expense	791000
Miscellaneous Expense	792000
Interest Expense	793000

The Winery at Chateau Americana
Price List

Inventory Code	Description	Standard Cost (per bottle)	Selling Price (per bottle)
R130064	Cabernet Franc	$ 4.50	$ 7.00
R130061	Cabernet Sauvignon	4.20	6.50
R130056	Merlot	4.62	6.00
R130072	Shiraz	4.58	6.25
W120080	Chardonnay	4.54	7.00
W120019	Chenin Blanc	3.34	5.25
W120015	Riesling	2.86	4.85
W120016	Sauvignon Blanc	2.86	4.85
S140000	Sparkling Brut	7.28	11.00

California Premium Beverage

39848 South Street
Santa Rosa, CA 95402
Phone (707) 555-7451 Fax (707) 555-7452

PURCHASE ORDER

To:
Chateau Americana
3003 Vineyard Way
Huntington, CA 95394

Ship To:
California Premium Beverage
39848 South Street
Santa Rosa, CA 95402

ABC Permit #: A59782

P.O. DATE	P.O. NUMBER	SHIPPED VIA	F.O.B. POINT	TERMS
12/13/03	8746	CA Express	Destination	3/15, net 30

ITEM NO	QTY	SIZE	DESCRIPTION	UNIT PRICE	TOTAL
W120015	1512	0.750	Riesling	4.85	7,333.20
W120016	504	0.750	Sauvignon Blanc	4.85	2,444.40
W120019	336	0.750	Chenin Blanc	5.25	1,764.00
R130061	1176	0.750	Cabernet Sauvignon	6.50	7,644.00
R130056	672	0.750	Merlot	6.00	4,032.00
S140000	240	0.750	Sparkling Brut	11.00	2,640.00
W120080	336	0.750	Chardonnay	7.00	2,352.00
				TOTAL	28,209.60

Jorge Gonzalez
Authorized by

12/13/03
Date

Seagate Technology
Disc Drive
Scotts Valley, CA 95067

Lone Star Bank
Dallas, TX 27540

23545

Date 12/15/03

PAY Eight Hundred Fifty and 00/100 Dollars -- $ 850.00

To the order of
Chateau Americana
3003 Vineyard Way
Huntington, CA 95394

- SAMPLE, DO NOT CASH -

⑆000000⑆ ⑈000000000⑈ 23545

Seagate Technology **23545**

Reference	Amount
Dividend (850 Seagate Technology common shares @ $1.00)	$850.00

Pacific Distribution Company
10034 Westborough Boulevard
San Francisco, CA 94080

Bank of America
San Francisco, CA 94104

69712

Date 12/16/03

PAY Nineteen Thousand Five Hundred Seventy Six and 80/100 Dollars ------------------ $ 19,576.80

To The Order Of
Chateau Americana
3003 Vineyard Way
Huntington, CA 95394

- SAMPLE, DO NOT CASH -

⑆000000⑆ ⑈000000000⑈ 69712

Pacific Distribution Company **69712**

Reference	Net Amount
Invoice #15243, customer # 0505	$19,576.80

PURCHASE ORDER

PO Number: 4376
Date: 12/19/03

To:
Chateau Americana
3003 Vineyard Way
Huntington, CA 95394

Ship To:
Ukiah Distributors
3224 Greenlawn Street
Ukiah, CA 95482
Phone (707) 555-1705 Fax (707) 555-1706

SHIPPED VIA	ABC #	F.O.B. POINT	TERMS
United Express	A557912	Huntington	Cash

ITEM NO	QTY	SIZE	DESCRIPTION	UNIT PRICE	TOTAL
W120015	480	0.750	Riesling	4.85	2,328.00
W120080	468	0.750	Chardonnay	7.00	3,276.00
W120019	300	0.750	Chenin Blanc	5.25	1,575.00
R130072	780	0.750	Shiraz	6.25	4,875.00
R130056	672	0.750	Merlot	6.00	4,032.00
				TOTAL	16,086.00

Chrystal Harrington — 12/19/03
Authorized by — Date

Ukiah Distributors
3224 Greenlawn Street
Ukiah, CA 95482

Humboldt Bank
Ukiah, CA 95482

17003

Date 12/19/03

PAY Sixteen Thousand Eighty Six and 00/100 Dollars -- $ 16,086.00

To the order of
Chateau Americana
3003 Vineyard Way
Huntington, CA 95394

- SAMPLE, DO NOT CASH -

⑆000000⑆ ⑈000000000⑈ 17003

Ukiah Distributors

17003

Reference	Discount	Net Amount
Payment for PO 4376		$16,086.00

CUSTOMER INVOICE

Invoice Number **M7634**

Invoice Date 12/20/2003

Mendocino Vineyards
8654 Witherspoon Way
Hopland, CA 95449
Phone: (707) 555-1890

Sold To:
Chateau Americana, Inc.
3003 Vineyard Way
Huntington, CA 95394

Credit Terms: 2/10, Net 30

Ship To:
Chateau Americana, Inc.
3003 Vineyard Way
Huntington, CA 95394

Customer I.D	Customer P.O. Number
CHATAM	9660

Description	Product Number	Quantity	Cost	Extended
Cabernet Sauvignon Grapes	CS1250	14,000 lbs.	$0.99	$13,860.00

Total Cost: $13,860.00

Comments:

Distribution: Copy 1 — Accounting; Copy 2 – Shipping; Copy 3 – Customer

Payment Coupon

Bill Date: 12/23/2003

Please Pay by 01/17/2004
$18,887.62

Amount Enclosed

Account No. 21790-1879

Chateau Americana, Inc.
3003 Vineyard Way
Huntington, CA 95394

Send Payment to:

Pacific Gas and Electric
P.O. Box 2575
San Francisco, CA 94103

Retain bottom portion for your records, detach and return stub with payment.

Service For:	Chateau Americana, Inc. 3003 Vineyard Way Huntington, CA 95394	Your Account Number **21790-1879**	Rate Class **Commercial**	Billing Date **12/23/2003**

Meter Number	Service Period	Days	Type of Reading	Multiplier	Units	Meter Readings Current	Meter Readings Past	Usage
68869800	**11/23/03 – 12/23/03**	**31**	**Actual**	**1**	**KWH**	**1098412**	**1001301**	**97111**

Previous Balance	16,895.53
Payment	16,895.53
Balance Forward	0.00
Current Charges	18,887.62

Due Date	Total Due
01/17/2004	18,887.62

Pacific Gas and Electric
1000 Energy Drive, San Francisco, CA 94103, (415) 973-8943

Edward Jones Financial Services

100 Market Street
San Francisco, CA 94109
(415)504-9000

Customer
Chateau Americana, Inc.
3003 Vineyard Way
Huntington, CA 95394

Account Number
02334-85763

Tax Identification #
23-7788954

SAVE THIS STATEMENT FOR TAX PURPOSES

Date	Description	Symbol	Fees and/or Commissions($)	Net Dollar Amount ($)	Share Price ($)	Transaction Shares
12/30/03	Microsoft Corporation Common Shares	MSFT	400.00	24,600.00	49.20	500.0000

California Premium Beverage
39848 South Street
Santa Rosa, CA 95402

Bay View Bank
Santa Rosa, CA 95407

21803

Date 12/29/03

PAY Twenty Seven Thousand Three Hundred Sixty Three and 31/100 Dollars ------------------ $ 27,363.31

To The Order Of
Chateau Americana
3003 Vineyard Way
Huntington, CA 95394

- SAMPLE, DO NOT CASH -

⑆000000⑆ ⑈000000000⑈ 21803

California Premium Beverage **21803**

Reference	Discount	Net Amount
# 0504 Invoice 15535	846.29	$27,363.31

Period Ending	December 19, 2003		
Employee Name	Thomas P. Bryan		
Signature	*Tom Bryan*		
Approved	*PJB*		
Out		7th Day	
In			
Out			
In			
Out	4	6th Day	04:00 PM
In			12:01 PM
Out	4		11:30 AM
In			07:29 AM
Out	4	5th Day	04:01 PM
In			12:00 PM
Out	4		11:30 AM
In			07:31 AM
Out	4	4th Day	04:02 PM
In			11:58 AM
Out	4		11:30 AM
In			07:30 AM
Out	4	3rd Day	04:03 PM
In			11:59 AM
Out	4		11:30 AM
In			07:31 AM
Out		2nd Day	
In			
Out			
In			
Out		1st Day	
In			
Out			
In			

Period Ending	December 26, 2003		
Employee Name	Thomas P. Bryan		
Signature	*Tom Bryan*		
Approved	*PJB*		
Out		7th Day	
In			
Out			
In			
Out	4	6th Day	
In			
Out	4		
In			*Holiday*
Out	4	5th Day	
In			
Out	4		
In			*Holiday*
Out	4	4th Day	04:00 PM
In			12:02 PM
Out	4		11:30 AM
In			07:29 AM
Out	4	3rd Day	04:00 PM
In			12:01 PM
Out	4		11:33 AM
In			07:30 AM
Out	4	2nd Day	04:04 PM
In			12:02 PM
Out	4		11:31 AM
In			07:28 AM
Out		1st Day	
In			
Out			
In			

Period Ending	December 31, 2003		
Employee Name	Thomas P. Bryan		
Signature	*Tom Bryan*		
Approved	*PJB*		
Out		7th Day	
In			
Out			
In			
Out		6th Day	
In			
Out			
In			
Out		5th Day	
In			
Out			
In			
Out	4	4th Day	04:02 PM
In			11:58 AM
Out	4.75		11:30 AM
In			06:45 AM
Out	4.5	3rd Day	04:33 PM
In			11:59 AM
Out	4		11:30 AM
In			07:31 AM
Out	5	2nd Day	05:00 PM
In			12:01 PM
Out	4		11:30 AM
In			07:29 AM
Out		1st Day	
In			
Out			
In			

Period Ending	December 19, 2003
Employee Name	Robert T. Hissom
Signature	*Bob Hissom*
Approved	*PJB*

Day		Hours	Time
7th Day	Out		
	In		
	Out		
	In		
6th Day	Out	4	04:02 PM
	In		12:01 PM
	Out	4	11:30 AM
	In		07:29 AM
5th Day	Out	4	03:59 PM
	In		12:02 PM
	Out	4	11:30 AM
	In		07:27 AM
4th Day	Out	4	04:00 PM
	In		11:59 AM
	Out	4	11:30 AM
	In		07:31 AM
3rd Day	Out	4	04:03 PM
	In		12:02PM
	Out	4	11:34 AM
	In		07:30 AM
2nd Day	Out		
	In		
	Out		
	In		
1st Day	Out		
	In		
	Out		
	In		

Period Ending	December 26, 2003
Employee Name	Robert T. Hissom
Signature	*Bob Hissom*
Approved	*PJB*

Day		Hours	Time
7th Day	Out		
	In		
	Out		
	In		
6th Day	Out	4	
	In		
	Out	4	
	In		*Holiday*
5th Day	Out	4	
	In		
	Out	4	
	In		*Holiday*
4th Day	Out	4	04:03 PM
	In		12:04 PM
	Out	4	11:30 AM
	In		07:29 AM
3rd Day	Out	4	04:00 PM
	In		12:00 PM
	Out	4	11:33 AM
	In		07:30 AM
2nd Day	Out	4	04:03 PM
	In		12:01 PM
	Out	4	11:31 AM
	In		07:31 AM
1st Day	Out		
	In		
	Out		
	In		

Period Ending	December 31, 2003
Employee Name	Robert T. Hissom
Signature	*Bob Hissom*
Approved	*PJB*

Day		Hours	Time
7th Day	Out		
	In		
	Out		
	In		
6th Day	Out		
	In		
	Out		
	In		
5th Day	Out		
	In		
	Out		
	In		
4th Day	Out	4	04:00 PM
	In		11:58 AM
	Out	4	11:32 AM
	In		07:32 AM
3rd Day	Out	4	04:01 PM
	In		11:59 AM
	Out	4	11:30 AM
	In		07:30 AM
2nd Day	Out	4	03:57PM
	In		11:55 AM
	Out	4	11:30 AM
	In		07:26 AM
1st Day	Out		
	In		
	Out		
	In		

GENERAL JOURNAL

Date		GL Acct #	Explanation	Post Ref*	Debit				Credit			

***Note: Posting reference is "GL and Page Number." For example, GL52.**

Initials ________
Date ________

GENERAL JOURNAL

Date	GL Acct #	Explanation	Post Ref*	Debit	Credit

*Note: Posting reference is "GL and Page Number." For example, GL52.

Initials ___________
Date ___________

SALES REGISTER

Date	Customer	Invoice/ Document Number	A/R Acct #	Accounts Receivable 121000	Sales 410000	Inventory 145000	Cost of Goods Sold 510000

Initials ___________
Date ____________

CASH RECEIPTS JOURNAL

				Accounts Receivable 121000			Other Account		
Date	Description	Cash 111000	Sales Discount 420000	A/R Acct #	Transaction Amount	Sales 410000	GL Acct #	Transaction Amount	Post Ref*

*Note: Posting reference is "GL and Page Number." For example, GL52.

Initials ____________
Date ____________

PURCHASES JOURNAL

Date	Vendor	Vendor Invoice #	Inventory 141000	Other Account			Accounts Payable 210000	
				G/L Acct #	Transaction Amount	Post Ref*	A/P Acct #	Transaction Amount

*Note: Posting reference is "GL and Page Number." For example, GL52.

Initials __________
Date __________

CASH DISBURSEMENTS JOURNAL

Date	Check Number	Description	Cash 111000	Inventory 141000	Accounts Payable 210000		Other Account		
					A/P Acct #	Transaction Amount	GL Acct #	Transaction Amount	Post Ref*

*Note: Posting reference is "GL and Page Number." For example, GL52.

Initials ________
Date ________

PAYROLL JOURNAL[1]

Date	Employee/ SSN	Hours: Regular/ Overtime	Pay: Regular/ Overtime	Gross Pay 601000	FICA Withheld 222200	Medicare Withheld 222300	Federal Income Tax 222100	Net Pay 112000	Check No.

[1] Use two lines for each employee. For example, for an hourly employee, the employee's name, regular hours and regular pay are written on the first line, while the social security number, overtime hours, overtime pay, and all other information are written on the second line.

Initials ________

Date ________

ACCOUNTS RECEIVABLE SUBSIDIARY LEDGER

0501	Bock Wines and Vines Pier 19, The Embarcadero San Francisco, CA 94111 Phone: (415) 834-9675	Terms: 3/15, net 30 Credit Limit:

Date		Description	Debit	Credit	Balance
12	15	Balance Forward			0 00

0504	California Premium Beverage 39848 South Street Santa Rosa, CA 95402 Phone: (707) 555-7451 Fax: (707) 555-7452	Terms: 3/15, net 30 Credit Limit:

Date		Description	Debit	Credit	Balance
12	15	Balance Forward			0 00

0505	Pacific Distribution Co. 10034 Westborough Boulevard San Francisco, CA 94080 Phone: (415) 555-1532	Terms: 3/15, net 30 Credit Limit:

Date		Description	Debit	Credit	Balance
12	15	Balance Forward (Invoice 15243, 11/13/03)	19 576 80		19 576 80

0506	Seaside Distributors, Inc. 9835 West Hills Road Ukiah, CA 94080 Phone: (707) 555-3102	Terms: 3/15, net 30 Credit Limit:

Date		Description	Debit	Credit	Balance
12	15	Balance Forward			0 00

Initials ________
Date ________

PERPETUAL INVENTORY SUBSIDIARY LEDGER

145000 - R130056 Merlot

Date		Description	Trans. Quantity	Cost		Extended Cost			Quantity on Hand	Total Balance			
Dec	15	Balance Forward							83484		385	696	08

145000 - R130061 Cabernet Sauvignon

Date		Description	Trans. Quantity	Cost		Extended Cost			Quantity on Hand	Total Balance			
Dec	15	Balance Forward							65784		276	292	80

145000 - R130064 Cabernet Franc

Date		Description	Trans. Quantity	Cost		Extended Cost			Quantity on Hand	Total Balance			
Dec	15	Balance Forward							5964		26	838	00

Initials ___________
Date ___________

145000 - R130072 Shiraz

Date		Description	Trans. Quantity	Cost		Extended Cost			Quantity on Hand	Total Balance			
Dec	15	Balance Forward							75888		347	567	04

145000 - W120015 Riesling

Date		Description	Trans. Quantity	Cost		Extended Cost			Quantity on Hand	Total Balance			
Dec	15	Balance Forward							118596		339	184	56

145000 - W120016 Sauvignon Blanc

Date		Description	Trans. Quantity	Cost		Extended Cost			Quantity on Hand	Total Balance			
Dec	15	Balance Forward							93636		267	798	96

Initials ___________
Date ___________

145000 - W120019 Chenin Blanc

Date		Description	Trans. Quantity	Cost		Extended Cost			Quantity on Hand	Total Balance			
Dec	15	Balance Forward							44532		148	736	88

145000 - W120080 Chardonnay

Date		Description	Trans. Quantity	Cost		Extended Cost			Quantity on Hand	Total Balance			
Dec	15	Balance Forward							420552	1	909	306	08

145000 - S140000 Sparkling Brut

Date		Description	Trans. Quantity	Cost		Extended Cost			Quantity on Hand	Total Balance			
Dec	15	Balance Forward							47064		342	625	91

Initials ___________
Date ___________

ACCOUNTS PAYABLE SUBSIDIARY LEDGER

P2538	**Delicio Vineyards** 12701 South Fernwood Livermore, CA 94550 Phone: (925) 555-1890	**Terms:** **2/10, net 30**

Date		**Description**	**Debit**				**Credit**				**Balance**			
11	4	Invoice No. 45354						14	563	56		14	563	56

P0652	**Mendocino Vineyards** 8654 Witherspoon Way Hopland, CA 95449 Phone: (707) 555-1890	**Terms:** **2/10, net 30**

Date		**Description**	**Debit**				**Credit**				**Balance**			

Initials ____________
Date ____________

EMPLOYEE PAYROLL SUBSIDIARY LEDGER

Employee Name (Last name, First Name, MI): Bryan, Thomas P.	**Social Security No:** 014-39-4215
Address: 35 Winchester Street	**Phone:** (707) 555-1495
Huntington, CA 95394	
	Date of Birth: 6/14/65
	Date of Employment: 4/25/95
	Date of Termination:

PAY RATE HISTORY

Effective Date	Pay Rate	Pay Type	Position	Filing Status	Withholding Allowances			
4/25/94	14.00	Hourly	Presses	Single	1			
4/25/95	15.00	Hourly	Presses	Single	1			

Date: Period Ending	Date: Payroll Date	Hours: Regular	Hours: Overtime	Gross Pay 601000	FICA Withheld 222200	Medicare Withheld 222300	Federal Income Tax 222100	Net Pay
11-30-03 Balance Forward				32 040 00	1 986 48	464 58	3 648 00	25 940 94
12 15	12 15	88 00	4 25	1 415 63	87 77	20 53	167 00	1 140 31

Initials ____________
Date ____________

Employee Name (Last name, First Name, MI): Hissom, Robert T.	**Social Security No:** 349-43-6417
Address: 3187 Heckert Way	**Phone:** (707) 555-1219
Apt. 4A	
Huntington, CA 95394	**Date of Birth:** 11-9-77
	Date of Employment: 1-4-98
	Date of Termination:

PAY RATE HISTORY

Effective Date	Pay Rate	Pay Type	Position	Filing Status	Withholding Allowances			
1-4-03	14.25	Hourly	Receiving	Single	0			

Date		Hours						
Period Ending	**Payroll Date**	**Regular**	**Overtime**	**Gross Pay 601000**	**FICA Withheld 222200**	**Medicare Withheld 222300**	**Federal Income Tax 222100**	**Net Pay**
11-30-03 Balance Forward				30 438 00	1 887 16	441 35	3 936 00	24 173 49
12 15	12 15	88 00	2 75	1 312 78	81 39	19 04	174 00	1 038 35

Initials ________
Date ________

Employee Name (Last name, First Name, MI): Johnson, Anna C.	**Social Security No:** 296-49-3438
Address: 175 Bunker Hill Lane	**Phone:** (707) 555-3856
Huntington, CA 95394	
	Date of Birth: 9-7-68
	Date of Employment: 2-14-01
	Date of Termination:

PAY RATE HISTORY

Effective Date	Pay Rate	Pay Type	Position	Filing Status	Withholding Allowances			
2-14-02	1,600	Salary	Payroll	Married	3			
2-16-03	1,750	Salary	Acct Sup	Married	3			

Date: Period Ending	Date: Payroll Date	Hours: Regular	Hours: Overtime	Gross Pay 601000	FICA Withheld 222200	Medicare Withheld 222300	Federal Income Tax 222100	Net Pay
11-30-03 Balance Forward				36 300 00	2 250 60	526 35	3 017 00	30 506 05
12 15	12 15			1 750 00	108 50	25 38	140 00	1 476 12

Initials ________
Date ________

Employee Name (Last name, First Name, MI): Rodriguez, José G.

Social Security No: 124-11-7755

Address: 2953 Whistler Hill Lane
Huntington, CA 95394

Phone: (707) 555-2024

Date of Birth: 7-7-71

Date of Employment: 11-3-93

Date of Termination:

PAY RATE HISTORY

Effective Date	Pay Rate	Pay Type	Position	Filing Status	Withholding Allowances			
1-1-03	2,550	Salary	Supervisor	Married	4			

Date: Period Ending	Date: Payroll Date	Hours: Regular	Hours: Overtime	Gross Pay 601000	FICA Withheld 222200	Medicare Withheld 222300	Federal Income Tax 222100	Net Pay
11-30-03 Balance Forward				56 100 00	3 478 20	813 45	5 302 00	46 506 35
12 15	12 15			2 550 00	158 10	36 98	241 00	2 113 92

Initials ________
Date ________

FIXED ASSET SUBSIDIARY LEDGER

Asset: Fork Lift	**Depreciation Method:** SL
Purchased from: Northern California Equipment	**Estimated Life:** 10 years
	Estimated Salvage Value: $ 0

Date			Asset Debit			Asset Credit			Asset Balance			Depreciation Debit			Depreciation Credit			Depreciation Balance			Net Book Value		
12	23	02	18	881	00				18	881	00										18	881	00
12	31	02														944	05		944	05	17	936	05
1	31	03														157	34	1	101	39	17	779	61
2	28	03														157	34	1	258	73	17	622	27
3	31	03														157	34	1	416	07	17	464	93
4	30	03														157	34	1	573	41	17	307	59
5	31	03														157	34	1	730	75	17	150	25
6	30	03														157	34	1	888	09	16	992	91
7	31	03														157	34	2	045	43	16	835	57
8	31	03														157	34	2	202	77	16	678	23
9	30	03														157	34	2	360	11	16	520	89
10	31	03														157	34	2	517	45	16	363	55
11	30	03														157	34	2	674	79	16	206	21
12	31	03														157	36	2	832	15	16	048	85

Initials ___________
Date ___________

Asset:	**Depreciation Method:**
Purchased from:	**Estimated Life:**
	Estimated Salvage Value:

	Asset			Depreciation			
Date	**Debit**	**Credit**	**Balance**	**Debit**	**Credit**	**Balance**	**Net Book Value**

Initials ________
Date ________

GENERAL LEDGER

111000 - General Checking Account			Ref	Debit	Credit	Debit Balance
Dec	15	Balance Forward				2 222 927 47

112000 - Payroll Checking Account			Ref	Debit	Credit	Debit Balance
Dec	15	Balance Forward				1 000 00

113000 - Money Market Account			Ref	Debit	Credit	Debit Balance
Dec	15	Balance Forward				782 546 49

114000 - Savings Account			Ref	Debit	Credit	Debit Balance
Dec	15	Balance Forward				51 745 56

119000 - Petty Cash			Ref	Debit	Credit	Debit Balance
Dec	15	Balance Forward				500 00

121000 - Accounts Receivable			Ref	Debit	Credit	Debit Balance
Dec	15	Balance Forward				5 366 670 86

*Note: Use the Reference column to refer to the applicable journal. For example, use SR and the page number (e.g., SR29) to refer to the appropriate page of the sales register. Similarly, use CD and the page number to refer to the appropriate page of the cash disbursements journal.

Initials __________
Date ___________

129000 – Allowance for Bad Debts			Ref	Debit	Credit	Credit Balance
Dec	15	Balance Forward				95 401 58

141000 – Inventory -- Production			Ref	Debit	Credit	Debit Balance
Dec	15	Balance Forward				11 564 851 56

145000 - Inventory – Finished Goods			Ref	Debit	Credit	Debit Balance
Dec	15	Balance Forward				4 044 046 31

150000 - Prepaid Expenses			Ref	Debit	Credit	Debit Balance
Dec	15	Balance Forward				142 465 96

160000 - Land and Buildings			Ref	Debit	Credit	Debit Balance
Dec	15	Balance Forward				16 358 487 34

170000 - Equipment			Ref	Debit	Credit	Debit Balance
Dec	15	Balance Forward				13 844 881 10

Initials ___________
Date ___________

180000 - Accumulated Depreciation			Ref	Debit	Credit	Credit Balance			
Dec	15	Balance Forward				15	233	662	97

191000 - Investments			Ref	Debit	Credit	Debit Balance			
Dec	15	Balance Forward				3	070	227	56

210000 - Accounts Payable			Ref	Debit	Credit	Credit Balance			
Dec	15	Balance Forward				4	987	975	79

222100 - Federal Income Tax Withheld			Ref	Debit	Credit	Credit Balance			
Dec	15	Balance Forward					66	739	08

222200 - FICA Withheld			Ref	Debit	Credit	Credit Balance			
Dec	15	Balance Forward					12	237	64

222300 - Medicare Withheld			Ref	Debit	Credit	Credit Balance			
Dec	15	Balance Forward					2	862	01

Initials __________
Date __________

223100 - FICA Payable – Employer			Ref	Debit				Credit				Credit Balance			
Dec	15	Balance Forward											12	237	64

223200 - Medicare Payable – Employer			Ref	Debit				Credit				Credit Balance			
Dec	15	Balance Forward											2	862	01

223300 - Unemployment Taxes Payable			Ref	Debit				Credit				Credit Balance			
Dec	15	Balance Forward												943	57

230000 – Other Accrued Expenses			Ref	Debit				Credit				Credit Balance			
Dec	15	Balance Forward											599	348	98

235000 - Federal Income Taxes Payable			Ref	Debit				Credit				Credit Balance			
Dec	15	Balance Forward												0	00

240000 - Mortgages Payable			Ref	Debit				Credit				Credit Balance			
Dec	15	Balance Forward										7	639	067	73

Initials ___________
Date ___________

261000 - Notes Payable			**Ref**	**Debit**	**Credit**	**Credit Balance**			
Dec	15	Balance Forward					841	000	00

310000 - Common Stock			**Ref**	**Debit**	**Credit**	**Credit Balance**			
Dec	15	Balance Forward					90	000	00

311000 - PIC in Excess of Par - Common			**Ref**	**Debit**	**Credit**	**Credit Balance**			
Dec	15	Balance Forward				3	567	265	00

312000 - Dividends - Common			**Ref**	**Debit**	**Credit**	**Credit Balance**			
Dec	15	Balance Forward						0	00

390000 - Retained Earnings			**Ref**	**Debit**	**Credit**	**Credit Balance**			
Dec	15	Balance Forward				22	064	134	78

410000 - Sales			**Ref**	**Debit**	**Credit**	**Credit Balance**			
Dec	15	Balance Forward				22	264	431	15

Initials ____________
Date ____________

420000 - Sales Discounts			Ref	Debit				Credit				Debit Balance			
Dec	15	Balance Forward											346	741	36

430000 - Sales Returns and Allowances			Ref	Debit				Credit				Debit Balance			
Dec	15	Balance Forward											15	588	47

452000 - Gain/Loss – Marketable Securities			Ref	Debit				Credit				Credit Balance			
Dec	15	Balance Forward												0	00

491000 - Dividend Income			Ref	Debit				Credit				Credit Balance			
Dec	15	Balance Forward											4	000	00

492000 - Interest Income			Ref	Debit				Credit				Credit Balance			
Dec	15	Balance Forward											23	482	56

510000 - Cost of Goods Sold			Ref	Debit				Credit				Debit Balance			
Dec	15	Balance Forward										11	514	092	11

Initials ___________
Date ___________

601000 - Wages and Salaries Expense			Ref	Debit	Credit	Debit Balance
Dec	15	Balance Forward				1 965 164 11

601500 - Sales Commission Expense			Ref	Debit	Credit	Debit Balance
Dec	15	Balance Forward				771 665 60

602100 - FICA Tax Expense			Ref	Debit	Credit	Debit Balance
Dec	15	Balance Forward				244 124 52

602200 - Medicare Tax Expense			Ref	Debit	Credit	Debit Balance
Dec	15	Balance Forward				57 093 62

602300 - FUTA Expense			Ref	Debit	Credit	Debit Balance
Dec	15	Balance Forward				7 392 00

602400 - SUTA Expense			Ref	Debit	Credit	Debit Balance
Dec	15	Balance Forward				22 176 00

Initials ___________
Date ___________

611000 - Utilities Expense			Ref	Debit	Credit	Debit Balance			
Dec	15	Balance Forward					307	067	05

611300 - Irrigation & Waste Disp. Expense			Ref	Debit	Credit	Debit Balance			
Dec	15	Balance Forward					230	910	91

612000 - Landscaping Expense			Ref	Debit	Credit	Debit Balance			
Dec	15	Balance Forward					142	475	69

621000 - Advertising Expense			Ref	Debit	Credit	Debit Balance			
Dec	15	Balance Forward					296	794	33

623000 - Marketing Expense			Ref	Debit	Credit	Debit Balance			
Dec	15	Balance Forward					192	865	67

624000 - Festivals & Competitions Expense			Ref	Debit	Credit	Debit Balance			
Dec	15	Balance Forward					238	654	75

Initials ________
Date ________

631000 - Telephone Expense			**Ref**	**Debit**	**Credit**	**Debit Balance**
Dec	15	Balance Forward				37 584 73

632000 - Internet & Computer Expense			**Ref**	**Debit**	**Credit**	**Debit Balance**
Dec	15	Balance Forward				14 475 00

633000 - Postage Expense			**Ref**	**Debit**	**Credit**	**Debit Balance**
Dec	15	Balance Forward				35 117 66

641000 - Legal & Accounting Fees			**Ref**	**Debit**	**Credit**	**Debit Balance**
Dec	15	Balance Forward				88 425 50

643000 - Other Consulting Fees			**Ref**	**Debit**	**Credit**	**Debit Balance**
Dec	15	Balance Forward				12 500 00

651000 - Office Supplies Expense			**Ref**	**Debit**	**Credit**	**Debit Balance**
Dec	15	Balance Forward				58 689 68

Initials ____________
Date ____________

660000 - Data Processing Expense			Ref	Debit				Credit				Debit Balance			
Dec	15	Balance Forward											9	743	89

670000 - Depreciation Expense			Ref	Debit				Credit				Debit Balance			
Dec	15	Balance Forward										1	092	832	66

680000 - Travel and Entertainment Expense			Ref	Debit				Credit				Debit Balance			
Dec	15	Balance Forward											169	405	86

691000 – Other Insurance Expense			Ref	Debit				Credit				Debit Balance			
Dec	15	Balance Forward											115	058	55

692000 – Medical Insurance			Ref	Debit				Credit				Debit Balance			
Dec	15	Balance Forward											192	154	80

693000 - Workmen's Compensation Insurance			Ref	Debit				Credit				Debit Balance			
Dec	15	Balance Forward											139	750	00

Initials __________
Date ____________

699000 - Other Employee Benefits Expense			Ref	Debit	Credit	Debit Balance		
Dec	15	Balance Forward				175	643	90

700000 - Dues and Subscriptions Expense			Ref	Debit	Credit	Debit Balance		
Dec	15	Balance Forward				32	076	00

711000 - Federal Income Tax Expense			Ref	Debit	Credit	Debit Balance		
Dec	15	Balance Forward				857	595	76

712000 - Property Tax Expense			Ref	Debit	Credit	Debit Balance		
Dec	15	Balance Forward				19	875	00

721000 - Repairs and Maintenance Expense			Ref	Debit	Credit	Debit Balance		
Dec	15	Balance Forward				71	974	93

731000 - Automobile Expense			Ref	Debit	Credit	Debit Balance		
Dec	15	Balance Forward				81	493	45

Initials ___________
Date ___________

740000 - Lease Expense			**Ref**	**Debit**				**Credit**				**Debit Balance**			
Dec	15	Balance Forward											113	607	56

791000 - Bad Debt Expense			**Ref**	**Debit**				**Credit**				**Debit Balance**			
Dec	15	Balance Forward												0	00

792000 - Miscellaneous Expense			**Ref**	**Debit**				**Credit**				**Debit Balance**			
Dec	15	Balance Forward											26	575	63

793000 - Interest Expense			**Ref**	**Debit**				**Credit**				**Debit Balance**			
Dec	15	Balance Forward											359	915	53

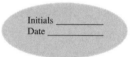

Initials __________
Date ____________

SPREADSHEET APPLICATIONS USING MICROSOFT® EXCEL 2002: The Winery at Chateau Americana

LEARNING OBJECTIVES

After completing and discussing this module, you should be able to:

- Recognize the managerial and technological issues and risks associated with designing and utilizing a spreadsheet application as the primary accounting information system
- Understand and evaluate data integrity issues associated with spreadsheet utilization
- Understand and perform data analysis techniques using spreadsheet applications
- Understand the advantages and disadvantages of various presentation formats
- Understand the advantages and disadvantages of database functions in spreadsheet applications

BACKGROUND

When Chateau Americana began operations in 1980, accounting records were maintained manually. As the winery grew, the former CFO decided it was time to computerize various aspects of the system. As an initial step, he decided to use a spreadsheet program to assist in preparing journal entries, the year-end worksheet, and the financial statements. He also wanted to be able to create a single set of financial statements that could be used to present differing amounts of information to the various users. His goal was to simplify the bookkeeping functions, while improving the accuracy and usefulness of the financial statements. He knew this could be done by reducing the amount of redundancy inherent in manual recordkeeping. If the data was entered once and was verified at that time, this data could then be transmitted to other spreadsheets without the risk of incurring clerical errors that might appear upon re-entering the same data. He, therefore, had created various spreadsheets for Chateau Americana that would assist in these goals.

Assume that you had been asked to create these spreadsheets for Chateau Americana, given the current year end data. The following exercises were written assuming that you would be working in *Microsoft® Excel 2002*. If this is not the case, some minor adjustments may need to be made to the instructions. In addition, a general tutorial consisting of basic information has been provided for novice Excel users at the end of the exercises. If you are not a novice user, you may skip that section entirely. Finally, tutorials follow many of the sections, providing hints and additional explanations for some of the more advanced Excel skill requirements. The symbol ⌘ denotes areas for which additional tutorial explanation is provided.

As with any other computer file, it is important to **save your work often** and to **back it up frequently** to another storage medium.

Download and save the Excel file entitled "CA_excel.xls" from the CAST web site (your instructor will provide you with the URL for this web site). This workbook contains several worksheets that will be necessary for the completion of the various exercises contained in the Spreadsheet assignment.

PROTECTING THE DATA

Open the **CA_excel** file you have downloaded. This file contains several worksheets including a blank year-end worksheet similar to the one you may have completed in the Manual AIS Module of *CAST* entitled **Y-E Worksheet**. Examine the set-up of the year-end worksheet, familiarizing yourself with the ways in which the creation of formulas in Excel can be used to minimize the amount of data input.

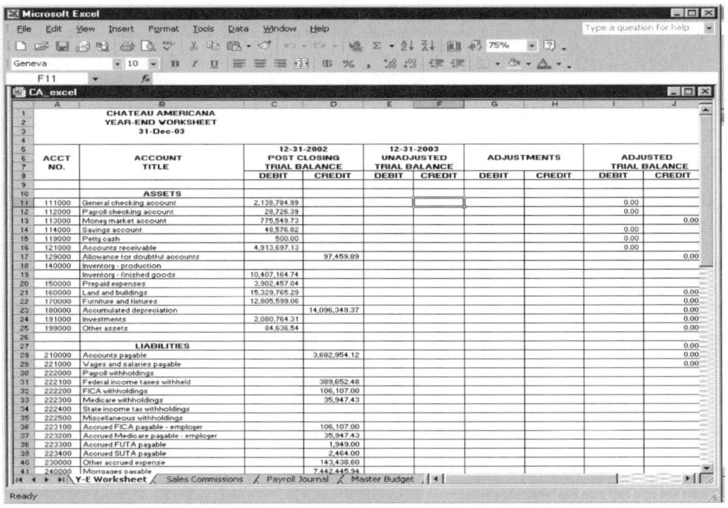

Figure 1

Requirements

1. Open the **CA_excel** file and enter on the **Y-E Worksheet**, the data for the 12-31-03 Unadjusted Trial Balance and the 12-31-03 Adjustments columns, allowing the formulas contained in the spreadsheet to calculate the totals and carry the figures from one column of the spreadsheet to the next (i.e., from those columns to the Adjusted Trial Balance, Balance Sheet, and Income Statement columns). The data for completion of this worksheet are available on the CAST web site.

2. Review the worksheet to be sure that your column totals are accurate and that you have entered the correct data for each account.

3. Once you have made certain that the embedded formulas are being calculated correctly, you should lock the cells that contain them so that no one can change the formulas at a later date. To do this, highlight cells **I9** through **N91** and then lock them ⌘.

4. Now protect ⌘ the locked cells.

5. Verify that the cells have been locked properly by attempting to alter any of the formulas contained in columns I through N.

Protecting the Data Tutorial
Highlight the cells to be locked. Click on **Format > Cells > Protection**. Click on the "Locked" box and click on "OK". Once you have locked all of the desired cells, click on **Tools > Protection > Protect Sheet**. The Protect Sheet pop-up window will appear with the "Protect worksheet and contents of locked cells" box checked. Enter a password that will enable you to unlock the cells at a later date, if necessary. You will then be prompted to confirm the password by reentering it. **NOTE:** If you do not enter a password, any user can unprotect the worksheet.

FORMULA AUDITING

The spreadsheet is now ready to be used for the creation of the financial statements and manipulation of the data for various managerial tasks. Before you begin, however, it is important to recognize that, despite the fact that you will be using a computer to deal with many of the clerical tasks previously done manually, the computer can do so accurately only insofar as the formulas are entered correctly. Statistics show that the number of errors on computer worksheets exceeds 25%.
Some of the more common errors are:

# NAME?	Occurs when Excel cannot evaluate a defined name used in the formula because the name may never have existed, may be misspelled, or may have been inadvertently deleted.
# N/A	Dependent upon the formula. For example, it may mean that no value was available in a vlookup function.
#REF!	Indicates a problem with a cell reference due, perhaps, to deleting cells, rows or columns used in a formula.
# VALUE!	Typically due to trying to use a cell containing text in a calculation or entering incorrect arguments.

The **Formula Auditing** tool in Excel enables the user to audit the worksheet to find and correct many of the errors that inevitably occur.

Requirements

As you work through the following steps, you will occasionally be asked questions. Please respond to these questions in the space provided in the **Sales Commissions** worksheet.

1. Open the **CA_excel** file and click on the **Sales Commissions** worksheet. Display the **Formula Auditing** toolbar by clicking on **Tools > Formula Auditing > Show Formula Auditing Toolbar**.

Figure 2

The following table describes some of the buttons on the toolbar:

Option	Description
Error Checking	Describes the error that has occurred and allows the user to obtain help on the error, to walk through the calculation steps, to ignore the error, or to edit the error in the formula bar.
Trace Precedents	Displays a blue arrow from all cells that supply data to the selected cell.
Remove Precedent Arrows	Removes all precedent arrows for each level displayed. The button must be pushed for each level from which the data is supplied.
Trace Dependents	Displays a red arrow that is dependent upon the selected cell for data.
Remove Dependent Arrows	Removes all dependent arrows for each level displayed. The button must be pushed for each level to which the data are supplied.
Remove All Arrows	Removes all tracer arrows throughout the worksheet.
Trace Errors	Allows the user to find the source of an error by displaying a blue arrow from the source of the error to the selected cell.
New Comment	Allows the user to add comments to a cell.
Circle Invalid Data	Displays a red circle around cells that break any validation rules the user stipulates.
Clear Validation Circles	Removes all validation circles.
Show Watch Window	Displays a window that enables the user to watch what happens to a chosen cell and its formula even when the cell may be off the screen.
Evaluate Formula	Allows the user to display the result of any underlined or italicized portion of a formula.

2. Go to cell **G30**. Click on **Trace Precedents** on the **Formula Auditing** toolbar. From what cell is cell **G30** obtaining its data? (Enter your response in cell **B48**.)

3. Now click on **Remove Precedent Arrows** on the **Formula Auditing** toolbar.

4. While cell **G30** is highlighted, click on **Error Checking** on the **Formula Auditing** toolbar. Obtain two possible causes for the error by clicking on **Help on this error** and enter the two causes in cell **B49**. Close the **Error Checking** window.

5. While cell **G30** is highlighted, click on **Evaluate Formula** on the **Formula Auditing** toolbar. Next, click on **Evaluate**. Why has the error occurred? (Enter your response in cell **B50**.)

6. Examine the cells surrounding **G30** and then fix the error in cell **G30**.

7. Go to cell **F35**. Click on **Trace Precedents** on the **Formula Auditing** toolbar. What happens? (Enter your response in cell **B51**.)

8. While cell **F35** is highlighted, click on **Trace Dependents** on the **Formula Auditing** toolbar. What happens? (Enter your response in cell **B52**.)

9. While cell **F35** is highlighted, click on **Evaluate Formula** on the **Formula Auditing** toolbar. Next, click on **Evaluate** and determine why the error has occurred and then fix it. (Enter your response in cell **B53**.)

10. Check to be sure that all errors on this worksheet have been fixed.

DATA INTEGRITY

Using the **Y-E Worksheet** you can create the Statement of Income and Retained Earnings and the Balance Sheet with very little additional data entry. This is beneficial because you have already verified the accuracy of the data on the **Y-E Worksheet**. If you use this data directly, you will only need to verify the logic on the other spreadsheets you are preparing. One method by which this can be accomplished is to utilize the "=" sign to tell Excel that a particular cell is equal to the amount in another cell on another spreadsheet. Another method is to create a Name for a particular amount to be used later in a formula. You will utilize both of these methods.

The Statement of Income and Retained Earnings is to be prepared as a **single-year, multi-step income statement**. This statement is to be formatted so that it can provide differing amounts of detail to the users when viewed or printed at a later date. To do this, you will need to pay careful attention to the formatting instructions provided below. Do not attempt to enter any amounts until you are finished formatting. Then carefully read the directions in step 8 to continue with the data entry. You may find it helpful to refer to *Figure 3* as you work through the income statement instructions.

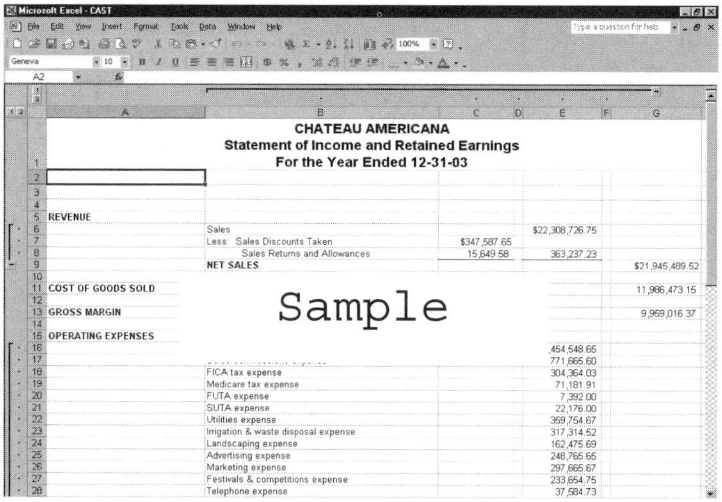

Figure 3

Requirements

1. Open the **CA_excel** file and insert a new worksheet. Format the columns for the following widths ⌘:

A	B	C	D	E	F	G
31	38	14	1	14	1	17

   Column A will contain the category headings. Column B will contain the account titles. Columns C, E and G will contain amounts. The single space columns (columns D and F) are to provide a slight space between the columns containing amounts.

   Set the row height for row 1 at 71 ⌘. It is not necessary to adjust the heights of the remaining rows.

2. Rename the newly inserted worksheet "**Income Statement**."

3. Column B will be used for individual revenue and expense account titles such as Sales, Wages and Salaries Expense, etc. Starting in row 6 of column B, enter the revenue and expense account titles listed on the **Y-E Worksheet**. (**HINT**: Be sure that you have copied and entered on the new worksheet all account titles needed to create the Statement of Income and Retained Earnings. The ordering and presentation of the account titles should be consistent with that commonly used on income statements, not that found on the **Y-E Worksheet**.)

4. Column A will be used for category headings. Beginning on row 5 in column A, enter the category heading "REVENUE." Enter the following headings in subsequent rows in column A: COST OF GOODS SOLD, GROSS MARGIN, OPERATING EXPENSES, INCOME FROM OPERATIONS, OTHER INCOME AND EXPENSES, INCOME (LOSS) BEFORE TAXES, FEDERAL INCOME TAX, NET

INCOME (LOSS), RETAINED EARNINGS - 12/31/2002, RETAINED EARNINGS - 12/31/2003, and EARNINGS PER SHARE.

5. Capitalize the main headings in column A using bold Arial 10. Use non-bold Arial 10 for the account titles in column B. Be sure to underline when appropriate using borders ⌘.

6. Column C should be used for amounts that must be added to arrive at subtotals. For example, the amounts for Sales Returns and Allowances and Sales Discounts should be placed in column C. These are combined to arrive at the amount that is subtracted from Sales to compute Net Sales, which is then presented in column G along with the other main category totals (see *Figure 3*).

7. Properly format your amounts for currency (i.e., with dollar signs, commas, decimal points, etc.) ⌘ where appropriate. REMEMBER: Decimal points are supposed to line up!

8. Create a heading ⌘ in cell **A1** as follows:

   Chateau Americana, Inc. (using bold Arial 14)
   Statement of Income and Retained Earnings (using bold Arial 12)
   For the Year ended 12/31/03 (using bold Arial 12)

   Center the heading across columns A through G.

9. Copy the appropriate amounts to the **Income Statement** bold worksheet by typing an "=," locating the appropriate cell on the **Y-E Worksheet** (**HINT**: Most of these amounts should be taken from columns M through P), and hitting **Enter**. Note, however, that Retained Earnings on the **Y-E Worksheet** has not yet been updated for the current year Net Income. Therefore, the amount in cell **N42** on the **Y-E Worksheet** represents Retained Earnings as of 12-31-02. You will have to use a formula on the **Income Statement** worksheet to calculate Retained Earnings as of 12-31-03.

10. Skip steps 11 through 13 if your instructor does not want you to calculate federal income taxes on the **Income Statement** worksheet using a nested "IF" statement.

11. You will need to calculate the amount to be entered into Federal Income Tax Expense using a nested "IF" ⌘ statement. To minimize future changes to the nested "IF" statement, insert a new worksheet and name it "**Reference Data.**" Create a heading in this worksheet for Corporate Tax Brackets and Rates. You should provide any text necessary for the bracket descriptions in column A (e.g., "Greater than or equal to," etc.), the amounts for the brackets in column B (e.g., $50,000, etc.) and the rates in column C (e.g., 15%, etc.). Creating the brackets and associated rates will take some thought on your part as they are to be used in your nested IF statement for the corporate tax

calculation to eliminate the need to recreate the formula if the brackets or rates are changed by Congress at a later date.

12. Create names ⌘ for the brackets and the rates (e.g., Bracket0, Rate0, Bracket1, Rate1, etc.)

13. Create the nested IF ⌘ statement using the cell names on the Reference Data sheet.

14. Create the following range names ⌘ for the Statement of Income and Retained Earnings:
    - Cost_Of_Goods_Sold
    - Net_Sales
    - Interest_Expense
    - NIBT (i.e., net income before tax)
    - Federal_Income_Tax
    - Net_Income

15. Use formulas to calculate subtotals and totals on the income statement.

16. Be sure to include Earnings Per Share on your income statement. There are 45,000 shares issued and outstanding.

17. Insert a new worksheet entitled "**Balance Sheet**" and create a **comparative, classified Balance Sheet** employing the same general formatting techniques and utilizing formulas as before (see *Figure 4).* Determine your column widths as you deem appropriate. Use a single column to present the various account balances for 2002 and 2003.

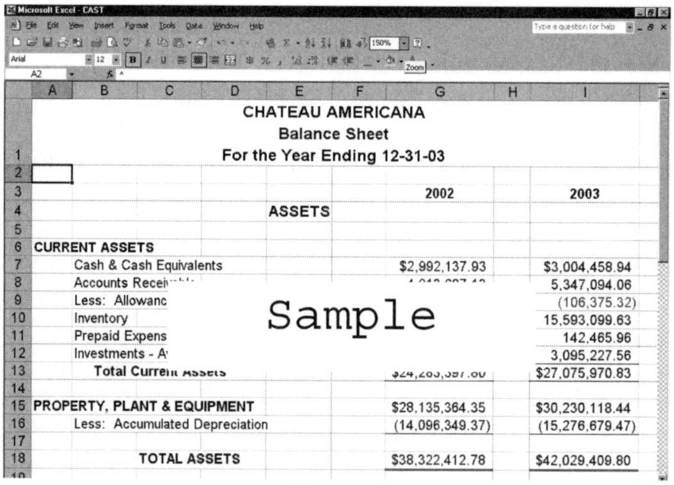

Figure 4

18. Create the following range names for the Balance Sheet:
    - Beginning_Inventory
    - Ending_Inventory
    - Current_Assets (for 2003 only)

- Beginning_Total_Assets
- Ending_Total_Assets
- Current_Liabilities (for 2003 only)
- Beginning_Stockholders_Equity
- Ending_Stockholders_Equity

Data Integrity Tutorial

Adjusting column width. Columns may be formatted using the **Format > Column > Width** menu or by adjusting the width using the cursor. Place the cursor on the line separating the heading for columns A and B on the gray bar above the cells. You will notice that the cursor turns to a cross and the column width is displayed in the box above the column separator. Drag the cursor to the desired width. Repeat for every column whose width should be changed.

Adjusting row height. Rows may be formatted using the **Format > Row > Height** menu or by adjusting the height using the cursor. Place the cursor on the line separating rows 1 and 2. You will notice that the cursor turns to a cross and the row height is displayed in the box above the row separator. Drag the cursor to the desired height. Repeat for every row whose height should be changed.

Heading. To enter a multiple line heading in one cell, type the first line. Hold down the **Alt** key and hit the **Enter** key to go on to the second line, and repeat this process for the third line. To center the heading across columns, highlight the cells in which you would like to center the heading and click on the **Merge and Center** button. Increase the font on each line to the desired size. Resize the height of the row.

Formatting numbers and currency. Click **Format > Cell**. Select **Number** and make sure the **Decimal places** box has "2" and the **Use 1000 Separator** (,) box has a check to format for commas with two decimal points or select **Currency** and make sure the **Decimal places** box has "2" and the **Symbol** box has "$" to format for currency with two decimal points.

Underlining. To underline totals and subtotals use the border Icon. After placing the cursor in the appropriate cell, pull down the border menu by placing the cursor on the arrow next to the Icon and select the dark solid line in the second row, second column.

Another way to place a border in a cell is to select the cell by clicking on it with the right mouse button to bring up the ShortCut Menu, select **Format Cells > Border > Bottom** and choose the heavy dark line under **Style**.

Cell name. When using cell names, you must use underlines ("_") rather than spaces between words. To enter a cell name, first highlight the cell or cells that you wish to name. Use only those cells that contain the numbers you want to name. It is not necessary to include the cells with the text describing those numbers. From the toolbar menu select **Insert > Name > Define** and use the appropriate cell or range name.

Data Integrity Tutorial (continued)

Entering and using formulas. A formula always begins with an "=" sign. Formulas use an operator (+ - / * > < % etc.) combined with values which can be cell references or range names. Note that the following are only examples of formulas you might need:

=Gross_Revenue-SUM(Sales_Adjustments)
=C15+C16
=$E9-$E19
=SUM(C24:C32)

Note the "**$**" in the third example above. This has the effect of holding the column **E** as an absolute reference; in other words, if this formula is moved to another place in the worksheet, it will still reference column **E** but the row number will change. If a dollar sign is placed on either side of the **E (E9)**, both the column and row reference will be absolute. Without the dollar signs, EXCEL treats cell references as relative; that is, when they are moved, the references will change relative to the new cell position.

To enter a formula in a cell:

a) Select the cell into which you want to enter the formula.
b) Type an "=" to activate the formula bar.
c) Type the formula. If you make a mistake, edit to correct it.
d) Press Enter or click on the enter box (the green checkmark) next to the formula bar.

Renaming a sheet. Double click on the Sheet tab at the bottom of the screen and enter Income Statement or other appropriate name.

Nested "IF" statement. An "IF" statement returns one of two values based on a specified logical condition. For example, if *X* is less than *Y* then return the value of 5 else return the value of 10. "IF" statements begin with the "=" sign and use comparison operators (=, >, <, >=, <=, <>) to specify the logical condition. The format for an "IF" statement is:

"=IF(**A1**<=**B1**,**C1**,**D1**)."

This "IF" statement specifies that if cell **A1** is less than or equal to cell **B1** (logical condition) then return the value in cell **C1** else return the value in cell **D1**. Note that numerical values, cell references or range names can be used in "IF" statements. A nested "IF" statement returns one of three or more values based on specified logical conditions. For example, if *X* is greater than *Y* then return the value of 10 else if *X* is greater than *Z* then return the value of 5 else return the value of 1. The format for a nested "IF" statement is:

"=IF(**A1**>=**B1**,**A2**, IF(**A1**>=**C1**,**B2**,**C2**))."

This "IF" statement specifies that if cell **A1** is greater than or equal to cell **B1** (first logical condition) then return the value in cell **A2** else if cell **A1** is greater than or equal to cell **C1** (second logical condition) then return the value in cell **B2** else return the value in cell **C2**.

DATA ANALYSIS

With the data you now have in the financial statements and with the cell names that you have created in those financial statements, it is very easy to calculate some common ratios.

Requirements

1. Open the **CA_excel** file and insert a new worksheet entitled "**Ratio Analysis.**"

2. On this new worksheet, calculate the ratios listed below by using formulas that refer to cell or range names that you have created. Do not use direct cell references (e.g., N42, G18, etc.) in these calculations.

    - Current ratio
    - Inventory turnover
    - Asset turnover
    - Return on equity
    - Debt to equity ratio
    - Times interest earned

    By using cell names only you increase the flexibility of your Excel workbook. For example, rows and columns can more easily be inserted and deleted without altering cell and range names, or formulas that refer to them.

3. Format your Ratio Analysis worksheet such that one column contains the ratio name and one column contains the ratio itself. In addition, the spreadsheet should include an appropriate heading.

INFORMATION NEEDS

Information needs vary among the users of the accounting information system and information overload is a very real problem in businesses. Spreadsheets are very flexible and have very powerful reporting capabilities. Using the spreadsheets and the financial statements you have prepared, you can easily report information to each user according to his or her needs by grouping and ungrouping data from a single spreadsheet without changing the format of the spreadsheet. For example, a company's president may only want to see the overall picture, rather than the detail of the accounts, while the vice president of sales might want to see details related to a specific product or line of products.

Spreadsheets can also be used to sort and query large bodies of data to extract only the desired information. For example, the controller may want to see a listing of only those expense accounts that exceed a certain dollar amount.

The following requirements will help you create an outline for the income statement that will let you show or hide varying levels of detail without changing the income statement format itself.

Requirements

1. Open the **CA_excel** file and click on the **Income Statement** worksheet. Highlight columns B through E.

2. Click on **Data > Group and Outline > Group**. Notice that a bar with a minus sign appears above the column letters.

3. Click on the minus sign to see what happens.

4. Highlight rows 6 through 8 and repeat the **Group** command.

5. Repeat the **Group** command for "OPERATING EXPENSES" and "OTHER INCOME AND EXPENSES" (see *Figure 5*).

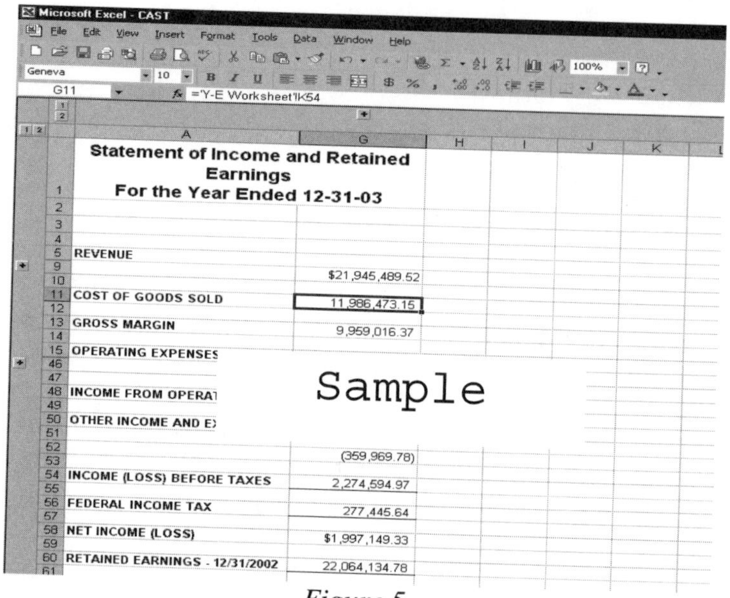

Figure 5

Now assume that the CFO has heard about your Excel skills and has asked you to help him determine which of the expense accounts for Chateau Americana, Inc. exceeded $200,000 for 2003. Filter the expense accounts to provide this information as follows:

6. Insert a new worksheet entitled "**Operating Expenses**" into the **CA_excel** file. For all operating expenses copy the account title and amount from the **Y-E Worksheet** to the new worksheet.

7. Insert a row at the top of the data and enter the column headings "**Operating Expenses**" in cell **A1** and "**Amount**" in cell **B1**.

8. Extract, or filter, all operating expenses in excess of $200,000 ⌘. Create an appropriate heading for the worksheet (see *Figure 6*).

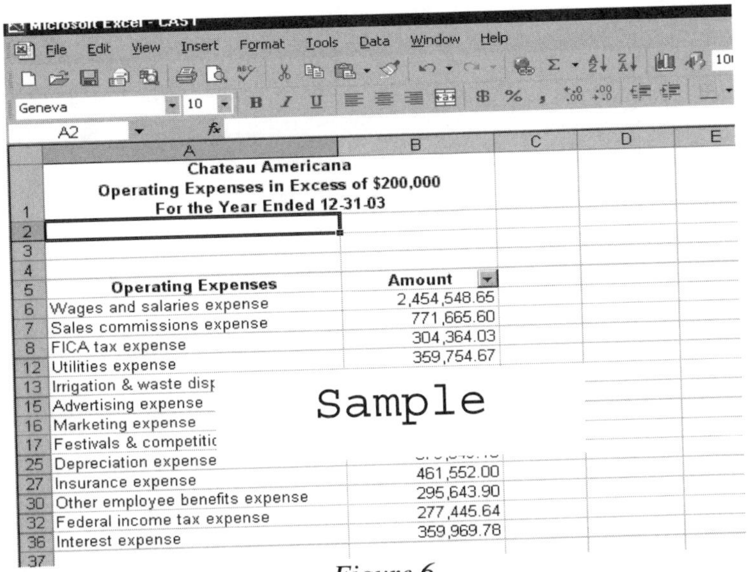

Figure 6

Information Needs Tutorial

Filtering data. Highlight the cells to be filtered including cells containing descriptions for other cells. Go to **Data > Filter > Auto Filter**. Notice that arrows for the pull-down menus appear in the top cells. Click on the arrow in the column to be filtered to obtain the appropriate pull-down menu. Select **Custom** from the pull-down menu. In the **Custom** window, click on the pull-down menu next to the box containing "equal" to select the appropriate logical condition and input the appropriate amount in the box to the right.

NOTE: You can restore the worksheet to its original format by selecting **Data > Filter** and removing the checkmark on **Auto Filter**. Therefore, it is not necessary to copy the data you are filtering to a new worksheet although it is advisable such that you are sure that you do not permanently alter the original format in any way.

DATABASE FUNCTIONS

One of the benefits of a database is the reduction or elimination of data redundancy, which in turn, reduces or eliminates data inconsistency. This is one of the reasons you have been instructed to use formulas whenever possible. **VLOOKUP** is an Excel function that queries data found on one or more worksheets and returns the query results to another worksheet, thus eliminating the need to reenter the data.

Requirements

1. Open the **CA_excel** file and insert a new worksheet. Name the new worksheet "**Payroll Master File.**"

2. On a blank the Payroll Master File, build a payroll rate table (beginning in cell **A1**) with the following headings: **ID**, **EMPLOYEE NAME**, **PAY TYPE**, **PAY RATE**, and **FIT W/H** (i.e., the amount of federal income tax to be withheld).

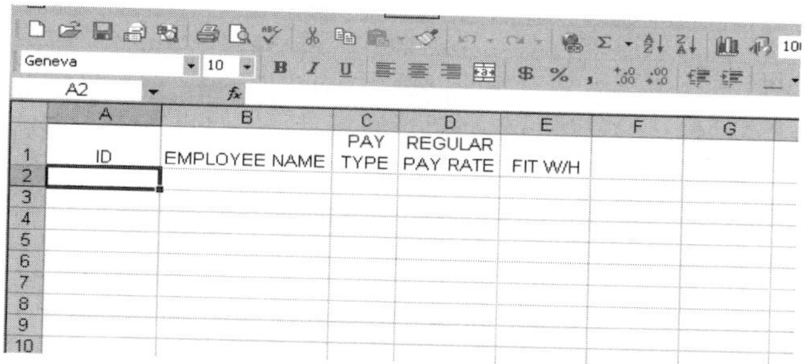

Figure 7

3. Use the following information to enter the data in the **Payroll Master File** worksheet:

Employee Name	Social Security Number	Pay Type	Regular Pay Rate	Filing Status	FIT W/H Allowance
Rodriguez, José G.	124-11-7755	Salaried	2550.00	Married	4
Johnson, Anna C.	296-49-3438	Salaried	1750.00	Married	3
Hissom, Robert T.	349-43-6417	Hourly	14.25	Single	0
Bryan, Thomas P.	014-39-4215	Hourly	15.00	Single	1

NOTE: The employee ID is the employee's social security number. The pay type is "S" for salaried employees or "H" for hourly employees. The FIT withholding should be the amount of federal income tax withheld for the pay period ending December 31, 2003. If you have not already completed the *Manual AIS Module*, you will need to determine the proper amount of federal income tax withheld for each employee by using the Wage Bracket Tables. This information can be found in IRS Publication 15.

4. The **Payroll Master File** worksheet will be used as a database for the **Payroll Journal** worksheet provided for you in the **CA_excel** file. To accomplish this, you must designate an array for the database (i.e., create a range name). To do this, highlight cells **A2:E5** and designate the range name (i.e., array) as **PAYROLL_MASTER**.

5. For each employee in the payroll subsidiary ledgers, enter the payroll pay date (December 31, 2003) and employee ID in cells **A3** through **B6** on the **Payroll Journal** worksheet.

   NOTE: The **Payroll Journal** worksheet has already been created and formatted, but does not contain any data, formulas, or functions. However, the worksheet does contain various range names which you must use in creating the required formulas and functions.

6. Use the **VLOOKUP** function ⌘ in cells **C3** and **D3** in the **Payroll Journal** worksheet to return the employee's name and pay type to these cells.

   NOTE: The **Payroll Journal** worksheet requires no entry for salaried employees in columns **E** or **H**. However, entries for the regular and overtime hours worked will be required later when entering the data for hourly employees.

7. Use the **VLOOKUP** function to return the pay rate in cell **F3** in the **Payroll Journal** worksheet.

8. In the **Payroll Journal** worksheet, create formulas to calculate the regular pay and overtime pay for cells **G3** and **I3**, respectively. **HINT:** These formulas must contain an **IF** statement based upon the time unit that accommodates salaried employees who do not have entries for number of hours worked.

9. In the **Payroll Journal** worksheet, create formulas in cells **J3** and **K3** to calculate gross pay and FICA, respectively.

10. Use the **VLOOKUP** function in cell **L3** in the **Payroll Journal** worksheet to return the amount of federal income tax to be withheld.

11. In the **Payroll Journal** worksheet, create a formula in cell **M3** to calculate net pay and enter the appropriate check number in cell **N3** beginning with check number **7111**.

12. For internal control purposes, a formula should also be created in cell **N4** in the **Payroll Journal** worksheet as a sequential number check for the check number (i.e., "=**N3** +1").

13. To facilitate the entry of payroll data for any other employees, you will need to copy the formulas and functions you created. For this assignment, you only need to copy them into the next 3 rows.

Database Functions Tutorial

VLOOKUP function. The VLOOKUP function in EXCEL searches a previously defined database (i.e., array designated by an appropriate range name) for a specified value and returns a desired field (i.e., a data value) from that database. The syntax for the VLOOKUP function is

=VLOOKUP(lookup_value,table_array,col_index_num,range_lookup)

where

lookup_value names the value to be matched in the database. The **lookup_value** is typically a value that is unique to each row of data. For example, in a customer database, the **lookup_value** might be the Customer ID number. Therefore, in an employee database, the **lookup_value** would be the Employee ID number.

table_array provides the name of the database that stores the data you want to bring into the current worksheet.

col_index_num specifies the column number in the database in which the desired data value is located (NOTE: you must count the columns beginning with A=1, etc., and enter the appropriate column number).

range_lookup is a logical value specifying whether or not you want an exact match; FALSE indicates an exact match is desired; TRUE indicates that an approximate match may be returned.

INTRODUCTION TO PIVOTTABLES

You have been asked to prepare Chateau Americana's budget for next year. You should create the budget in a way that takes advantage of Excel's ability to simplify data analysis. You decide to utilize a PivotTable to assist in this effort.

A PivotTable is an interactive table that enables you to quickly sift through and summarize large amounts of data. You can rotate rows and columns to see different summaries of the source data, filter the data by displaying different pages, or display details for certain areas of interest.

Before creating a PivotTable, you must prepare the data source. An excerpt from the Chateau Americana budget has been provided for you. You will find it on the "**Master Budget**" worksheet contained in the CA_excel file. Certain assumptions have been made and constraints have been imposed to facilitate your handling of the budget and the PivotTable, as detailed below.

The budget contains data for the first 6 months and contains only selected accounts. For purposes of this assignment, only three departments have been selected and the number of employees per department has been limited, as follows:

Administration (Edward and Rob)
Marketing (Taylor, Daniel and Cameron)
Operations (Jacques and Paul)

Review the **Master Budget** worksheet. Notice that the worksheet has the following headings: **ACCT_TYPE**, **ACCT_CODE**, **ACCT_TITLE**, **DEPT**, **COST_CENTER**, **YR**, **MON**, **BUDGET**, **EXPLANATIONS**. These represent the fields that you will use to create the PivotTable.

Requirements

1. Open the **CA_excel** file and click on the **Master Budget** worksheet. Be sure that the cursor is placed somewhere in the data on the worksheet. From the main menu at the top of the screen, select **Data > PivotTable and PivotChart Report**. The PivotTable Wizard, Step 1 of 3 screen appears (see *Figure 8*). Be sure that the radio buttons for "Microsoft Excel list or database" and for "PivotTable" are selected. Click on **Next**.

2. Step 2 of 3: Be sure that the entire master budget has been selected (the range should be **A1** to **I151**). Click on **Next**.

3. Step 3 of 3: Be sure that the radio button for "New worksheet" is selected. Click on **Finish**.

Figure 8

4. Notice that Excel has generated (and moved you to) a new worksheet to create the PivotTable. You should see a **Drop** table and a **PivotTable Field List** that contains the column headings from your **Master Budget** spreadsheet (see *Figure 9*).

   Drag these headings into the box as follows:

   > **ACCT_CODE** into the **Drop Row Fields Here** area.
   >
   > **BUDGET** into the **Drop Data Items Here** area. (**NOTE:** The tab above **ACCT_CODE** should now say "**Sum of BUDGET**" rather than **BUDGET**. A list of general ledger codes should appear with a total beside it. The total at the bottom of the sheet should be $2,266,066. Excel has now generated a PivotTable that summarized the master budget by GL code.

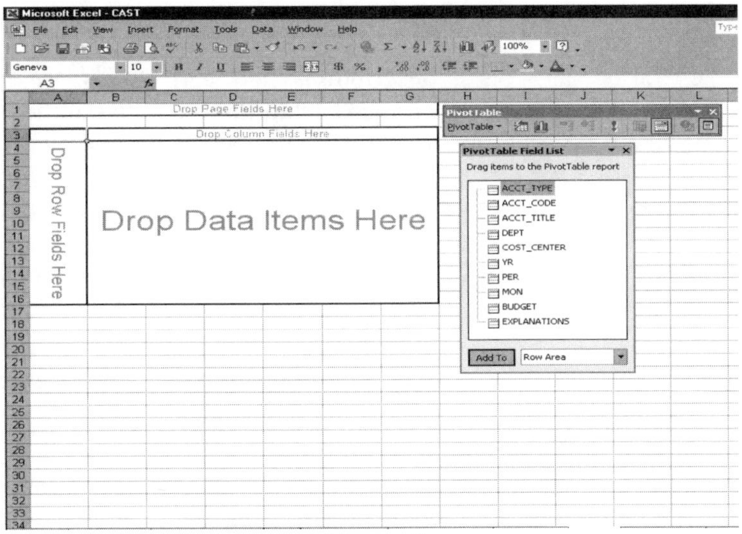

Figure 9

5. Notice that the **Master Budget** worksheet is still intact. Now rename the new worksheet "**Pivot**".

6. General ledger codes do not provide much information without the account titles. To add the general ledger account titles, right click anywhere within the PivotTable that you just created to access the short-cut menu.

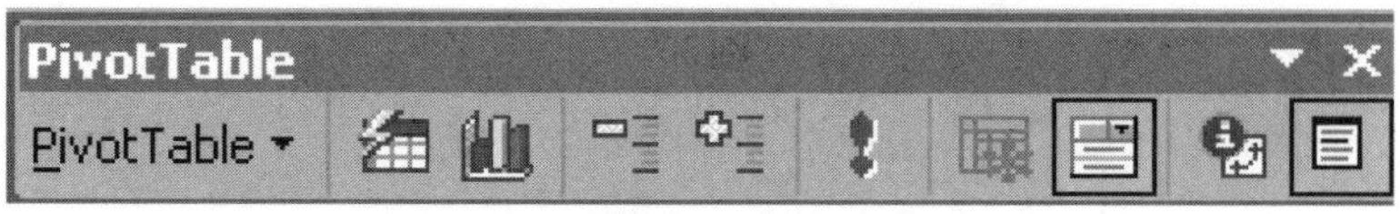

Figure 10

In the **PivotTable** short-cut menu, click on the **PivotTable** pull-down menu. From this menu, select **Wizard**. A window containing Step 3 of 3 of the Wizard should appear. Click on **Layout**. The **Column-Row-Data** box re-appears (see *Figure 11*).

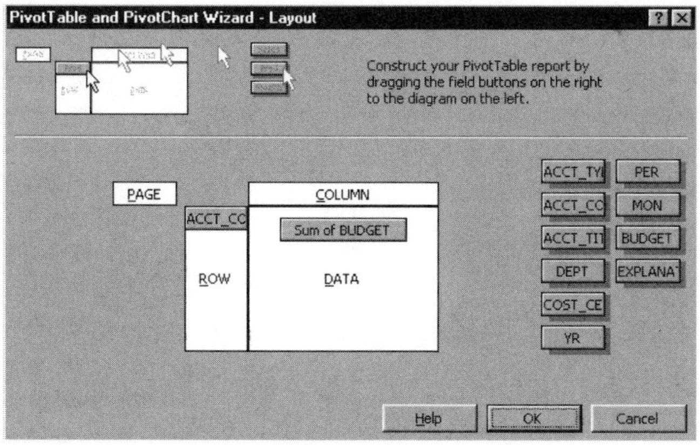

Figure 11

7. Drag and drop **ACCT_TITLE** below **ACCT_CODE** in the **Row** area. Then click **OK** and click on **Finish.**

8. The general ledger codes, descriptions and their totals are now in the PivotTable. This contains much more detail than we need in the budget. For example, the total lines are repetitious and should be removed. To do this, right click on the **ACCT_CODE** field button (this should be in Cell **A4**) to access the short-cut menu. Select **Field Settings** to pull up the **PivotTable Field** window. In the **Subtotals** area on the left, click on the radio button for **None.** This should deselect the **Automatic** button. Click on **OK** and the subtotals disappear.

9. Left justify the GL account codes by highlighting column **A** (left click on the **A** at the top of the column) and clicking the **Align Left** icon.

10. To provide managers with more detailed budget information, the period should be added to the PivotTable. Right click anywhere within the

PivotTable. Select **Wizard**. Click on **Layout**. The **Column-Row-Data** box re-appears. Drop **MON** into the **Column** area. Then click **OK** and click on **Finish**. The PivotTable should now break down the GL account totals by month.

11. Pull up the **Column-Row-Data** box again. Drag and drop **ACCT_TYPE** above **ACCT_CODE** (the **Row** area now contains **ACCT_TYPE**, **ACCT_CODE** and **ACCT_TITLE**). Click **OK** and click on **Finish**. The PivotTable should now be divided into "**601 – Salaries**", "**602 – Payroll Taxes**," "**610 – Occupancy**," etc, each with a total.

12. The PivotTable allows you to easily compare values in the same category or field through the use of structured selection by highlighting each of the total lines. To see how this works, go to cell **B6** and right click in that cell. Click on **Select – Enable Selection** (see *Figure 12*).

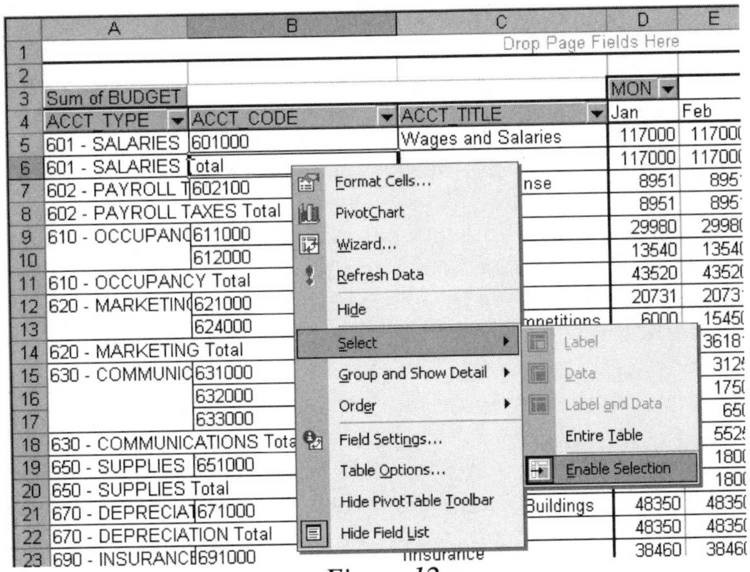

Figure 12

13. Then click on the yellow "**Fill Color**" icon. Now click anywhere on the table. The "**Total**" lines are now shaded yellow (see *Figure 13*).

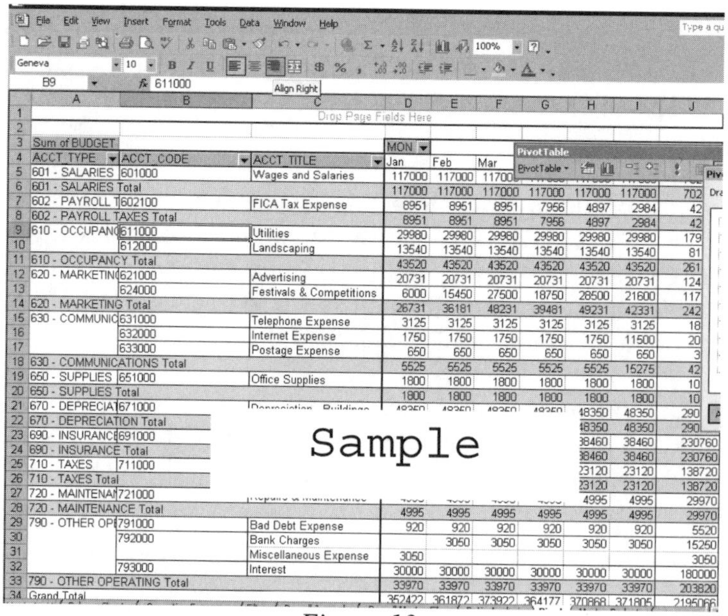

	ACCT_TYPE	ACCT_CODE	ACCT_TITLE	Jan	Feb	Mar				
5	601 - SALARIES	601000	Wages and Salaries	117000	117000	11700[illegible]	[illegible]	[illegible]	[illegible]	[illegible]
6	601 - SALARIES Total			117000	117000	117000	117000	117000	117000	702
7	602 - PAYROLL T	602100	FICA Tax Expense	8951	8951	8951	7956	4897	2984	42
8	602 - PAYROLL TAXES Total			8951	8951	8951	7956	4897	2984	42
9	610 - OCCUPANC	611000	Utilities	29980	29980	29980	29980	29980	29980	179
10		612000	Landscaping	13540	13540	13540	13540	13540	13540	81
11	610 - OCCUPANCY Total			43520	43520	43520	43520	43520	43520	261
12	620 - MARKETIN	621000	Advertising	20731	20731	20731	20731	20731	20731	124
13		624000	Festivals & Competitions	6000	15450	27500	18750	28500	21600	117
14	620 - MARKETING Total			26731	36181	48231	39481	49231	42331	242
15	630 - COMMUNIC	631000	Telephone Expense	3125	3125	3125	3125	3125	3125	18
16		632000	Internet Expense	1750	1750	1750	1750	1750	11500	20
17		633000	Postage Expense	650	650	650	650	650	650	3
18	630 - COMMUNICATIONS Total			5525	5525	5525	5525	5525	15275	42
19	650 - SUPPLIES	651000	Office Supplies	1800	1800	1800	1800	1800	1800	10
20	650 - SUPPLIES Total			1800	1800	1800	1800	1800	1800	10
21	670 - DEPRECIAT	671000	[illegible]	[illegible]	[illegible]	[illegible]	[illegible]	48350	48350	290
22	670 - DEPRECIATION Total							48350	48350	290
23	690 - INSURANCE	691000						38460	38460	230760
24	690 - INSURANCE Total							38460	38460	230760
25	710 - TAXES	711000						23120	23120	138720
26	710 - TAXES Total							23120	23120	138720
27	720 - MAINTENAN	721000	[illegible]	[illegible]	[illegible]	[illegible]	[illegible]	4995	4995	29970
28	720 - MAINTENANCE Total			4995	4995	4995	4995	4995	4995	29970
29	790 - OTHER OP	791000	Bad Debt Expense	920	920	920	920	920	920	5520
30		792000	Bank Charges		3050	3050	3050	3050	3050	15250
31			Miscellaneous Expense	3050						3050
32		793000	Interest	30000	30000	30000	30000	30000	30000	180000
33	790 - OTHER OPERATING Total			33970	33970	33970	33970	33970	33970	203820
34	Grand Total			352422	361872	373922	364177	370868	371805	2195066

Figure 13

DETAIL IN REPORTING

The PivotTable allows the user to query or "drilldown" into a particular value in the PivotTable report to examine that item more closely. This provides a great deal of power and flexibility to the PivotTable report, whether the report is for budgeting applications, reporting monthly costs to department managers, or for reporting the results of sales to territory managers. The user can query a balance to view any of the underlying detail by simply double clicking on the entry in question.

The CFO has asked you to identify any unusual items in the budgeted amounts and report them to him. A quick review of the budget reveals two months under **Festivals and Competitions** and one month under **Internet and Computer** that appear to have unusual amounts of expenditures.

Requirements

1. Open the **CA_excel** file and click on the **Pivot** worksheet. To determine what has caused this spike in costs, query one of the amounts in question by double clicking on grand total amount. A new worksheet appears that provides detail for the amount in question (see *Figure 14*).

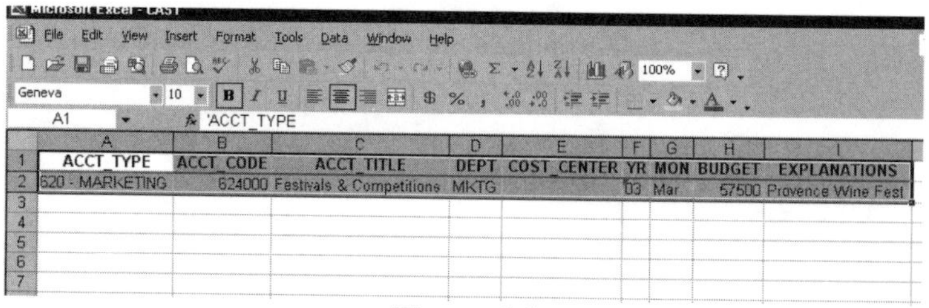

ACCT_TYPE	ACCT_CODE	ACCT_TITLE	DEPT	COST_CENTER	YR	MON	BUDGET	EXPLANATIONS
620 - MARKETING	624000	Festivals & Competitions	MKTG		03	Mar	57500	Provence Wine Fest

Figure 14

2. Return to the **Pivot** worksheet. Examine the amounts in the other questioned account. Double click on the grand total amount to investigate the cause.

   Return to the **Pivot** worksheet again. You may also want to limit other users' abilities to drilldown into the data. This is done by right-clicking anywhere in the PivotTable report, selecting **Table Options** from the shortcut menu, and deselecting the **Enable drill to details** box.

3. As you've seen, the PivotTable can be used to display only the data of interest. You might, for example, want to view the data for a particular department rather than for all departments or view data by cost centers. Either of these views can be obtained by dropping a particular field of interest in the **Column** area of the PivotTable or by filtering the entire PivotTable report to display data for a single item or all the items, using the **Page** field.

   Access the **Column-Row-Data** box again. Remove **MON** from **Column** by dropping it anywhere outside the box. Drag and drop **DEPT** into the **Column** area. Click **OK** and click on **Finish**. Notice that the departmental totals for the Administrative, Marketing, and Operations departments now appear.

4. You can also view the data by department and month by using the "**Page**" fields. Open the **COLUMN-ROW-DATA** box again. Drag **DEPT** to the **Page** area and drop it. Drag and drop **MON** back into the **Column** area. Click **OK** and click on **Finish**. Notice that the data is now broken down by period again. Notice also that cell **A1** now contains a grey box entitled "**DEPT**" and cell **B1** says, "**All**" and has a pull-down menu. **DEPT** is now a **Page** field. It allows the user to see the information for the entire organization or by department (see *Figure 15*).

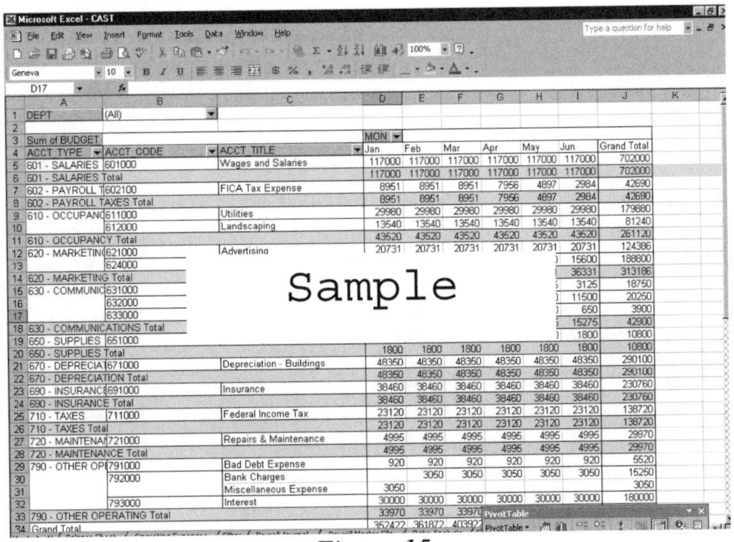

Figure 15

5. Click on the down arrow in the right of cell **B1** and notice that the choices **ADMIN**, **MKTG**, and **OPS** appear. Click on **ADMIN**. The PivotTable now

shows the costs for the Administrative department. You can click on the pull-down arrow again to look at the budgets for the Marketing department and for Operations. Note that the **(All)** option allows you to view the company totals.

6. View the **ADMIN** data again. This data can broken down further into individual cost centers. To do this, access the **Column-Row-Data** box again. Drag and drop **COST_CENTER** below **ACCT_TITLE** and remove the subtotals. The PivotTable is now broken down further to show the costs attributed to the individual cost centers in the Administrative department (i.e., Rob and Edward). Some of the cells in the **COST_CENTER** column contain "**(blank)**." This indicates that the costs for these accounts were not allocated to individual cost centers within the Administrative department, but were allocated instead to the entire Administrative department.

7. As more data is included in a worksheet, the threat of *information overload* or *analysis paralysis* increases. In addition, as more data is included, the PivotTable will likely require more levels to facilitate analysis of the data. However, increasing levels also increases complexity making data analysis more difficult. To address the issue of complexity, the PivotTable can be expanded or collapsed between different levels of detail using the **Hide Detail** and **Show Detail** commands. Click on cell **B1** and select **(All)**. The entire budget is now displayed. Right click on **A4**, **ACCT_TYPE**. Select **Group and Show Detail - Hide Detail** from the short-cut menu. Only the top level data (i.e., the account types) should now be visible (see *Figure 16*).

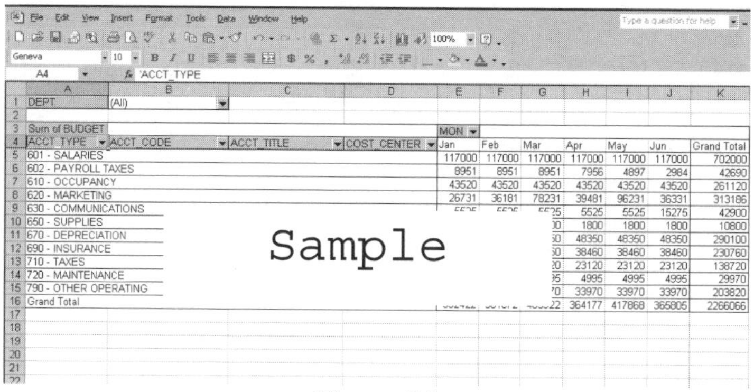

Figure 16

8. The detail can then be expanded for one or more account types. However, before you can access the detail you will need to re-enable the drilldown option that you previously deselected in step 3 above. Show the detail for the costs associated with Communications by double clicking on the "630 – Communications" title in column **A**. The Communications detail is now shown down to the **COST_CENTER** level (see *Figure 17*).

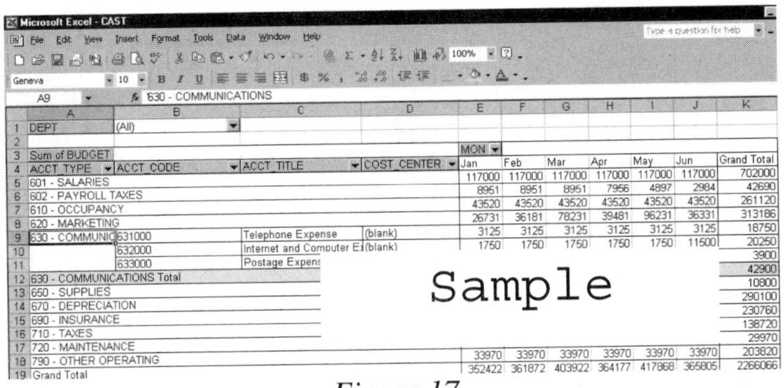

Figure 17

9. To return to the more concise view, double click in the space below the "630 – Communications" title.

10. Return the entire PivotTable to its full detail again by right clicking **ACCT_TYPE**. From the short-cut menu, select **Group and Show Detail - Show Detail**.

11. It is also sometimes desirable to focus on certain periods in a budget. The PivotTable enables you to hide the detail for some periods while leaving the detail for others showing and simultaneously recalculate the cumulative totals to show totals for just the periods of interest. Look at the data for the second quarter only by left clicking on the **MON** title. Uncheck January, February and March and click **OK**. The PivotTable now contains the data only for April, May and June and the cumulative totals for each **ACCT_CODE** have been recalculated to include only the amounts from the second quarter months (see *Figure 18*).

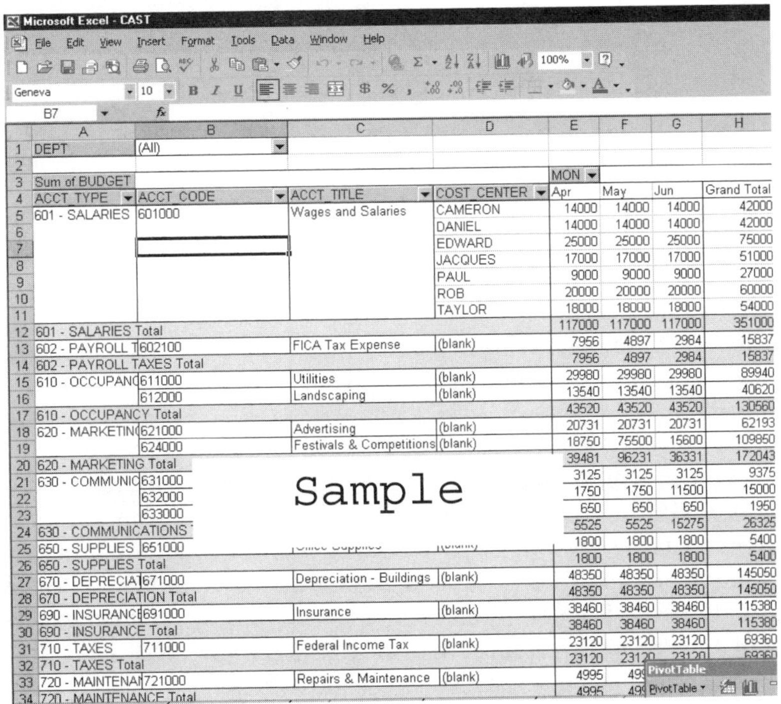

Figure 18

12. Unhide the first quarter months by left clicking on **MON** and reselecting January, February and March and click on **OK**.

FLEXIBLE BUDGETING USING PIVOTTABLES

Flexible budgets are an important tool in accounting. PivotTables facilitate flexible budgeting. It is very easy to make changes, the results appear immediately, and any formulas that are affected are automatically updated. To see how revisions work, perform the following independent steps.

1. Open the **CA_excel** file and click on the **Pivot** worksheet.

2. After the budget was established, it was decided that Daniel would transfer from Marketing to Administration as of March 1. At that time, his salary will increase by $1,000. To adjust the budget for this change, click onto the **Master Budget** worksheet. Since the **ACCT_CODE** filter is still on, click the pull-down menu in that column and select **(All)** to show all the records. Now click on the **Cost Center** pull-down menu and select Daniel. Six records for Daniel should appear. Change Daniel's department for the appropriate periods and increase his salary for those periods (see *Figure 19*).

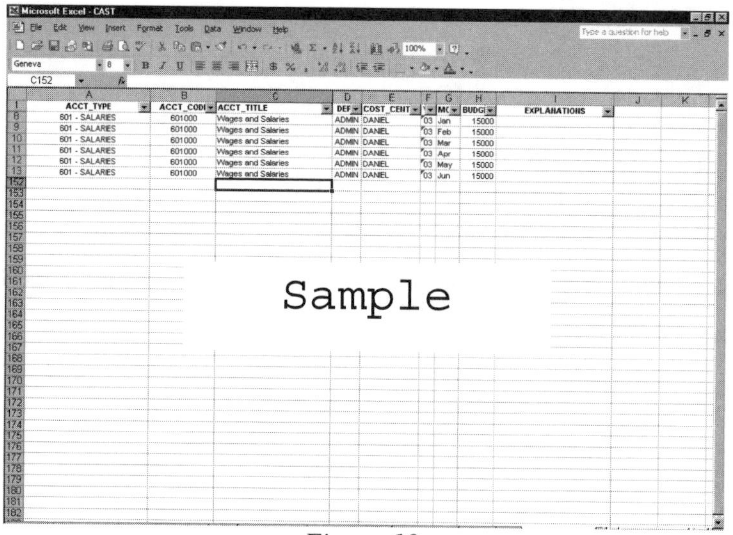

Figure 19

3. Go to the **Pivot** worksheet. Notice that Daniel's salary has not changed. Right click anywhere on the worksheet and click on **Refresh Data** (see *Figure 20*).

4. Go back to the **Master Budget** worksheet. Turn off the **Autofilter** by selecting **Data - Filter - Autofilter** from the menu and clicking on **Autofilter** to deselect it. Insert a new column before the **EXPLANATIONS** column. Copy the **BUDGET** values into the new column **I** by selecting the entire **BUDGET** column and copying and pasting it to the new column. Change the column heading **BUDGET** to **REV_BUDGET**. You should now have the original and revised budgets side by side.

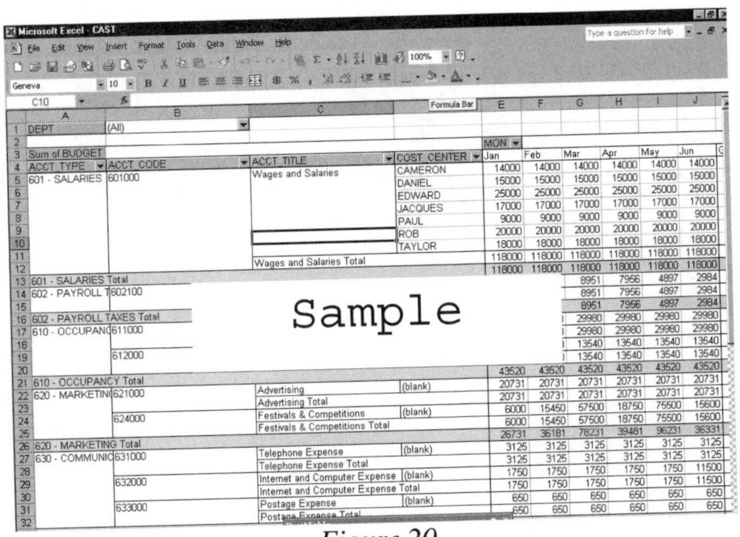

Figure 20

5. Turn on the **Autofilter** again. Select Cameron and update her salary to reflect a $1,000 raise in the **REV_BUDGET** column for June. Click onto the **Pivot** worksheet. Right click on the PivotTable, and select **Refresh Data** from the short-cut menu.

6. Note what happens. Nothing happens because the PivotTable was set up to display the sum of **BUDGET**. Now access the **Column-Row-Data** box and drag and drop **REV_BUDGET** below **BUDGET** in the **Data** area. Click on **OK** and then click on **Finish**. The PivotTable should now display both the original and the revised budget. After comparing the revised budget numbers to the original budget numbers access the **Column-Row-Data** window and remove the **BUDGET** numbers from **Data**.

7. Once the first budget has been created using PivotTables, it can be used to produce others very quickly. In the **PivotTable** worksheet, show all departments. In the **PivotTable** short-cut menu**,** click on the **PivotTable** pull-down menu. From this menu, select **Show Pages** and click **OK**. The three departmental budget PivotTables (one for **ADMIN**, one for **MKTG** and one for **OPS**) were created as three new worksheets in your workbook. Open the **ADMIN** worksheet. You will notice that columns **A** and **C** need to be widened in this and the other two new worksheets. Adjust these two columns to the appropriate width.

   You can widen the columns for all of these new worksheets at one time. To do this, depress the **Shift** key and highlight the departmental sheets by clicking on the **Pivot** worksheet *OR* hold down the **CTRL** key and select each of the departmental sheets individually. Widen columns **A** and **C** by highlighting the columns and selecting **Format - Column - AutoFit Selection**.

8. You have now completed the Excel assignment. Save your work. Your instructor will provide you with the appropriate file naming convention.

EXCEL GENERAL TUTORIAL

The following information provides the novice Excel user with some basic terminology utilized by Excel. If you have not used Excel previously, you should take the time to read through this information.

Excel Workbook

Each Excel file is called a "workbook". Each workbook contains several worksheets. Each of these sheets can be accessed (i.e., you can switch back and forth between them) by clicking on the tabs at the bottom of the Excel window (e.g., switch from "Sheet 1" to "Sheet 2"). Each of these sheets can also be renamed by double-clicking on the appropriate sheet tab.

Help

In addition to the information provided in this assignment, Excel has an excellent Help facility which allows you to learn more about a variety of topics, to see demonstrations on the topic, and to facilitate a transition to Excel for Lotus users. The Help facility also allows you to keep the information on top of the worksheet as you attempt to apply its information to your application (click on the "**On Top**" button in the Help window). Help may be accessed by using the **Menu Bar** or by clicking on the **Help** icon.

Menu Bar

The menu bar contains pull-down menus for all Excel commands. Examine the commands which are located in the pull-down menus under the following broad categories:

File
Edit
View
Insert
Format
Tools
Data
Window
Help

Moving Around a Worksheet

You can move around a worksheet by selecting a cell using the cursor (i.e., pointing at a new cell) or using the arrow keys until you have arrived at the desired cell. You can also use the **Menu Bar** (i.e., **Edit** - **Go To**) and type in the desired cell address.

Entering Data

Data is entered in a cell by selecting the cell itself, typing the desired data, and (1) hitting the "**Enter**" key or (2) clicking on the enter box (a green "➽ " located on the edit bar). You may change your mind about the data you have entered by hitting the "**Escape**" key prior to (1) or (2) above.

Editing Data

Previously entered data may be edited by accessing the edit bar. This may be done by selecting the desired cell, hitting the "**F2**" key, using the arrow keys or the cursor to arrive at the point in the cell which needs to be edited and making the changes, and hitting the "**Enter**" key or the enter box. Alternatively, editing may be done by double-clicking on the desired cell to bring up the edit line, using the cursor to arrive at the point of insertion, and proceeding as above. You may exit the edit mode without making any changes by hitting the "**Escape**" key.

Moving Data

Data can be moved by copying it from one cell to another or by cutting it out of one cell and pasting it in a new cell.

Copying data - Data can be copied by selecting the desired cell or cells and (1) using the **Menu Bar** (i.e., **Edit** - **Copy**); (2) clicking on the right mouse button to bring down the shortcut menu and selecting "**Copy**"; or (3) if you are copying the data to an adjacent cell, you can use the "**Fill Handle**" and drag the cursor to the adjacent cell.

Moving data - Data can be moved by selecting the desired cell or cells and (1) using the **Menu Bar** (i.e., **Edit** - **Cut**), moving to the new desired cell and accessing the **Menu Bar** again (i.e., **Edit** - **Paste**); (2) clicking on the right mouse button to bring down the shortcut menu and selecting "**Cut**" and then repeating the process at the new desired cell and selecting "**Paste**"; and (3) positioning the pointer over the border of the selected cell or cells and dragging the border to the new location.

Selecting Multiple Cells

You may wish to have your commands apply to more than one cell. Multiple cells may be selected in several ways.

Highlighting a range of cells - Position your cursor in the cell in the upper left hand corner of the range of cells you wish to manipulate and drag it down to the lower right hand corner of the range. Then apply whatever command you wish for that range of cells.

Highlighting a column or a row - You may apply your command to an entire column or row by positioning the cursor on the column or row header and clicking on the letter or number (you will notice that the entire column/row is then highlighted).

Arithmetic Operations on Data Cells

You may add, subtract, multiply, or divide the data in two or more cells by selecting an empty cell and typing an "=" sign, clicking on the first cell you want to be included in the arithmetic formula, selecting the operation's sign (i.e., +, -, *, /), clicking on the second cell to be included, followed by another operation sign if applicable, etc.

You may also use the SUM function to add a group of cells together and use that total in an arithmetic operation (e.g., =SUM(A1:A5)/A7).

NOTE: Excel utilizes the normal order of arithmetic procedures; i.e., multiplication and division operations take precedence over addition and subtraction operations. For example, let's look at possible answers for combinations of operations for the following information:

A1 = 5
A2 = 3
A3 = 15
A4 = 17
A5 = 20
A7 = 4

If your formula reads:	Excel's answer is:
= A1+A2+A3+A4+A5/A7	45
= (A1+A2+A3+A4+A5)/A7	15
=SUM(A1:A5)/A7	15

Other Helpful Information

Row/Column Insertion and deletion - To insert or delete an entire row or column, click on that row's/column's header (i.e., row number/column letter) using the right mouse button and select **Insert** or **Delete**.

Erasing the contents of a cell - Click on the desired cell(s) and hit the **Delete** key.

GENERAL LEDGER APPLICATIONS USING *PEACHTREE COMPLETE ACCOUNTING 2004®*: The Winery At Chateau Americana

LEARNING OBJECTIVES

After completing and discussing this assignment, you should be able to:

- Recognize the managerial and technological issues associated with the implementation of a general ledger package
- Complete sample transactions
- Understand the implications of the design of the user interface
- Recognize and evaluate the strengths and weaknesses of controls embedded in a general ledger package
- Compare and contrast a general ledger package with a manual accounting information system

BACKGROUND

As the winery has grown, Rob Breeden, the chief financial officer, has realized that management does not have timely information about the financial condition of the company. This has resulted in several instances in which the decisions made were not optimal. Therefore, he has determined that it is time to convert the current system to a general ledger package. After investigating the possibilities, he has decided to utilize *Peachtree Complete Accounting 2004®*. Chateau Americana has hired you to convert the system.

REQUIREMENTS

Using the *Peachtree Complete Accounting 2004®* software program contained in your *CAST* package or in your school computer lab, you are to convert Chateau Americana from a manual system to a general ledger software package. If you are working on this assignment on your home computer, load the software following the instructions contained on the CD envelope.

As with any other computer file, it is important to **back up frequently** to another storage medium.

SETTING UP A NEW COMPANY

Requirements

1. Start *Peachtree Complete Accounting 2004®* and click on **Set up a new company**.

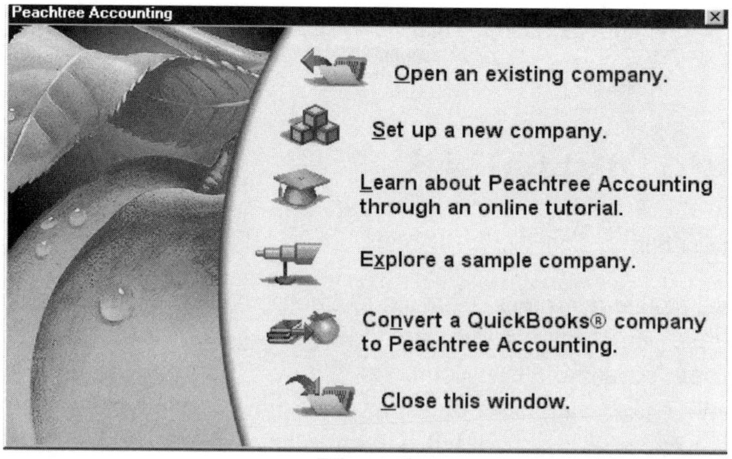

Figure 1

2. The Welcome screen that appears next alerts the user to information that will be required throughout the set-up procedure. Click on **Next**.

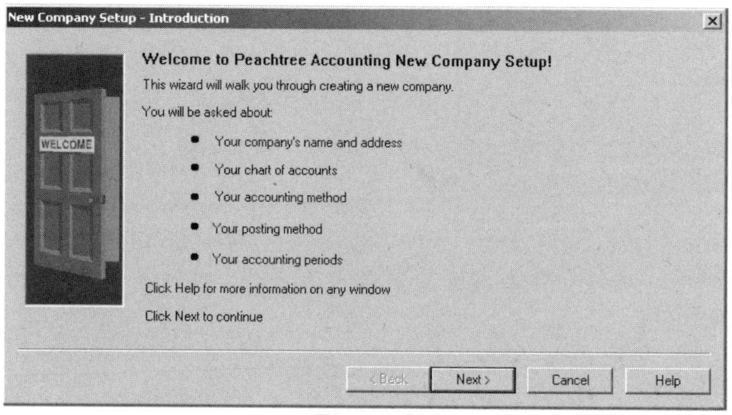

Figure 2

3. Enter the following company information and then click on **Next:**

.

The Winery at Chateau Americana, Inc.
3003 Vineyard Way
Huntington, CA 95394
Phone: (707) 368-8485
Fax: (707) 368-8486

Do not enter any information in the remaining input boxes.

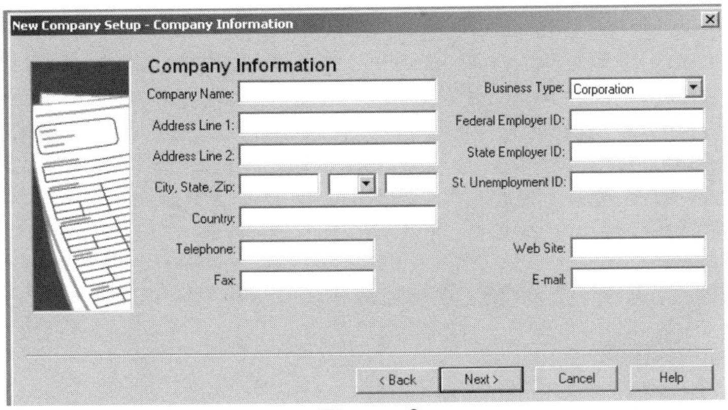

Figure 3

4. You are now asked to select an option for setting up the Chart of Accounts. Peachtree provides you with sample charts of accounts in the event that you are setting up a start-up company. Because Chateau Americana already has a Chart of Accounts select **Build your own company** and click on **Next**.

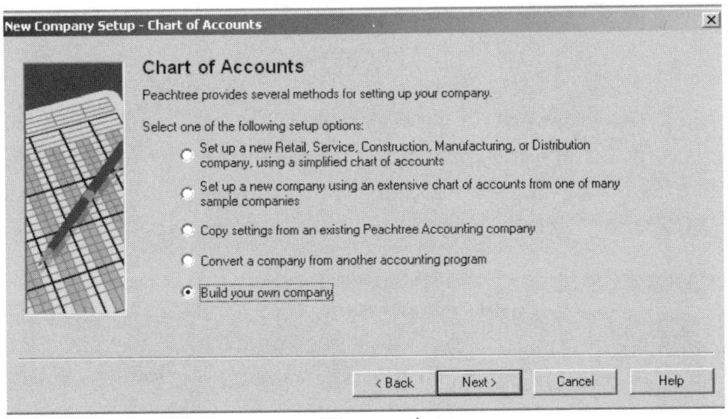

Figure 4

5. The next screen provides options for the company's accounting method. If you examine the Chart of Accounts you will notice various accounts that provide evidence that Chateau Americana utilizes the accrual method of accounting. Therefore, just click on **Next**.

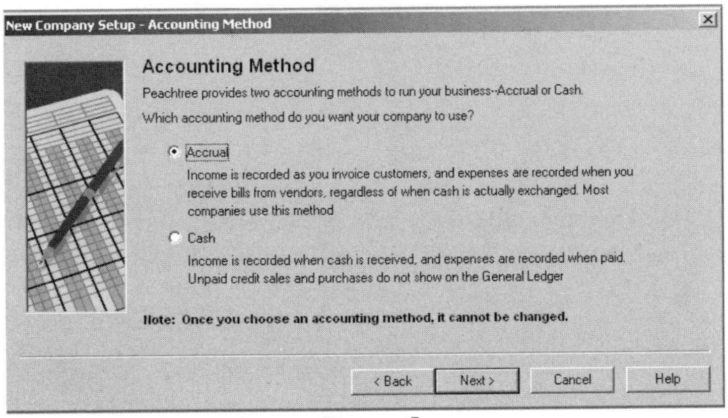

Figure 5

6. Peachtree offers two posting methods. In Real Time mode, each transaction is posted as it is written and the General Ledger is always up to date. In Batch mode, transactions are posted in batches or groups, resulting in processing efficiencies but delaying the updating of the General Ledger. Since one of Rob Breeden's concerns is that of timely information, select the **Real Time** posting method and click on **Next**.

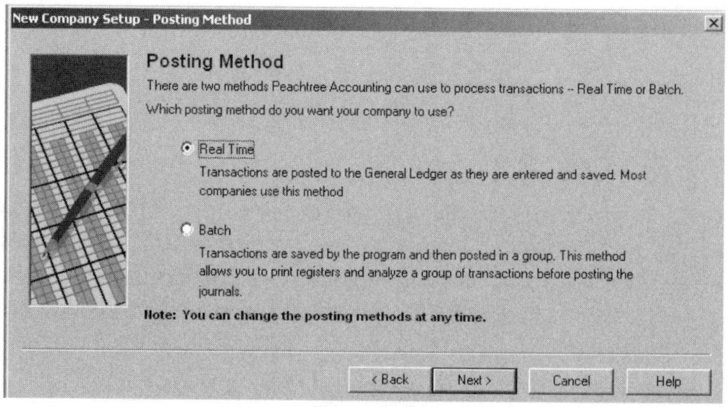

Figure 6

7. The next two screens address the company's accounting period. The first asks you to select the number of accounting periods within a year. The company's fiscal year is a calendar year with 12-monthly accounting periods. Make sure the correct accounting period is selected and click on **Next**.

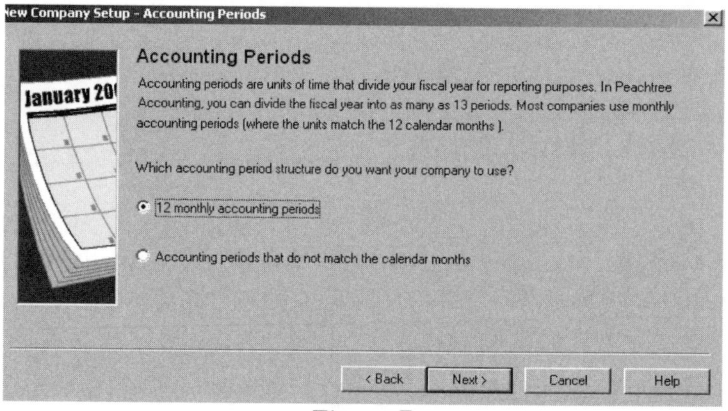

Figure 7

8. Now you are prompted to provide the month and year that the fiscal year begins (i.e., January 2003) and for the first month in which data will be entered. You have been given the general ledger balances as of December 15, 2003. Therefore, the first data will be entered as of December 2003 and payroll will begin as of 2003. Make sure the correct information is input and click on **Next**.

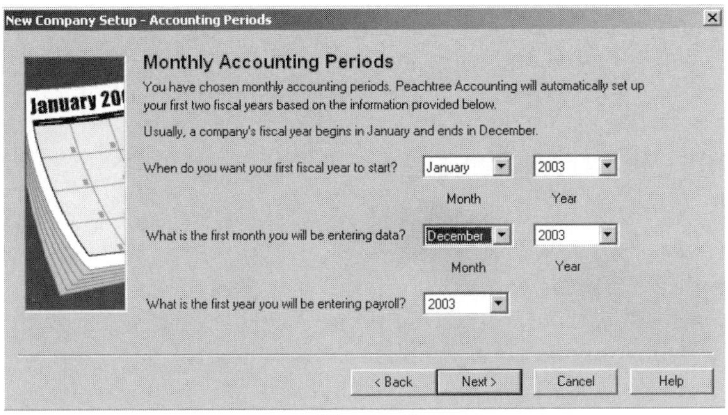

Figure 8

9. You have now completed the set-up procedures for converting Chateau Americana to Peachtree. Click on **Finish**.

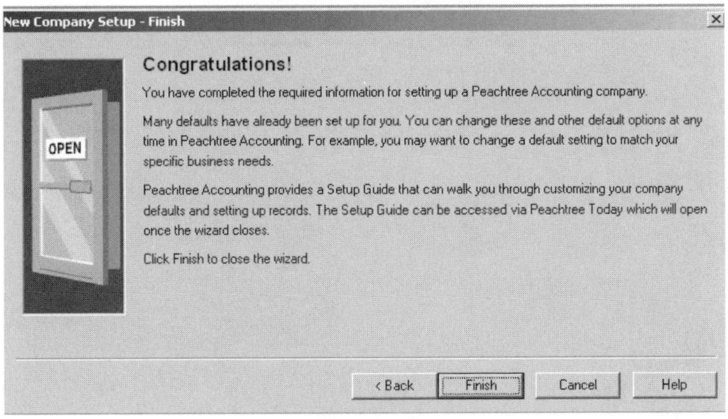

Figure 9

10. The **Peachtree Today** window appears with an arrow pointing to the **Setup Guide**. Click on the **Setup Guide** to proceed.

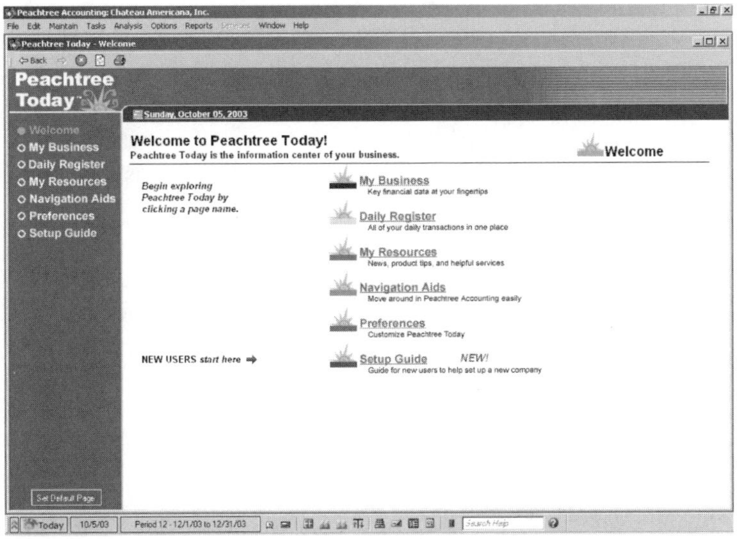

Figure 10

11. If you wish, you may close the file at this time and Peachtree will automatically save the contents.

SETTING UP THE GENERAL LEDGER

Requirements

1. Open the Chateau Americana file. (Note: Peachtree will automatically save the file you created in the first portion of this assignment with the company name you provide. For simplicity, we refer to the company, and file, as Chateau Americana.) Once you click on the **Setup Guide**, you will have access to the General Ledger, Accounts Receivable, Accounts Payable, Payroll, Inventory, and Jobs.

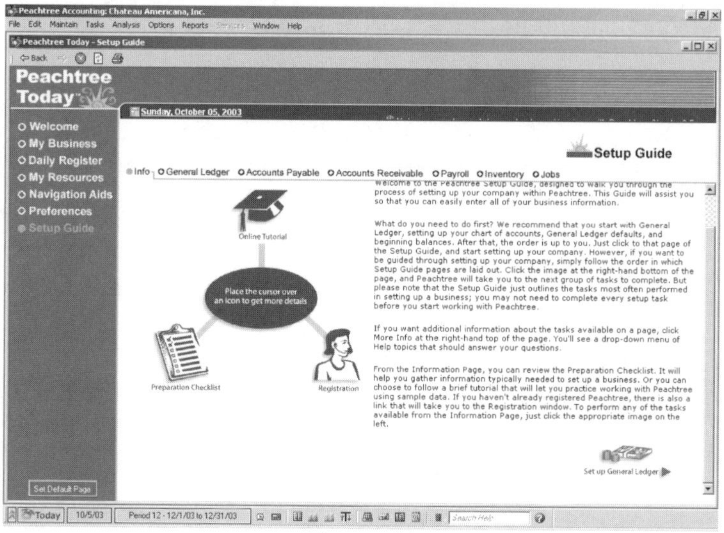

Figure 11

2. You will begin by setting up the **General Ledger.** Click on the **General Ledger** menu selection at the top of the page.

3. You can now set up your **Chart of Accounts**. It is extremely important that you set up the chart of accounts properly. Use the account numbers and related descriptions that follow. (Note: All of the accounts have normal balances)

Account Title	Account #	12/15/03 Balance
Assets (100000)		
General Checking Account	111000	$ 2,222,927.47
Payroll Checking Account	112000	1,000.00
Money Market Account	113000	782,546.49
Savings Account	114000	51,745.56
Petty Cash	119000	500.00
Accounts Receivable	121000	5,366,670.86
Allowance for Bad Debts	129000	95,401.58

Inventory – Production	141000	$ 11,564,851.56
Inventory – Finished Goods	145000	4,044,046.31
Prepaid Expenses	150000	142,465.96
Land and Buildings	160000	16,358,487.34
Equipment	170000	13,844,881.10
Accumulated Depreciation	180000	15,233,662.97
Investments	191000	3,070,227.56
Liabilities (200000)		
Accounts Payable	210000	4,987,975.79
Federal Income Tax Withheld	222100	66,739.08
FICA Withheld	222200	12,237.64
Medicare Withheld	222300	2,862.01
FICA Payable – Employer	223100	12,237.64
Medicare Payable – Employer	223200	2,862.01
Unemployment Taxes Payable	223300	943.57
Other Accrued Expenses	230000	599,348.98
Federal Income Taxes Payable	235000	0.00
Property Taxes Payable	236000	0.00
Mortgages Payable	240000	7,639,067.73
Notes Payable	261000	841,000.00
Owners' Equity (300000)		
Common Stock	310000	90,000.00
Paid-in Capital in Excess of Par – Common	311000	3,567,265.00
Dividends – Common	312000	0.00
Retained Earnings	390000	22,064,134.78
Income (400000)		
Sales	410000	22,264,431.15
Sales Discounts	420000	346,741.36
Sales Returns and Allowances	430000	15,588.47
Gain/Loss – Marketable Securities	452000	0.00
Dividend Income	491000	4,000.00
Interest Income	492000	23,482.56
Cost of Goods Sold	510000	11,514,092.11
Expenses (600000 – 700000)		
Wages and Salaries Expense	601000	1,965,164.11
Sales Commission Expense	601500	771,665.60
FICA Tax Expense	602100	244,124.52
Medicare Tax Expense	602200	57,093.62
FUTA Expense	602300	7,392.00
SUTA Expense	602400	22,176.00
Utilities Expense	611000	307,067.05
Irrigation & Waste Disposal Expense	611300	230,910.91
Landscaping Expense	612000	142,475.69
Advertising Expense	621000	296,794.33
Marketing Expense	623000	192,865.67
Festivals & Competitions Expense	624000	238,654.75
Telephone Expense	631000	37,584.73
Internet & Computer Expense	632000	14,475.00
Postage Expense	633000	35,117.66
Legal & Accounting Fees	641000	88,425.50
Other Consulting Fees	643000	12,500.00

Office Supplies Expense	651000	$ 58,689.68
Data Processing Expense	660000	9,743.89
Depreciation Expense	670000	1,092,832.66
Travel and Entertainment Expense	680000	169,405.86
Other Insurance	691000	115,058.55
Medical Insurance	692000	192,154.80
Workmen's Compensation Insurance	693000	139,750.00
Other Employee Benefits Expense	699000	175,643.90
Dues and Subscriptions Expense	700000	32,076.00
Federal Income Tax Expense	711000	857,595.76
Property Tax Expense	712000	19,875.00
Repairs and Maintenance Expense	721000	71,974.93
Automobile Expense	731000	81,493.45
Lease Expense	740000	113,607.56
Bad Debt Expense	791000	0.00
Miscellaneous Expense	792000	26,575.63
Interest Expense	793000	359,915.53

Begin by entering the Cash account. Type the account number (111000) in the field entitled **Account ID** field. Then enter "General Checking Account" in the **Description** field. The pull-down menu next to the **Account Type** field requires you to select the type of account for each account number. **Do not enter balance information** for the accounts at this time.

Click the **Save** button after you enter each account's information**.** As you enter the account titles, notice that the full title does not always fit in the space provided and you will, therefore, need to abbreviate the descriptions slightly. In addition, the **Account Type** for many of these accounts is obvious. For those which are not obvious, you will need to refer to the information provided below.

- Common Stock and Paid-In Capital in Excess of Par are "Equity-doesn't close" accounts
- Dividends is an "Equity-gets closed" account type
- "Income" accounts include Sales, Sales Returns and Allowances, Sales Discounts Taken, Gain/Loss on Sale of Assets, Gain/Loss on Sale of Securities, Interest/Dividend Income, and Miscellaneous Revenue

You can go back and view or edit your work at any time by clicking on the **View** button and selecting the account that you want to edit.

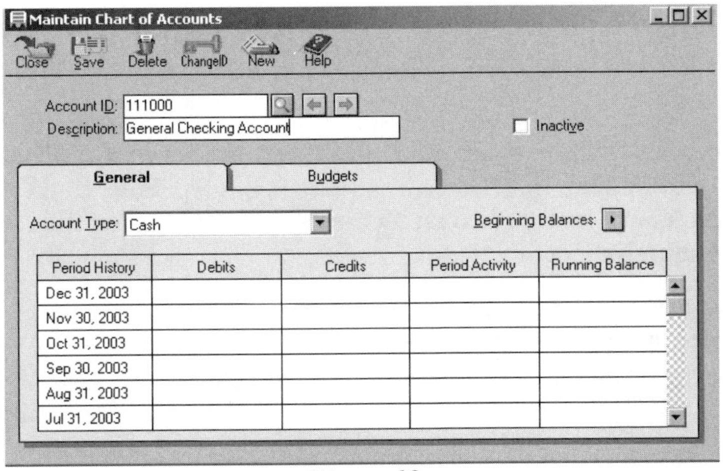

Figure 12

4. When you have finished entering all of the accounts, click the **Close** button. A window will appear asking if you would like to mark the **Setup Guide** as complete. Click **Yes**.

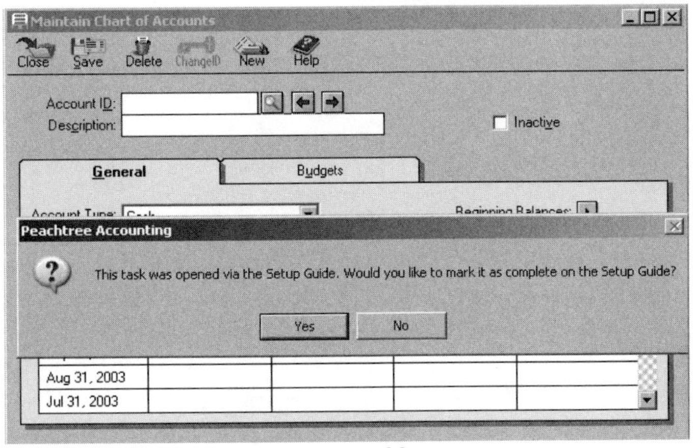

Figure 13

5. If you wish, you may close the file at this time.

SETTING UP BEGINNING ACCOUNT BALANCES

Requirements

1. Open the Chateau Americana file. Click on **Setup Guide** and select the **General Ledger**. Skip Steps 2 and 3 (i.e., **Set Up Your Bank Accounts** and **Select Your General Ledger Defaults**). Click on **Enter Your G/L Account Beginning Balances**.

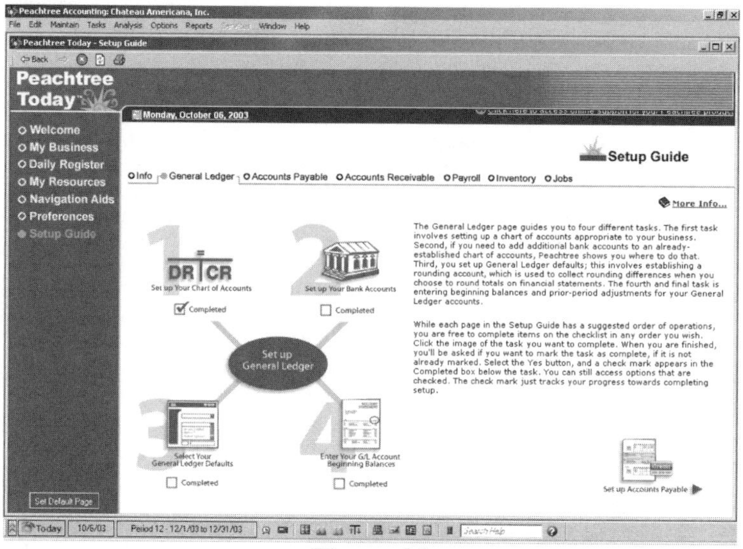

Figure 14

2. Use the balances as of **December 15** provided in the prior section to enter the beginning balances. Select "**From 12/1/2003 through 12/31/2003**" as the period in which to enter beginning balances.

   IMPORTANT: When entering beginning balances, Peachtree classifies the balances as either "Assets, Expenses" accounts that have debit balances or "Liabilities, Equities, Income" accounts that have credit balances. Thus, it is imperative that you watch for contra accounts (e.g., allowance for doubt accounts) and enter them as negative numbers if necessary, since, in most instances, Peachtree will not recognize them as contra accounts.

3. When you are finished entering the beginning balances for all accounts, you should see that the trial balance equals "**0.**" If the trial balance does not equal "**0,**" Peachtree will provide a prompt such as that shown in Figure 15 below.

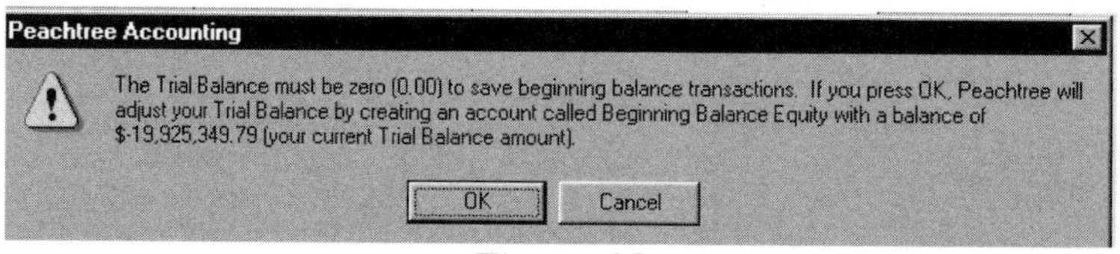

Figure 15

Peachtree will create a temporary equity account for any unaccounted for difference. This amount will have to be investigated and adjusted for at a later time.

4. Click the **OK** button after you have entered all of the account balances and mark the task as completed.

5. If you wish, you may close the file at this time.

SETTING UP ACCOUNTS PAYABLE

Requirements

1. Open the Chateau Americana file. Click on **Setup Guide** and select **Accounts Payable**. You will notice that **Select Your Vendor Defaults** has already been checked off as completed. This is because Peachtree has default settings that you may or may not want to accept for your company. Click on **Select Your Vendor Defaults** to see these defaults. Since the terms vary for each vendor, leave the default set to "Due in number of days." Using the pull-down menu, select the Inventory - Production account for the default Purchases account. The default Discount GL account should also be set to the Inventory - Production account. This sets up the debit for purchases to default to Production Inventory and will similarly credit any discounts to Production Inventory. Clear all remaining default values on the **Payment Terms** tab.

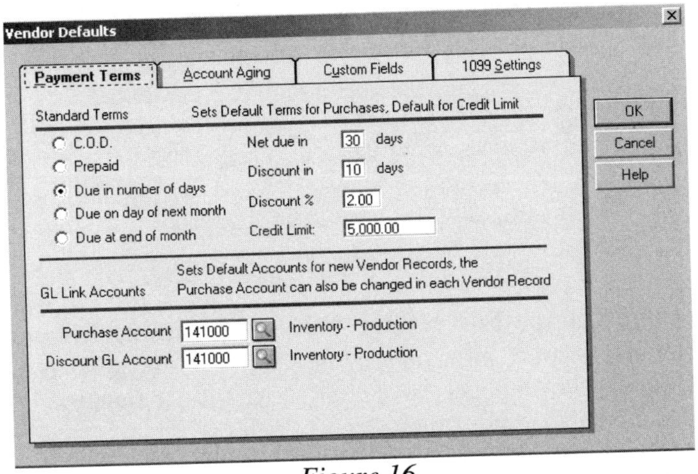

Figure 16

2. Continuing with the vendor defaults menu, click on **Account Aging**. Notice that the default in Peachtree is to age by due date. Change the aging to invoice date and click **OK**. Make certain the task is marked as completed. It will not be necessary to modify any of the fields on the remaining tabs.

3. Click on **Set Up Your Vendors**. Set up the following three vendor accounts using the information provided below along with the vendor invoices provided at the end of this module:

Vendor Name	Vendor ID	Address/Phone
Delicio Vineyards	P2538	12701 South Fernwood Livermore, CA 94550 (925)555-1890
Mendocino Vineyards	P0652	8654 Witherspoon Way Hopland, CA 95449 (707)555-1890
Pacific Gas and Electric	P8325	P.O. Box 2575 San Francisco, CA 94103 (415)973-8943

The **General** data is self-explanatory. If information is not provided above or on the vendor invoices leave the cell blank. Click on the **Purchase Defaults** tab. Make certain that the Production Inventory is shown as the "Purchase Account" for Delicio Vineyards and Mendocino Vineyards. Utilities Expense should be selected as the "Purchase Account" for Pacific Gas and Electric. Select "Best Way" for type of shipping for all vendors. Click **Close** and mark the task as completed. Do not enter any balance information.

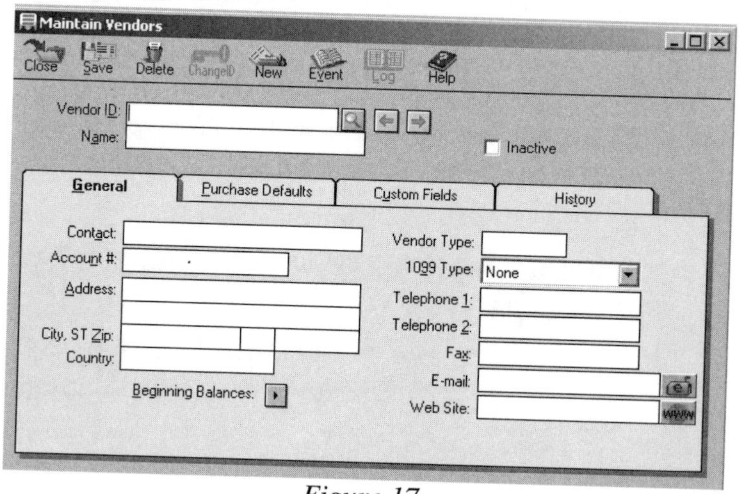

Figure 17

4. Now click on the **Enter Your Vendor Beginning Balances** and enter the beginning balance information for Delicio Vineyards as of December 15. The other two vendors have zero beginning balances. Delicio Vineyards beginning balance information is:

Vendor Name	Invoice Number	Invoice Date	P.O. Number	Amount
Delicio Vineyards	45354	11/04/03	9607	$14,563.56

When you are finished, click **Close** and mark the task as completed.

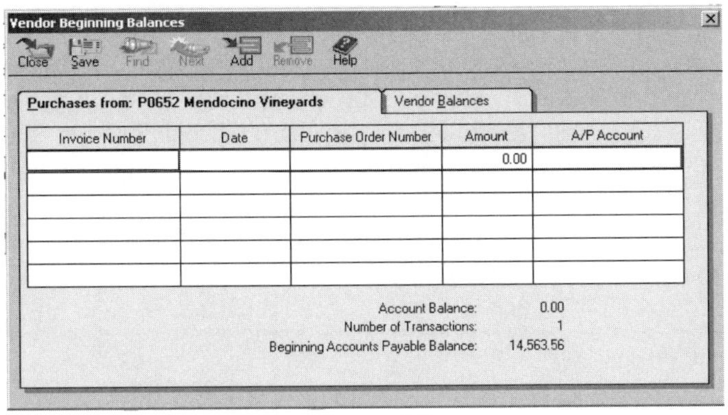

Figure 18

5. If you wish, you may close the file at this time.

SETTING UP ACCOUNTS RECEIVABLE

Requirements

1. Open the Chateau Americana file. Click on **Setup Guide** and select **Accounts Receivable. Next,** click on **Select Your Customer Defaults**. Leave the Standard Terms as "Due in number of days." Remove the Credit Limit since you have not been provided credit limits for any of Chateau Americana's customers. Change the Discount Terms to "0" percent and "0" number of days. Set the defaults for the Sales account and the Sales Discounts account using the pull-down menu as you did for Accounts Payable.

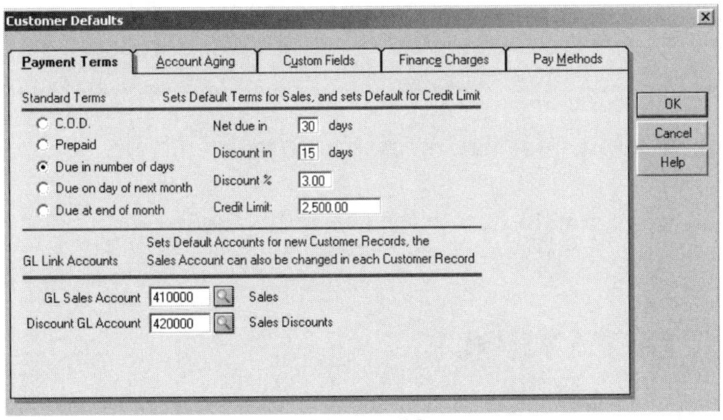

Figure 19

2. Click on the **Account Aging** tab. Change the aging to Invoice date and click **OK**. Mark the task as completed. There is no need to modify any information on the remaining tabs.

3. You do not need to enter anything under **Select Your Statement** and **Invoice Defaults**.

4. Click on **Set Up Your Customers**. Most of the general information required for each of the customers is self-explanatory and can be found below. You may have to refer to purchase orders for any missing information. Chateau Americana makes only wholesale sales to distributors. Therefore, no sales tax is applied to any sales transactions. Do not enter any balance information at this time. Be sure to save each customer as they are entered. After all customers have been entered, click **Close** and mark the task as completed. There is no need to modify any information on the remaining tabs.

Customer Name	Customer ID	Address/Phone	Terms
Bock Wines and Vines	0501	Pier 19, The Embarcadero San Francisco, CA 94111 Phone: (415) 834-9675	3/15, net 30
California Premium Beverage	0504	39848 South Street Santa Rosa, CA 95402 Phone: (707) 555-7451 Fax: (707) 555-7452	3/15, net 30
Pacific Distribution Co.	0505	10034 Westborough Boulevard San Francisco, CA 94080 Phone: (415) 555-1532	3/15, net 30
Seaside Distributors, Inc.	0506	9835 West Hills Road Ukiah, CA 94080 Phone: (707) 555-3102	3/15, net 30

5. Return to the **Setup Guide** and click on **Enter Your Customer Beginning Balances** and enter the beginning balances (as of December 15). The only customer that has a beginning balance is Pacific Distribution Co. Enter the following beginning balance information for Pacific:

Customer Name	Invoice #	Invoice Date	P.O. #	Amount
Pacific Distribution Co.	15243	11/13/03	123033	$19,576.80

   Click on **Close** and mark the task as completed.

6. If you wish, you may close the file at this time.

SETTING UP PAYROLL

Requirements

1. Open the Chateau Americana file. Click on **Setup Guide** and select **Payroll**. Set up the initial payroll fields by clicking on **Select Your Employee Defaults**. The Payroll Setup Wizard window pops up. Go ahead and click **Next**.

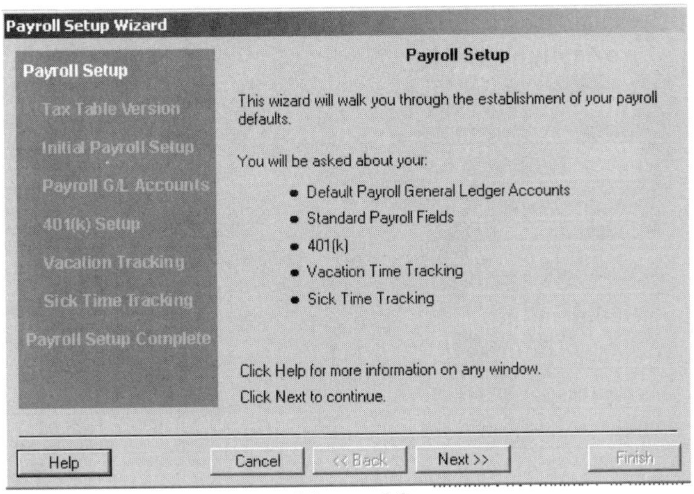

Figure 20

2. The following screen informs you of the Tax Table version currently installed on your computer. Click on **Next**. Employees will be paid in California. Assume the unemployment tax rate is 3.2%. Do not record meals and tips. Click on **Next**.

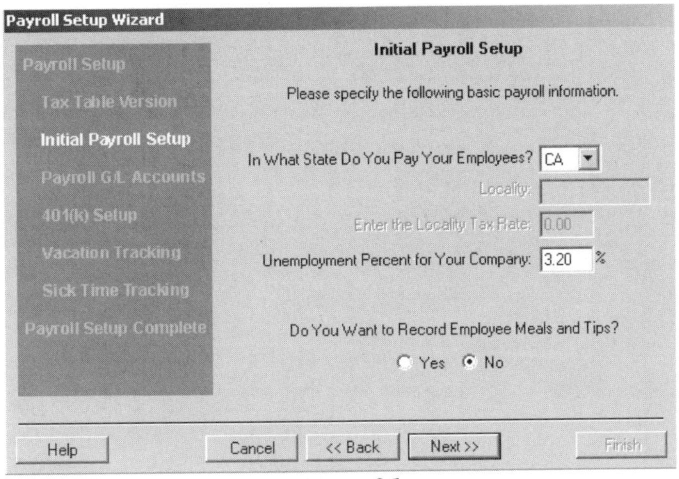

Figure 21

3. You are now prompted to enter the Gross Pay, Tax Liability, and Tax Expense accounts. Select the Wages and Salaries Expense account for the default Gross Pay account. Notice that only one default account can be chosen for the Tax Liability account, despite the fact that companies typically separate the payroll tax liabilities. You will, therefore, have to adjust the default accounts for the payroll tax liabilities later. Select the Federal Income Tax Withheld account for the Tax Liability account and the FICA Tax Expense account for the Tax Expense account. Click on **Next**.

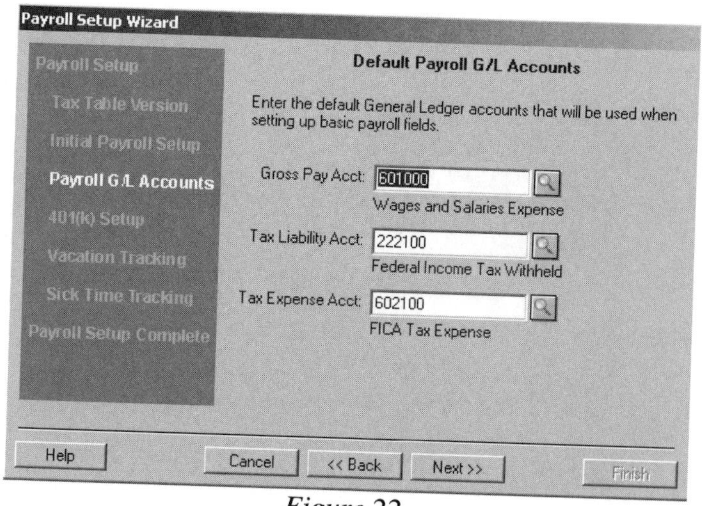

Figure 22

4. You will not set up 401(k) information nor track vacation or sick time so click on **Next** for each of those three windows and then click **Finish**. Notice that the **Employee Defaults** window pops up.

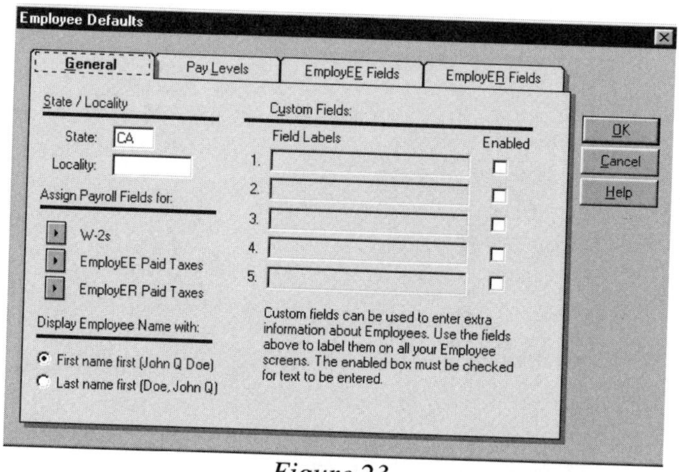

Figure 23

5. Enter the employee default information (**EmployEE Fields**). You will have to select the proper GL accounts for the employee's portion of FICA and Medicare or the amounts will not be properly posted to the correct payable accounts. Be sure to reference Chateau Americana's general ledger to ensure that you understand which payroll accounts are the expense accounts and which are the payable accounts. Remove the check marks from all fields not being used, but do not delete any fields. (**Hint: Remember that Chateau Americana employees only have FIT, FICA, and Medicare withheld from their gross pay**).

6. Enter the employer default information (**EmployER Fields**). Again, be sure that the proper payroll tax payable and expense accounts are being referenced. Remove the check mark from SETT_ER as the state unemployment taxes will be included in SUI_ER. When you are finished, click **OK** and mark the task as completed.

7. Click on **Set up Your Employees** to enter the individual employee's payroll information. Enter the employee's social security number without hyphens as the "Employee ID." Additional information for each employee can be found below:

Name: Thomas P. Bryan			
Social Security No:	014-39-4215	**Pay rate:**	$15.00
Address:	35 Winchester Street, Huntington, CA 95394	**Pay type:**	Hourly
Phone:	(707) 555-1495	**Position:**	Presses
Date of Birth:	6/14/65	**Filing Status:**	Single
Date of Employment:	4/25/95	**Withholding Allowances**	1
Date of Last Raise:	4/25/95		
Name: Robert T. Hissom			
Social Security No:	349-43-6417	**Pay rate:**	$14.25
Address:	3187 Heckert Way, Apt. 4A, Huntington, CA 95394	**Pay type:**	Hourly
Phone:	(707) 555-1219	**Position:**	Receiving
Date of Birth:	11/9/77	**Filing Status:**	Single
Date of Employment:	1/4/98	**Withholding Allowances**	0
Date of Last Raise:	1/4/03		
Name: Anna C. Johnson			
Social Security No:	296-49-3438	**Pay rate:**	$1,750
Address:	175 Bunker Hill Lane, Huntington, CA 95394	**Pay type:**	Salary
Phone:	(707) 555-3856	**Position:**	Acct Sup
Date of Birth:	9/7/68	**Filing Status:**	Married
Date of Employment:	2/14/01	**Withholding Allowances**	3
Date of Last Raise:	2/16/03		
Name: José G. Rodriquez			
Social Security No:	124-11-7755	**Pay rate:**	$2,550
Address:	2953 Whistler Hill Lane, Huntington, CA 95394	**Pay type:**	Salary
Phone:	(707) 555-2024	**Position:**	Supervisor
Date of Birth:	7/7/71	**Filing Status:**	Married
Date of Employment:	11/3/93	**Withholding Allowances**	4
Date of Last Raise:	1/1/03		

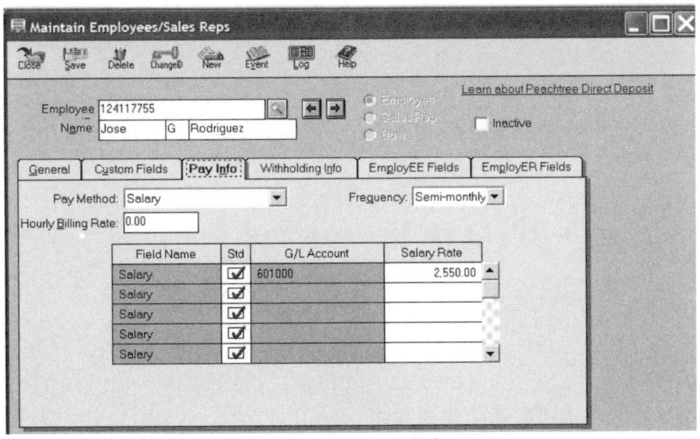

Figure 24

8. Click on the **Pay Info** tab to enter the employee type and pay rate information. The **Pay Method** for the hourly employees is "Hourly - Hours per Pay Period" and for salaried employees is "Salary." You will need to enter the Regular Hourly Rate and the Overtime Hourly Rate (1.5 times the regular hourly rate) for hourly employees. All employees are paid on the 15th and the last day of each month. Enter the withholding information on the **Withholding Info** tab. Make sure you save each employee as they are

entered. When you are finished entering the data for all four employees, click on **Close** and mark the task as completed.

9. Click on **Enter Your Employee Beginning Balances**, and enter the payroll information for each employee as of December 15, 2003. You will use the first column only and enter the following year-to-date information (**Hint: You will need to enter those amounts which represent deductions from gross pay as negative amounts.)**

Name	Gross Pay	Federal Income Tax	FICA Withheld	Medicare Withheld	Net Pay
Bryan, T	33,455.63	3,815.00	2,074.25	485.11	27,081.27
Hissom, R	31,750.78	4,110.00	1,968.55	460.39	25,211.84
Johnson, A	38,050.00	3,157.00	2,359.10	551.73	31,982.17
Rodriquez, J	58,650.00	5,543.00	3,636.30	850.43	48,620.27

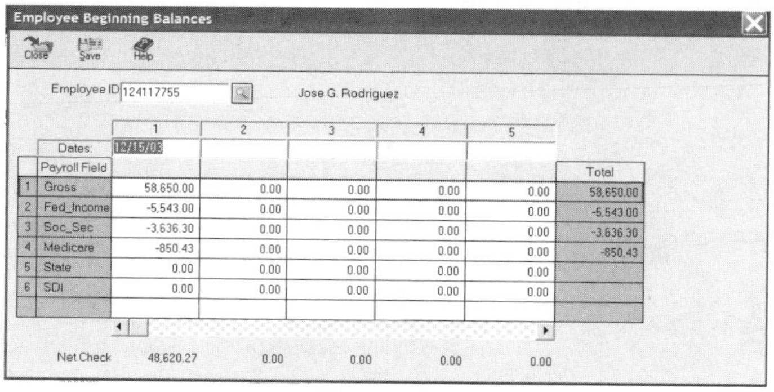

Figure 25

When you are finished entering the data for all four employees, click on **Close** and mark the task as completed.

10. If you wish, you may close the file at this time.

SETTING UP INVENTORY

Requirements

1. Open the Chateau Americana file. Click on **Setup Guide** and select **Inventory**. Set up the initial inventory fields by clicking on **Select Your Inventory Defaults**. Do not change any of the defaults under the **General** tab.

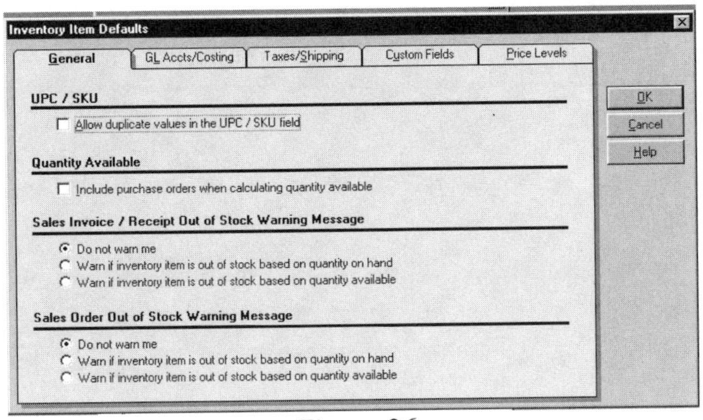

Figure 26

2. Click on the **GL Accts/Costing** tab. Set up the default accounts as follows: GL/Sales Inc should be set to Sales - 410000, GL Invtry/Wage should be set to Inventory – Finished Goods - 145000, and GL Cost Sales should be set to Cost of Goods Sold — 510000 (only for stock items). You will also need to set the GL Freight Account to Cost of Goods Sold - 510000. Leave the costing method as FIFO. Click **OK** and mark the task as completed. Do not modify settings on the other tabs.

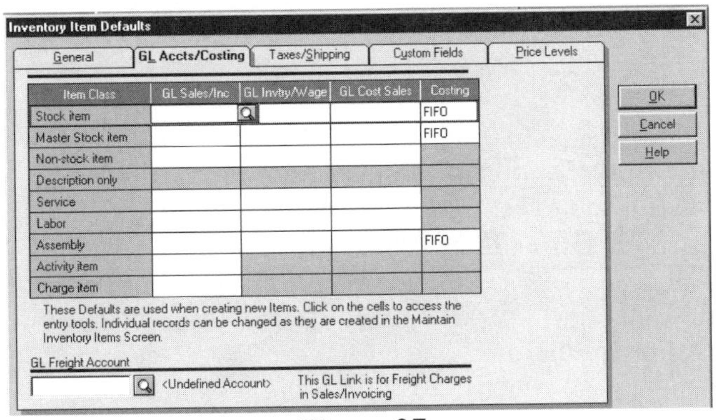

Figure 27

3. Click on **Set up Your Inventory Items**. On the **General** tab enter the following information for each inventory item: Item ID, Description, Price, Item Tax Type (select 2 - Exempt), and Last Unit Cost. Be sure to save after inputting each inventory item. Do not enter any information below the heavy black line at this time. Information regarding finished goods inventory is as follows:

Inventory ID	Description	Price	Last Unit Cost	Quantity On Hand	Beginning Balance
R130064	Cabernet Franc	$7.00	$4.50	5,964	$ 26,838.00
R130061	Cabernet Sauvignon	6.50	4.20	65,784	276,292.80
R130056	Merlot	6.00	4.62	83,484	385,696.08
R130072	Shiraz	6.25	4.58	75,888	347,567.04
W120080	Chardonnay	7.00	4.54	420,552	1,909,306.08
W120019	Chenin Blanc	5.25	3.34	44,532	148,736.88
W120015	Riesling	4.85	2.86	118,596	339,184.56

W120016	Sauvignon Blanc	4.85	2.86	93,636	$ 267,798.96
S140000	Sparkling Brut	11.00	7.28	47,064	342,625.91

When you are finished entering all of the inventory items, click **Close** and mark the task as completed.

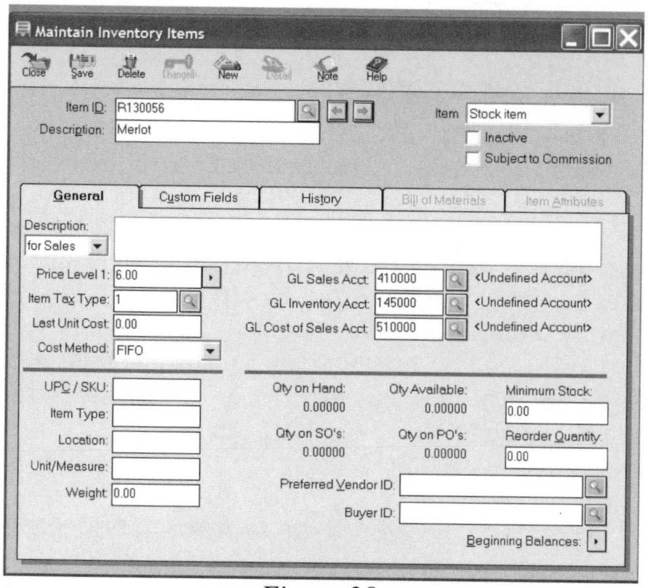

Figure 28

4. Click on **Enter Your Inventory Beginning Balances**. Enter the quantity on hand and the unit cost for each inventory item (last unit cost). When you are finished click **OK** and mark the task as completed.

5. The last item in the Setup Guide is Jobs. You do not need to enter information for this area.

6. If you wish, you may close the file at this time.

ENTERING TRANSACTIONS

Requirements

1. Open the Chateau Americana file. Click on **Navigation Aids**.

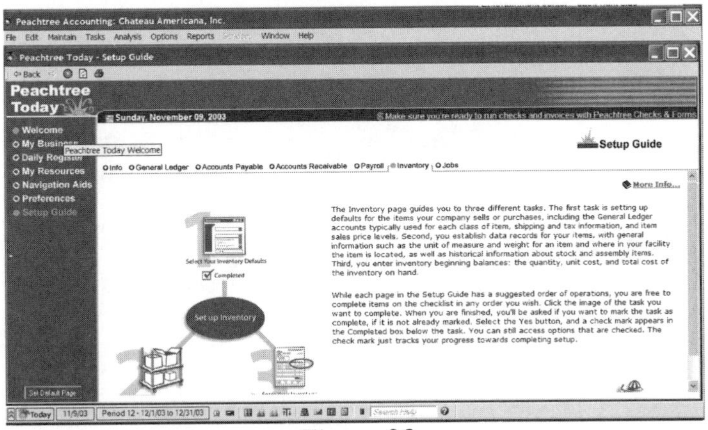

Figure 29

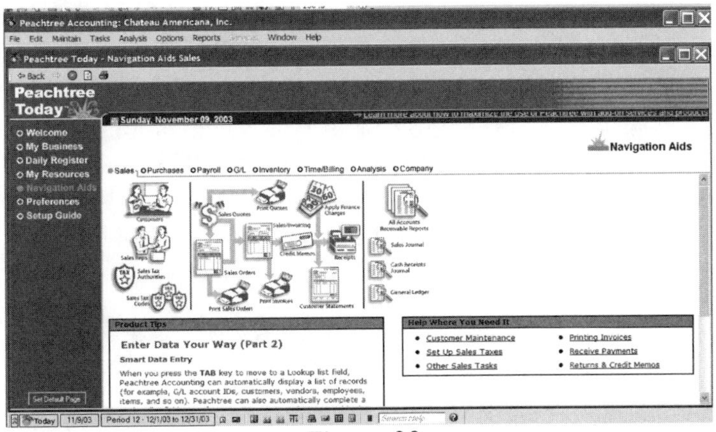

Figure 30

You can use the icons and menu bar in the **Navigation Aids** window to enter transactions and perform various maintenance activities (e.g., create new suppliers, customers, etc.). You can find the same selections on the **Tasks** menu bar at the top of the window.

2. Using the transactions listed below examine the first transaction for December 16. (Note: Documents supporting the transactions are provided behind the Year-End Procedures and Summary.) You will notice that it is a sale to California Premium Beverage. Enter this transaction in Peachtree by clicking on **Sales/Invoicing**.

   Using the **View**  button, select the customer name. Notice that the Customer ID number appears next to the **View** button and the customer name and address appear below. Enter the Invoice # and the transaction date and complete the remainder of the form. Do not enter the sales account representative since you have not set up these individuals as employees of the company. Do not enter any of the shippers for these transactions. Click **Save** after you have entered all information pertaining to the transaction.

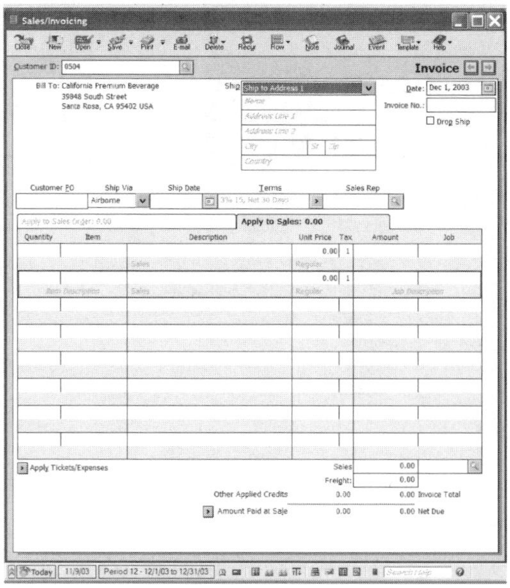

Figure 31

Notice that when you click on **Save** you get a warning telling you that the customer balance will exceed the credit limit. This occurs because you did not set up credit limits. This is a very useful internal control. We will, however, ignore this message for purposes of this assignment. Click **OK** and close the window.

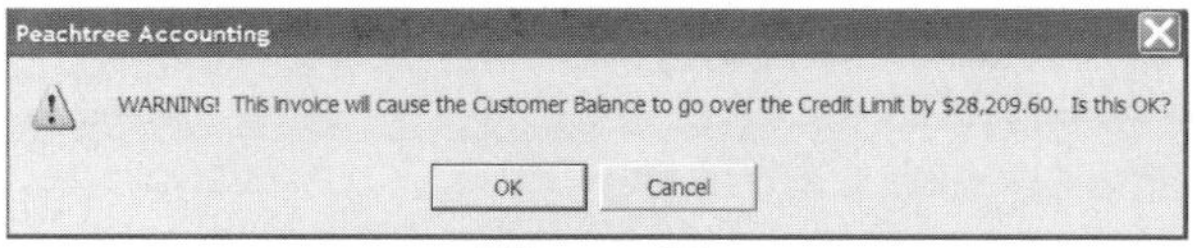

Figure 32

December	Transaction
16	Receive a purchase order from California Premium Beverage. Fill and ship the order. Complete Invoice No. 15535 and record the sale in the journals and ledgers (do not complete the "Sales Rep" field).
16	Order 18,000 lbs. white grapes at $1.05 per pound from Mendocino Vineyards. Complete Purchase Order No. 9682 (do not complete the "Item" field).
16	Purchase a 2002 Ford truck for $26,750.00. The terms include a $4,750.00 down payment and a 3-year, 6% promissory note to Ford Credit for the remaining $22,000.00. Principal and interest on the note are due monthly beginning January 4, 2004. The company expects the truck to have a useful life of 5 years and no salvage value. Prepare Check No. 19257 payable to Potter Valley Ford for the down payment and record the transaction in the journals and ledgers (do not complete the "Vendor ID" field).

17	Receive a phone complaint from Seaside Distributors about a case of Chenin Blanc that was damaged in shipment. The case was part of Invoice No. 15175, dated November 5, 2003, in the amount of $20,438.40. Seaside paid the invoice on November 19, 2003 and took advantage of the discount (terms 3/15, net 30). Prepare Credit Memo No. 2753 to write-off the damaged inventory that was not returned (do not complete the "Sales Rep" or "Item" fields), and prepare Check No. 19286 to reimburse Seaside for the damaged goods (do not complete the "Vendor ID" field).
19	Receive $850 dividend income from investment in Seagate shares. The cash receipt was included in Cash Receipts Summary No. 5712 which is not shown here. Record the cash receipt in the journals and ledgers (do not complete the "Customer ID" field).
19	Receive payment in full from Pacific Distribution Co. on Invoice No. 15243 dated November 13, 2003, in the amount of $19,576.80. The receipt was included in Cash Receipts Summary No. 5712 which is not shown here. Record the cash receipt in the journals and ledgers.
19	Receive a purchase order with payment from Ukiah Distributors. Fill and ship the order. The receipt was included in Cash Receipts Summary No. 5712 which is not shown here. Record the sale in the journals and ledgers (do no complete the "Customer ID" or "Sales Rep" fields).
22	Receive 14,000 lbs. red grapes at $0.99 per pound from Mendocino Vineyards. Also received Invoice No. M7634 from Mendocino Vineyards with the shipment. Terms on the invoice are 2/10, net 30. The receipt was included on Receiving Report No. 17251. Record the inventory in the journals and ledgers using the gross method (do not complete the "Item" field).
26	Receive utility bill from Pacific Gas and Electric in the amount of $18,887.62. Prepare Check No. 19402 and record the payment in the journals and ledgers.
30	Receive Brokerage Advice from Edwards Jones for purchase of 500 shares of Microsoft at $49.20 per share plus $400 broker's commission. Prepare Check No. 19468 and record the purchase in the journals and ledgers (do not complete the "Vendor ID" field).
31	Receive payment in full for the December 15 purchase from California Premium Beverage. The receipt was included in Cash Receipts Summary No. 5718 which is not shown here. Record the cash receipt in the journals and ledgers.
31	Prepare Check No. 19473 payable to Mendocino Vineyards for the shipment received on December 22 and record the payment in the journals and ledgers.
31	Prepare Payroll Checks (Nos. 7111-7114) for Anna Johnson, José Rodriguez, Tom Bryan, and Bob Hissom and record the payroll transactions in the journals and ledgers. Time cards for Tom and Bob are provided. Prepare Check No. 19474 to transfer cash from the general cash account to the payroll account (do not complete the "Vendor ID" field).

31	Prepare Check No. 19475 to repay $50,000 of the principal on long-term debt to Bank of Huntington and record the payment in the journals and ledgers (do not complete the "Vendor ID" field).

3. Continue working through the transactions listed above, selecting **Sales/Invoicing**, **Receipts**, **Purchases Orders**, **Payments** or **Payroll Entry**, as appropriate. Be sure the default accounts being used by the Peachtree Journals are the appropriate accounts for the particular transaction you are entering. You can check the accounts being debited and credited by each transaction by clicking on the **Journal** icon once you have entered the information needed at the top of the transaction screen. If necessary, you can then change the GL account. However, if the defaults have been set up properly, the Sales Journal will post to Sales and Accounts Receivable; the Cash Receipts Journal will post to Cash, Sales Discounts, and Accounts Receivable.

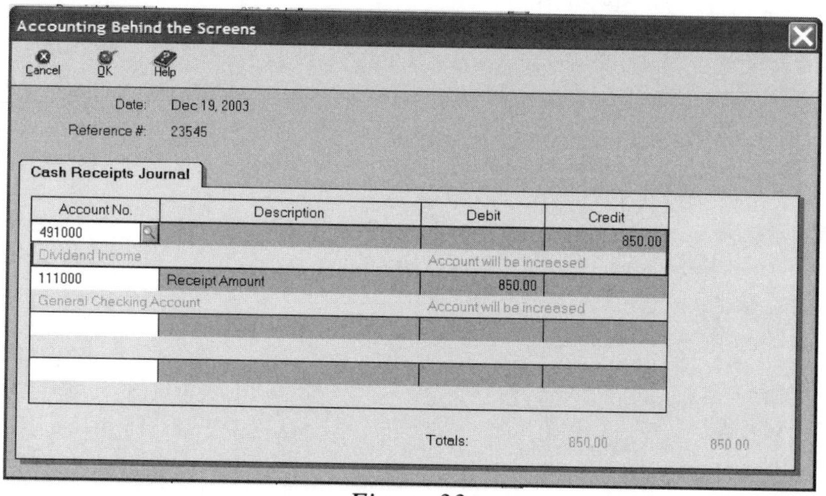

Figure 33

Remember that not all customers receive credit terms. For those customers who have remitted a check along with their order, you will need to use the **Receipts** task. If a customer number is not available, tab past the Customer ID field, enter the customer name and address, and enter the details of the sales transaction.

You will also use the **Receipts** task for other miscellaneous cash receipts.

Note that when you enter the payroll data the net pay is slightly different from the net pay you calculated if you prepared the payroll checks in the *CAST Manual AIS Module*. This is because Peachtree uses the Percentage Method for calculating federal income tax withheld whereas the *CAST Manual AIS Module* uses the Wage Bracket Method tables.

MONTH-END PROCEDURES

1. Calculate monthly accrued interest expense for the $22,000 installment note to Ford Credit (based on 365 days per year and interest starting to accrue on December 17, 2003). Make the appropriate adjusting entry. The payable is posted to Other Accrued Expenses Payable.

2. For your convenience, depreciation in the amount of $105,341.50 has been calculated on all assets for the month of December **except** for the Ford Pickup. Calculate the depreciation for the truck and add that amount to the $105,341.50 to determine the total depreciation expense for December. Record the appropriate adjusting entry in the General Journal.

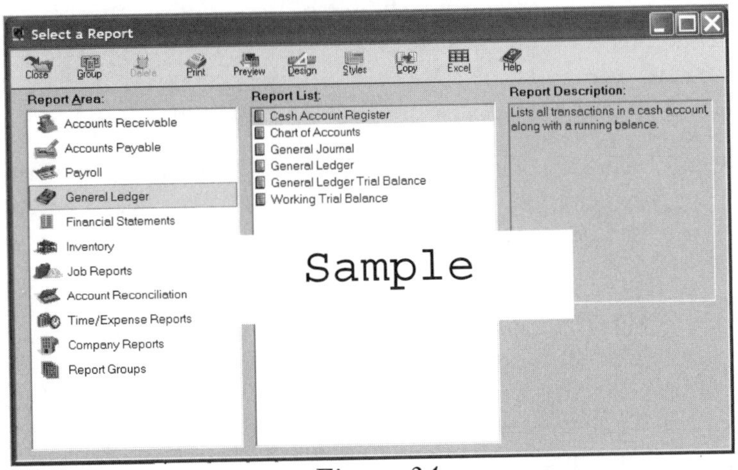

Figure 34

3. Your account balances can be verified at this time by clicking on **G/L – All General Ledger Reports** and selecting **Working Trial Balance**. The transactions for the Payroll Journal, Accounts Receivable, and Accounts Payable can also be verified through the **Reports** menu.

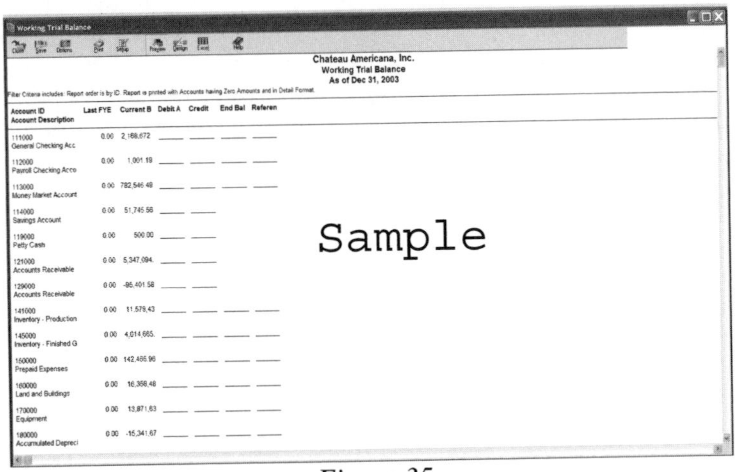

Figure 35

4. Take some time and examine some of the journals provided for you in Peachtree. If you completed the *CAST Manual AIS Module*, think about the similarities and differences of these journals to those you prepared manually. For example, compare and contrast the processes required to create and post a sales entry in Peachtree to those required in the *CAST Manual AIS Module*. You should observe that the defaults you created during set-up have simplified the posting process, but also have obscured part of the double-entry process.

YEAR-END PROCEDURES

1. Year-end adjusting entries should be recorded in the general journal after reconciling the unadjusted trial balance (the beginning balances in the working trial balance). **DO NOT** close the books for the end of the year. Prepare the following year-end adjusting journal entries:

    a. Calculate the allowance for bad debts using the net sales method. Experience indicates that 0.05% of net sales should be set aside for bad debts. Record the appropriate adjusting entry.

    b. The calculation of federal income tax expense is a year-end adjusting entry but it cannot be made until all other entries have been made and net income before taxes has been determined. Therefore, you must first calculate net income before taxes. Then calculate federal income tax expense and record the adjusting entry. (**HINT:** Use rates in effect as of January 2003.)

    Adjusting entries should be verified through the working trial balance as was done previously.

2. Print, and prepare to submit, the financial statements (including the **Balance Sheet**, the **Income Statement**, and the **Statement of Cash Flows**), the **Aged Receivables Report,** and the **Aged Payables Report**. (Note that there is no Fixed Assets Trial Balance.) These reports are accessed by clicking on **All General Ledger Reports** and then clicking on: (1) **Financial Statements** and selecting each of the financial statements to be printed; (2) **Accounts Receivable** and selecting Aged Receivables; or (3) **Accounts Payable** and selecting Aged Payables.

California Premium Beverage

PURCHASE ORDER

39848 South Street
Santa Rosa, CA 95402
Phone (707) 555-7451 Fax (707) 555-7452

To:
Chateau Americana
3003 Vineyard Way
Huntington, CA 95394

Ship To:
California Premium Beverage
39848 South Street
Santa Rosa, CA 95402

ABC Permit #: A59782

P.O. DATE	P.O. NUMBER	SHIPPED VIA	F.O.B. POINT	TERMS
12/13/03	8746	CA Express	Destination	3/15, net 30

ITEM NO	QTY	SIZE	DESCRIPTION	UNIT PRICE	TOTAL
W120015	1512	0.750	Riesling	4.85	7,333.20
W120016	504	0.750	Sauvignon Blanc	4.85	2,444.40
W120019	336	0.750	Chenin Blanc	5.25	1,764.00
R130061	1176	0.750	Cabernet Sauvignon	6.50	7,644.00
R130056	672	0.750	Merlot	6.00	4,032.00
S140000	240	0.750	Sparkling Brut	11.00	2,640.00
W120080	336	0.750	Chardonnay	7.00	2,352.00
				TOTAL	28,209.60

Jorge Gonzalez — 12/13/03

Authorized by — Date

Seagate Technology
Disc Drive
Scotts Valley, CA 95067

Lone Star Bank
Dallas, TX 27540

23545

Date 12/15/03

PAY Eight Hundred Fifty and 00/100 Dollars ---------- $ 850.00

To the order of
Chateau Americana
3003 Vineyard Way
Huntington, CA 95394

- SAMPLE, DO NOT CASH -

⁝:000000⁝: :000000000: 23545

Seagate Technology **23545**

Reference	Amount
Dividend (850 Seagate Technology common shares @ $1.00)	$850.00

Pacific Distribution Company
10034 Westborough Boulevard
San Francisco, CA 94080

Bank of America
San Francisco, CA 94104

69712

Date 12/16/03

PAY Nineteen Thousand Five Hundred Seventy Six and 80/100 Dollars ------------------ $ 19,576.80

To The Order Of
Chateau Americana
3003 Vineyard Way
Huntington, CA 95394

- SAMPLE, DO NOT CASH -

⑆000000⑆ ⑈000000000⑈ 69712

Pacific Distribution Company **69712**

Reference	Net Amount
Invoice #15243, customer # 0505	$19,576.80

PURCHASE ORDER

PO Number: 4376
Date: 12/19/03

To:
Chateau Americana
3003 Vineyard Way
Huntington, CA 95394

Ship To:
Ukiah Distributors
3224 Greenlawn Street
Ukiah, CA 95482
Phone (707) 555-1705 Fax (707) 555-1706

SHIPPED VIA	ABC #	F.O.B. POINT	TERMS
United Express	A557912	Huntington	

ITEM NO	QTY	SIZE	DESCRIPTION	UNIT PRICE	TOTAL
W120015	480	0.750	Riesling	4.85	2,328.00
W120080	468	0.750	Chardonnay	7.00	3,276.00
W120019	300	0.750	Chenin Blanc	5.25	1,575.00
R130072	780	0.750	Shiraz	6.25	4,875.00
R130056	672	0.750	Merlot	6.00	4,032.00
				TOTAL	16,086.00

Chrystal Harrington — 12/19/03

Authorized by — Date

Ukiah Distributors
3224 Greenlawn Street
Ukiah, CA 95482

Humboldt Bank
Ukiah, CA 95482

17003

Date 12/19/03

PAY Sixteen Thousand Eighty Six and 00/100 Dollars -- $ 16,086.00

To the order of
Chateau Americana
3003 Vineyard Way
Huntington, CA 95394

- SAMPLE, DO NOT CASH -

⑆000000⑆ ⑈000000000⑈ 17003

Ukiah Distributors **17003**

Reference	Discount	Net Amount
Payment for PO 4376		$16,086.00

CUSTOMER INVOICE

Invoice Number **M7634**

Mendocino Vineyards
8654 Witherspoon Way
Hopland, CA 95449
Phone: (707) 555-1890

Invoice Date 12/20/2003

Sold To:
Chateau Americana, Inc.
3003 Vineyard Way
Huntington, CA 95394

Credit Terms: 2/10, Net 30

Ship To:
Chateau Americana, Inc.
3003 Vineyard Way
Huntington, CA 95394

Customer I.D	Customer P.O. Number
CHATAM	9660

Description	Product Number	Quantity	Cost	Extended
Cabernet Sauvignon Grapes	CS1250	14,000 lbs.	$0.99	$13,860.00

Total Cost: $13,860.00

Comments:

Distribution: Copy 1 — Accounting; Copy 2 – Shipping; Copy 3 – Customer

Payment Coupon

Bill Date: 12/23/2003

Please Pay by 01/17/2004
$18,887.62

Amount Enclosed

Account No. 21790-1879

Chateau Americana, Inc.
3003 Vineyard Way
Huntington, CA 95394

Send Payment to:

Pacific Gas and Electric
P.O. Box 2575
San Francisco, CA 94103

- -

Retain bottom portion for your records, detach and return stub with payment.

Service For:	Chateau Americana, Inc. 3003 Vineyard Way Huntington, CA 95394	Your Account Number **21790-1879**	Rate Class **Commercial**	Billing Date **12/23/2003**

Meter Number	Service Period	Days	Type of Reading	Multiplier	Units	Meter Readings Current	Meter Readings Past	Usage
68869800	**11/23/03 – 12/23/03**	**31**	**Actual**	**1**	**KWH**	**1098412**	**1001301**	**97111**

Previous Balance	16,895.53
Payment	16,895.53
Balance Forward	0.00
Current Charges	18,887.62

Due Date	**Total Due**
01/17/2004	18,887.62

Pacific Gas and Electric
1000 Energy Drive, San Francisco, CA 94103, (415) 973-8943

Edward Jones Financial Services

100 Market Street
San Francisco, CA 94109
(415)504-9000

Customer
Chateau Americana, Inc.
3003 Vineyard Way
Huntington, CA 95394

Account Number
02334-85763

Tax Identification #
23-7788954

SAVE THIS STATEMENT FOR TAX PURPOSES

Date	Description	Symbol	Fees and/or Commissions($)	Net Dollar Amount ($)	Share Price ($)	Transaction Shares
12/30/03	Microsoft Corporation Common Shares	MSFT	400.00	24,600.00	49.20	500.0000

California Premium Beverage **21803**
39848 South Street
Santa Rosa, CA 95402

Bay View Bank
Santa Rosa, CA 95407

Date 12/29/03

PAY Twenty Seven Thousand Three Hundred Sixty Three and 31/100 Dollars ------------------ $ 27,363.31

To The Order Of
Chateau Americana
3003 Vineyard Way
Huntington, CA 95394

- SAMPLE, DO NOT CASH -

⑆000000⑆ ⑈000000000⑈ 21803

California Premium Beverage **21803**

Reference	Discount	Net Amount
#0504 Invoice 15535	846.29	$27,363.31

Period Ending	December 19, 2003		
Employee Name	Thomas P. Bryan		
Signature	*Tom Bryan*		
Approved	*PJB*		
Out		7th Day	
In			
Out			
In			
Out	4	6th Day	04:00 PM
In			12:01 PM
Out	4		11:30 AM
In			07:29 AM
Out	4	5th Day	04:01 PM
In			12:00 PM
Out	4		11:30 AM
In			07:31 AM
Out	4	4th Day	04:02 PM
In			11:58 AM
Out	4		11:30 AM
In			07:30 AM
Out	4	3rd Day	04:03 PM
In			11:59 AM
Out	4		11:30 AM
In			07:31 AM
Out		2nd Day	
In			
Out			
In			
Out		1st Day	
In			
Out			
In			

Period Ending	December 26, 2003		
Employee Name	Thomas P. Bryan		
Signature	*Tom Bryan*		
Approved	*PJB*		
Out		7th Day	
In			
Out			
In			
Out	4	6th Day	
In			
Out	4		
In			*Holiday*
Out	4	5th Day	
In			
Out	4		
In			*Holiday*
Out	4	4th Day	04:00 PM
In			12:02 PM
Out	4		11:30 AM
In			07:29 AM
Out	4	3rd Day	04:00 PM
In			12:01 PM
Out	4		11:33 AM
In			07:30 AM
Out	4	2nd Day	04:04 PM
In			12:02 PM
Out	4		11:31 AM
In			07:28 AM
Out		1st Day	
In			
Out			
In			

Period Ending	December 31, 2003		
Employee Name	Thomas P. Bryan		
Signature	*Tom Bryan*		
Approved	*PJB*		
Out		7th Day	
In			
Out			
In			
Out		6th Day	
In			
Out			
In			
Out		5th Day	
In			
Out			
In			
Out	4	4th Day	04:02 PM
In			11:58 AM
Out	4.75		11:30 AM
In			06:45 AM
Out	4.5	3rd Day	04:33 PM
In			11:59 AM
Out	4		11:30 AM
In			07:31 AM
Out	5	2nd Day	05:00 PM
In			12:01 PM
Out	4		11:30 AM
In			07:29 AM
Out		1st Day	
In			
Out			
In			

Period Ending	December 19, 2003
Employee Name	Robert T. Hissom
Signature	*Bob Hissom*
Approved	*PJB*

Punch	Hours	Day	Time
Out		7th Day	
In			
Out			
In			
Out	4	6th Day	04:02 PM
In			12:01 PM
Out	4		11:30 AM
In			07:29 AM
Out	4	5th Day	03:59 PM
In			12:02 PM
Out	4		11:30 AM
In			07:27 AM
Out	4	4th Day	04:00 PM
In			11:59 AM
Out	4		11:30 AM
In			07:31 AM
Out	4	3rd Day	04:03 PM
In			12:02PM
Out	4		11:34 AM
In			07:30 AM
Out		2nd Day	
In			
Out			
In			
Out		1st Day	
In			
Out			
In			

Period Ending	December 26, 2003
Employee Name	Robert T. Hissom
Signature	*Bob Hissom*
Approved	*PJB*

Punch	Hours	Day	Time
Out		7th Day	
In			
Out			
In			
Out	4	6th Day	
In			
Out	4		
In			*Holiday*
Out	4	5th Day	
In			
Out	4		
In			*Holiday*
Out	4	4th Day	04:03 PM
In			12:04 PM
Out	4		11:30 AM
In			07:29 AM
Out	4	3rd Day	04:00 PM
In			12:00 PM
Out	4		11:33 AM
In			07:30 AM
Out	4	2nd Day	04:03 PM
In			12:01 PM
Out	4		11:31 AM
In			07:31 AM
Out		1st Day	
In			
Out			
In			

Period Ending	December 31, 2003
Employee Name	Robert T. Hissom
Signature	*Bob Hissom*
Approved	*PJB*

Punch	Hours	Day	Time
Out		7th Day	
In			
Out			
In			
Out		6th Day	
In			
Out			
In			
Out		5th Day	
In			
Out			
In			
Out	4	4th Day	04:00 PM
In			11:58 AM
Out	4		11:32 AM
In			07:32 AM
Out	4	3rd Day	04:01 PM
In			11:59 AM
Out	4		11:30 AM
In			07:30 AM
Out	4	2nd Day	03:57PM
In			11:55 AM
Out	4		11:30 AM
In			07:26 AM
Out		1st Day	
In			
Out			
In			

DATABASE APPLICATIONS USING MICROSOFT® ACCESS 2002: The Winery at Chateau Americana

LEARNING OBJECTIVES

After completing and discussing this material, you should be able to:

- Recognize and explain the purpose of the elements of a relational database
- Build selected elements of a database management system
- Recognize and evaluate the strengths and weaknesses of the controls embedded in a database management system
- Compare and contrast a database package with a general ledger package and with a manual accounting information system

BACKGROUND

Before you begin the database assignments, it is important to understand a little about a database management system and its terminology and to understand the scope of these assignments. A database management system (DBMS) is based on a logical data model. The majority of DBMSs in existence today (*Access*, *MySQL*, *Oracle*, *FoxPro*, etc.) are based on the relational data model. A relational database (which will be the only type of database to which we refer) represents all of the data about the entity in a collection of tables. The following exercises are specific to *Microsoft® Access 2002*, but the theory discussed herein applies to any relational database.

The structures and methods used to manage the data are called objects. There are seven types of objects in *Access*. They are tables, queries, forms, reports, pages, macros, and modules.

Tables are the fundamental storage entity of a relational database. Therefore, all database data is stored in one or more tables comprised of rows and columns. A row, or **record**, contains all the data about a specific instance, or item, in the table.

A column, or **field**, in a table represents characteristics or attributes of the data. Most tables will contain one field that represents the **primary key** (i.e., a value that uniquely identifies each record). In *Figure 1* below, CustomerNo is the primary key. Each field can contain only one data type. Data types constrain the type of data that can be entered into a field (e.g., text, number, counter, currency, date/time).

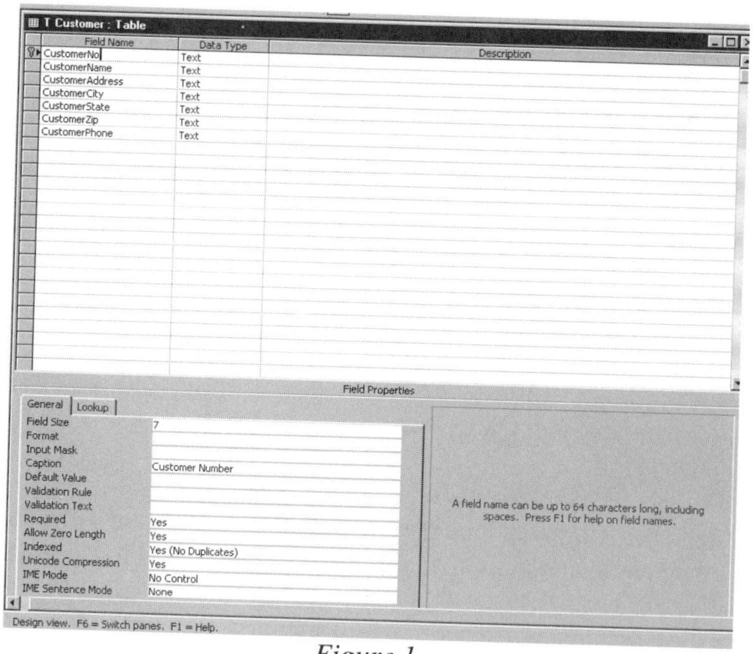

Figure 1

A record's fields contain individual values for each attribute that characterizes that particular record, as shown in *Table 1*.

CustomerNo	CustomerName	CustomerAddress	CustomerCity
WD564	Wine Distributors, Inc.	1285 Napa Ave.	Mendocino

Table 1

Queries are used for asking questions about the data in one or more tables in a database. Queries can be used to locate and display a subset of the records of a table (the **select query**), modify data (using one of four types of **action queries**) such as combining information from several tables into a single result (the **append query**), or perform calculations on fields, or specify criteria for searching the data (the **parameter query**).

Queries can be created in *Access* using SQL (structured query language), a text-based query language. Syntax is very important and very specific in creating SQL statements. The SQL in *Figure 2* uses a field (SupplierNo) common to two tables that might exist in an organization's database (i.e., a Purchase Order table and a Supplier table) to present several fields from the two tables in one form.

Queries can also be created in *Access* using QBE (query by example), a graphical query language in which the user selects one or more tables to query and then selects the columns which should be included in the query response. Because of its graphical interface, QBE is typically the technique of choice because it is easier to use. QBE allows the user to place values or expressions, called selection criteria, below particular field names, thereby limiting the records that are retrieved. Thus, queries are used to reduce the amount of displayed information, summarizing it, and giving it meaning. *Figure 3* presents the same query using the QBE technique as was described in *Figure 2*.

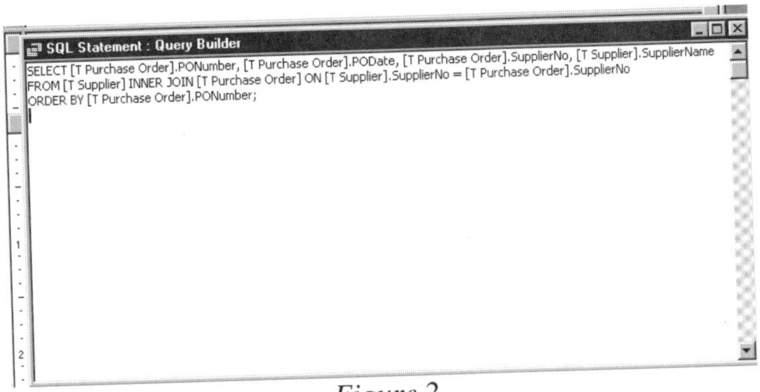

Figure 2

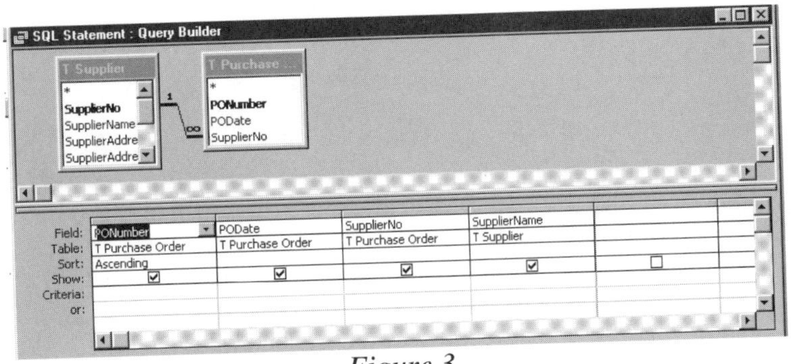

Figure 3

Forms allow the user to see data from tables in a more convenient format. Forms can be customized so that they precisely match an existing paper form, making it easier to move from hard copy to soft copy. Forms contain **labels** and **controls**. **Controls** display data, perform actions, or make forms easier to read. Text boxes are examples of bound controls. A bound control is one that obtains its data from a field in an underlying table or query. An unbound control is not connected to a field. Lines, shapes, and instructions regarding the use of a form are examples of unbound controls. **Labels** can be attached to controls, in which case they are pre-specified by the **Caption**, or they can be stand-alone, in which case they are created using the **Label** icon in the Toolbox. Both of these will be discussed later). Forms can also include other forms, or subforms, to allow data entry into more than one table at a time.

Embedded aids and prompts are other useful tools that aid in the creation of forms. Some of these can be created by the database designer and some of them are provided by the program itself. For example, **Form Navigation** buttons, located at the bottom of the screen, enable the user to move to another record by moving up or down one record at a time, selecting a particular record number, or moving to the first or last record in the table.

Reports utilize data from one table or several tables linked together to provide the user with meaningful information. Reports can be used to sort, group, and summarize data in almost limitless ways. As a result, reports can appear as invoices, purchase orders, sales summaries, or financial statements. However, whereas the user can enter, edit, and interact with the data in a **Form**, he or she can not interact with the data in a **Report**.

Pages, or data access pages, are similar to forms. They also have the benefit of being able to accommodate live data from the Internet or an intranet outside of an Access database.

Macros are more advanced *Access* objects. They contain sets of instructions that automate frequently performed tasks, such as opening a form, printing a report, or processing an order. They can also assist in the creation of turnkey applications that anyone can use, whether or not they have experience with *Access*.

Modules are even more advanced *Access* objects than macros. They are similar to macros in that they allow for automation and customization. However, these tools require knowledge of *Visual Basic* programming and give the user more precise control over the actions taken.

REQUIREMENTS

These assignments will be limited to familiarizing you with tables, queries, forms, and reports. The objective of this assignment is not to provide you with expertise in the development of a database, but to provide you with an initiation in and an appreciation of both the complexity and the power of a database when used to create an accounting information system.

Good programming procedures require a certain amount of standardization. For example, when saving tables, queries, forms, and reports created in a database, it is often useful to use a naming convention (i.e., a method which names the objects in a way that will let the user know to which classification the object belongs). Therefore, the naming convention indicated in *Table 2* will be used throughout this assignment:

Table	T *tablename*
Queries	Q *queryname*
Forms	F *formname*
Reports	R *reportname*

Table 2

Please read the following sections carefully. They are intended to be tutorial in nature as well as providing you with the information necessary to complete your *Access* assignments. In some instances, the assignment provides you with explicit instructions about creating the necessary tables, forms, queries and reports. However, in other instances, the assignment allows you to make choices about design considerations such as form style, size, font size, etc. Therefore, it is imperative to follow the directions carefully **AND** to critique the forms and reports you create from a user's perspective.

Note: Words or characters that you are asked to type are commonly displayed in bold with quotation marks. The quotation marks should not be typed unless otherwise specified.

Finally, as always, it is important to **back your work up frequently**!

CREATING A NEW DATABASE AND NEW TABLE

Requirements

1. Create a new database by launching *Access*. On the right hand side of your screen, click on **Blank Database** under **New**.

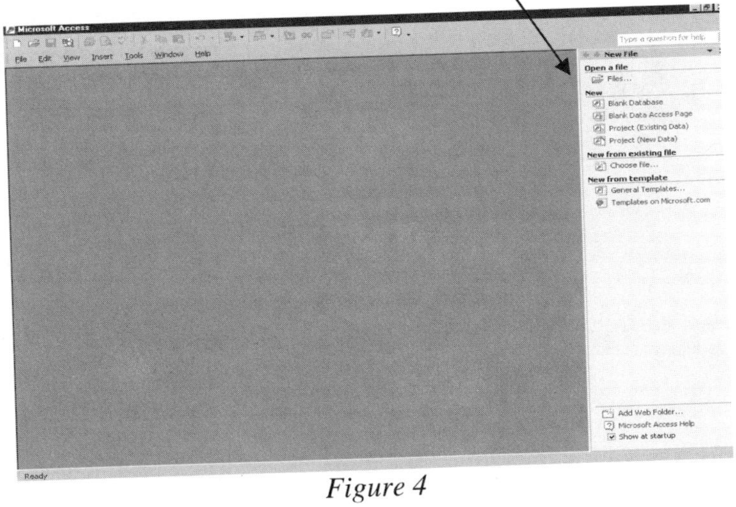

Figure 4

Notice that you are now prompted to name the new database (the default name is "db1"). Check with your instructor to determine the appropriate file naming convention.

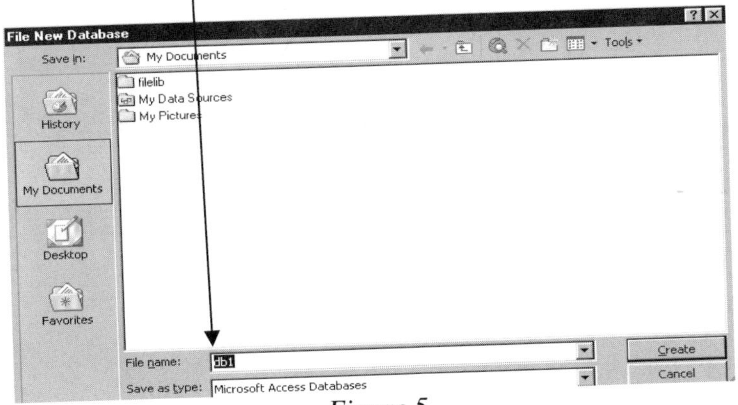

Figure 5

After you have entered the appropriate file name click **Create**. The file is automatically created. You are now ready to design the database. As discussed previously, tables are the fundamental storage entity of a relational database so we will begin there.

2. Using your newly created database, generate a table for your database. Select the **Tables** tab in the **Database** window. Click on the **Design** icon or click on **Create table in Design view**. See *Figure 6*.

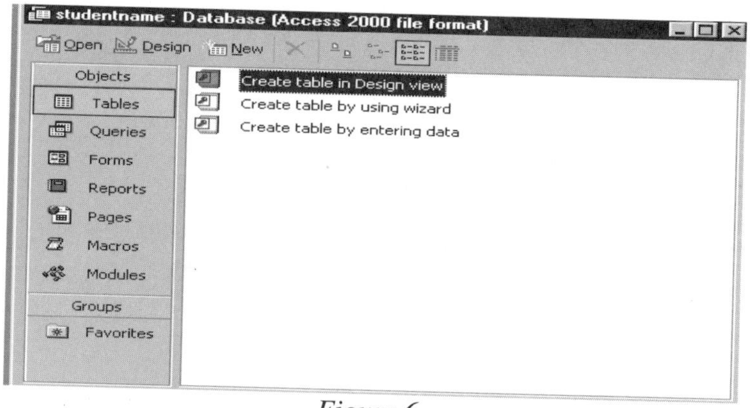

Figure 6

A **Table** window is displayed which contains three columns: **Field Name, Data Type,** and **Description**. You may move among these columns by either clicking in various fields with the mouse or by clicking in a field and then using the **Tab** key.

Field Names can be up to 64 characters and can include almost any combination of letters, numbers, spaces, and special characters. **Field Names** may not include a period, an exclamation point, a backquote character, or brackets. In addition, a **Field Name** cannot contain leading spaces. When the cursor is in the **Data Type** column, you will see a button to pull down a menu. This button allows you to select the **Data Type** for the given **Field Name**. Take some time to explore the various data types. The **Description** property is optional and is used to provide useful information about the table or query and its fields. Check with your instructor to determine whether you are to complete the description field for this assignment.

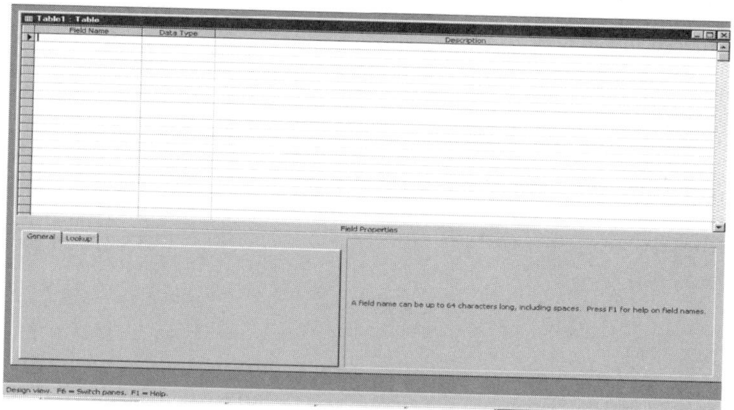

Figure 7

3. Type "**SupplierNo**" in the first Field Name space.

*At this point, it is very important that you check your work. Before you tab out of the Field Name, make it a habit to check your spelling. Field Names are recorded in the **data dictionary**. The data dictionary contains information about the entire structure of the database. Thus, for each data element, the data dictionary might include the data element name, its description, the records in which it is contained, its source, its field* *length and type, the program in which it is used, the outputs in which it is contained, and its authorized users.*

It is often very difficult to remove data elements from the data dictionary. Therefore, it is critical that you check your work very carefully when you are creating fields in tables.

4. Once you have verified the field name, press **Enter** or the **Tab** key. Make **SupplierNo** the primary key by clicking the **Primary Key** icon.

   As we discussed earlier, a primary key is a value that uniquely identifies each record. By defining a primary key, Access does three things:
   a. It insures that no two records in that table will have the same value in the primary key field.
   b. It keeps records sorted according to the primary key field.
   c. It speeds up processing.

5. Set its data type to **Text** since Chateau Americana uses a combination of letters and numbers to identify their suppliers.

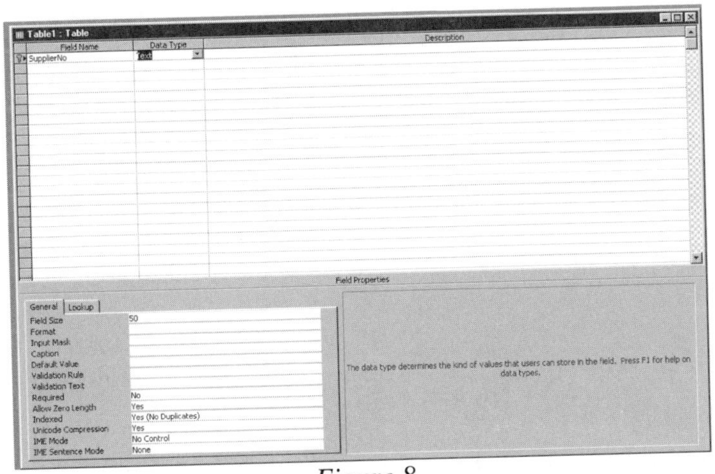

Figure 8

When you move from the **Field Name** column to the **Data Type** column, a **Field Properties** pane is displayed at the bottom of the screen. You can toggle to the **Field Properties** pane by pressing **F6** or you can move to the **Field Properties** pane by moving your mouse to the desired field. This pane allows the user to specify the properties for the chosen field and type. *Table 3* describes the most important field properties.

Field Property	Description
Field Size	Sets the maximum size for data stored in a Text, Number or AutoNumber field. In a text field the default size is 50, but size may range from 1 to 255. In Number fields, the default is set to Long Integer.
Format	Specifies how data is to be displayed in a field. It is particularly useful in specifying the format for numbers, currency, dates, and times.
Decimal Places	Specifies the number of digits to the right of the decimal point. "**Auto**" allows the Format property to determine the number of decimal places automatically.
Input Mask	Makes data entry easier by adjusting the data entered so that it conforms to the standard set in the Input Mask. It is also used to control the values users can enter.
Caption	Specifies the text for labels attached to controls created by dragging a field from the field list and serves as the heading for the field when the table or query is in Datasheet view.
Default Value	Specifies a default value for a field (e.g., Napa can be set as the Default Value for a City field; the user then has the option of accepting the Default Value or inputting different data).
Validation Rule	Specifies the requirements for data entry. For example, you can create a rule that specifies that all entries must contain five numeric characters as might be the case with zip codes.
Validation Text	Text input in the Validation Text property specifies the message to be displayed to the user when the Validation Rule is violated. For example, when a record is added for a new employee, you can require that the entry in the **Start Date** field fall between the company's founding date and the current date. If the date entered is not in this range, you can display a message such as, "**Start date is incorrect**."
Required	Specifies whether or not a value is required in a field. If **Yes**, the field requires a value. If **No**, no entry is required.
Allow Zero Length	Indicates whether an empty string (i.e., a string containing no characters) is a valid entry. If **Yes**, the field will accept an empty string even when the Required property is set to **Yes**.
Indexed	Sets a single-field index (i.e., a feature which speeds the sorting and searching of a table). The primary key is always indexed. When a record is indexed, it is also necessary to specify whether duplicates will be allowed. For example, when creating a purchase order table, the primary key might be "PO #" and you would not want to allow duplicates. However, when creating a table to add the inventory purchased on a particular purchase order, you might still want to be able to sort and search based upon the PO # (which would require that field to be indexed), but you would expect that a particular purchase order might have several items of inventory. Therefore, duplicates would be allowed.

Table 3

6. Press **F6** to switch to the **Field Properties** pane of the **Table** window and establish the following properties for **SupplierNo** (No entries are required for other properties for **SupplierNo.**):

Field Size	**5**
Caption	**Supplier Number**
Validation Rule	**Like "?####"** (Note: Include quotation marks)
Validation Text	**Invalid entry. The Supplier Number must consist of two letters and three numbers.**
Required	**Yes**
Indexed	**Yes (No duplicates)**

Table 4

7. All Data Types for all subsequent fields in this table should be set to **Text**. The second Field Name should be **SupplierName**, the Field Size is **35**, and the Caption should be **Supplier Name**. The third Field Name should be **SupplierAddress1**, the Field Size is **35**, and the Caption should be **Supplier Address**. The fourth Field Name should be **SupplierAddress2** and the field size is **35**. There is no caption for this field. The fifth Field Name should be **SupplierCity** with a Field Size of **25** and an appropriate Caption.

8. The sixth Field Name should be **SupplierState**. The Field Size is **2**. Set the Input Mask property for the **SupplierState** field by typing "**>LL**," and use an appropriate Caption.

9. The seventh Field Name should be **SupplierZip**. Set the Field Size to **10** and use an appropriate Caption. Activate the **Input Mask Wizard** (the button with three small dots located in the Input Mask Property) to aid in making a template for the Zip Code. You will have to save the table before proceeding. Save the table as **T Supplier** (Remember the naming convention discussed earlier). Select **Zip Code** from the menu, click **Next** twice, and choose to store the Zip Code with the hyphen. See *Figure 9*. Click on **Finish.**

10. The last field name is **SupplierTelephone**. Set the Field Size to **14** and use an appropriate Caption. Use the Input Mask Wizard to set the Input Mask property to the pre-defined Phone Number setting.

11. You are now finished with the table. When you close this object and all objects in the future, use the **X** in the upper right hand corner of the screen to save and close the object. By doing this, you will avoid having to provide names to queries that are underlying the database that should not appear in the Query window, thus limiting the possibility that users may gain unauthorized access.

12. If you wish to quit *Access* at this time, simply close the program and your database will be saved with the name you used to create it.

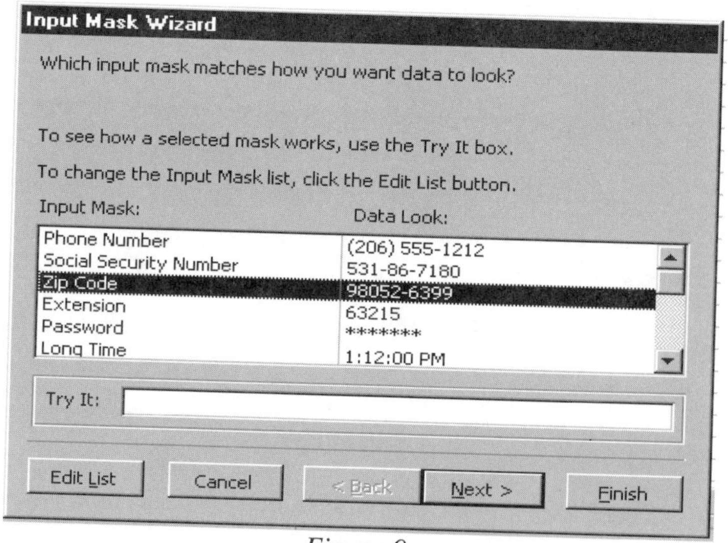

Figure 9

CREATING A FORM

Although data can be entered from the datasheet view of a table, the utilization of forms makes data entry easier and the database more user friendly. A form can display data in almost any format. A very simple form can be designed to display one record at a time. More complex forms can be created as 'fill-in-the-blanks' forms that resemble paper documents used within a company.

Requirements

1. Open your database. You will now enter relevant data into the Supplier Table (i.e., T Supplier) after you create a form utilizing the **Form Wizard**.

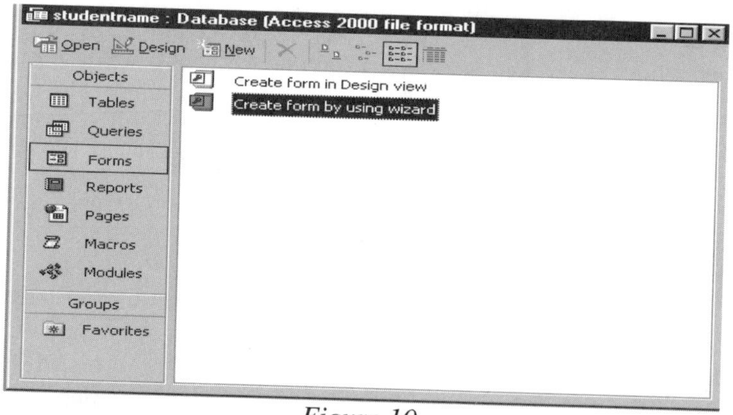

Figure 10

2. Select the **Forms** tab in your **Database** window and double click on the **Design** icon. Be sure that **T Supplier** is highlighted in the **Tables/Queries** box.

3. Select all the fields you created in the table for inclusion in the new form by clicking on the >> button in the middle of the window and click on **Next**. See *Figure 11*.

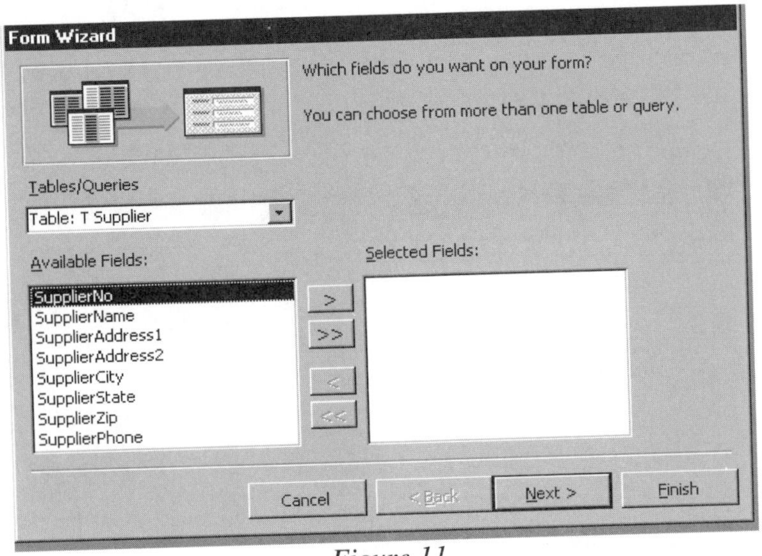

Figure 11

4. The next window allows you to choose a layout. Take some time to view each of the various layouts and then select the **Columnar** format. Click **Next**.

5. You are now presented with a selection of styles or backgrounds from which to choose. Again take some time to view each of the styles. Keep your users in mind when you choose a style and pick one that will be pleasing to the users. Click **Next**.

6. Recalling the naming convention discussed earlier, entitle the form **F Supplier**. Select **Modify the form's design**. Click **Finish**.

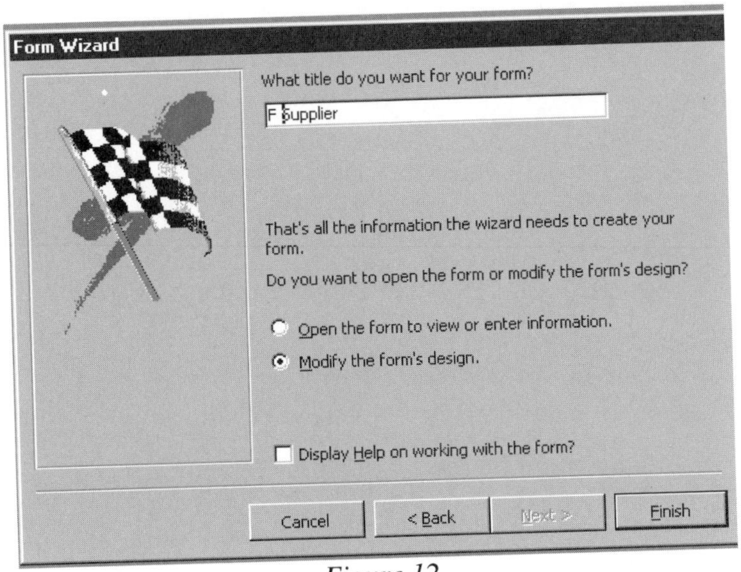

Figure 12

7. To enlarge the form's work area, place the mouse on the right side of the work area (i.e., the area that shows the background of the style you chose for your form) until the crosshairs appear. Click and drag the mouse to the right enlarging the work area approximately one to two inches. Similarly, add space for a form title by placing the mouse between the **Form Header** bar and the **Detail** bar until the crosshairs appear. Click and drag the **Detail** bar down approximately one-half inch.

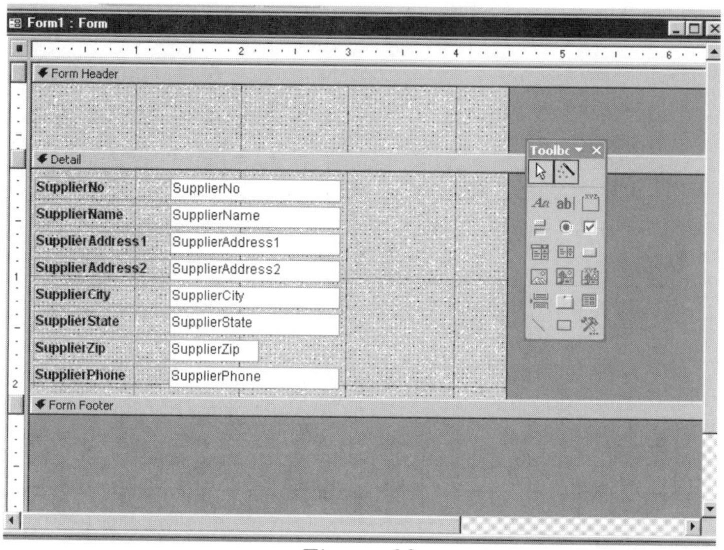

Figure 13

8. Click the **Label** icon on the **Toolbox** toolbar and then click in the form header area to create a stand-alone label for inclusion in the **Header** window. Type the label "**Supplier Form**." Click outside the label once and then click the label once again. Notice that the **Formatting** toolbar is enabled. Format the label using a **bold font of your choosing with a font size of 18**. Adjust the label text box as needed to properly display the label. Close the form and select **Yes** to save it.

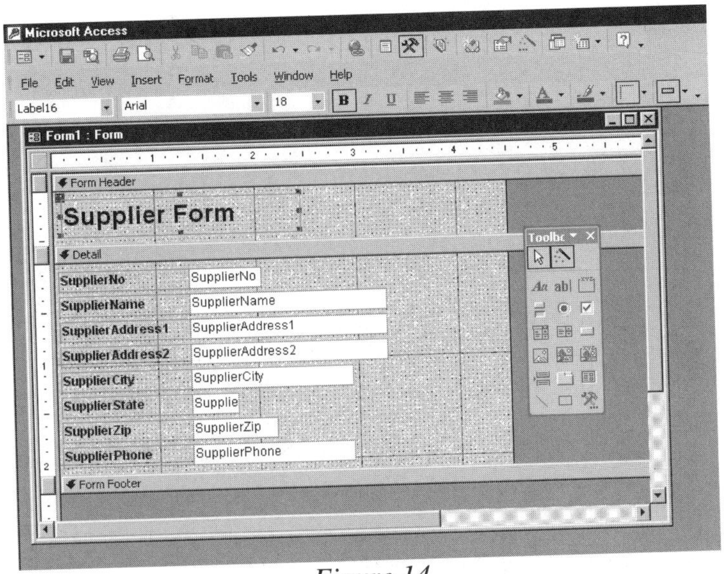

Figure 14

9. Now you are ready to begin entering data using your newly created Supplier form. Open the Supplier Form by double clicking on **F Supplier** in the **Database** window. Enter data for each of Chateau Americana's suppliers listed below:

Vendor Name	Vendor Number	Vendor Address	Vendor Phone
Delicio Vineyards	P2538	12701 South Fernwood Livermore, CA 94550	(925)555-1890
Mendocino Vineyards	P0652	8654 Witherspoon Way Hopland, CA 95449	(707)555-1890

As you enter the supplier information, pay attention to the size of the fields. You can adjust the size by clicking on the **Design View** and stretching or shrinking the field and then toggling back to the form by clicking on the **Form View** icon. After you have entered the first supplier's information press the **Enter** key to input the next supplier's information.

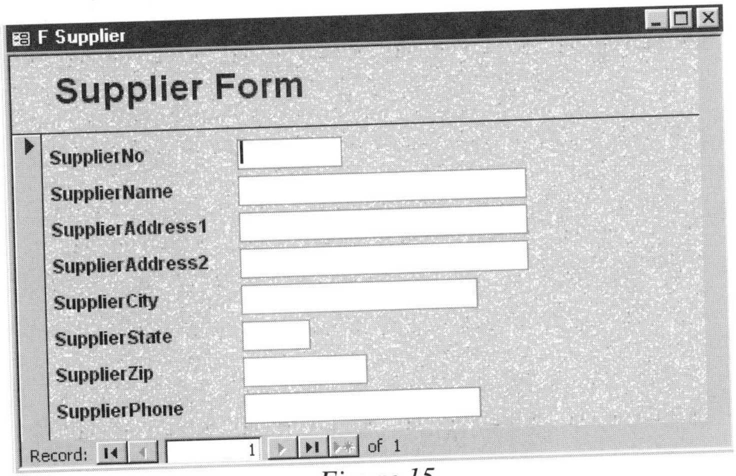

Figure 15

10. Close the form by clicking on the **X** in the upper right hand corner of the form.

11. If you wish to quit *Access* at this time, simply close the program and your database will be saved with the name you used to create it.

ENSURING SEQUENTIAL INTEGRITY

Completeness is an important aspect of internal control. Completeness suggests not only that all data in a transaction are captured, but also that all transactions are recorded. Therefore, it is important to ensure that no documents are lost or misplaced. One way to accomplish this is to pre-number documents and verify the sequential integrity of the completed documents.

Requirements

1. Open your *Access* database used for the previous assignments and create a new table.

2. The first Field Name in this new table is **PONumber**. Choose **AutoNumber** as the Data Type and enter **PO #** as the Caption. Do not change any other default values for this or other Field Names in the **Field Properties** pane unless instructed to do so.

3. The second Field Name is **PODate**. The Data type is **Date/Time**. Use the Input Mask Wizard to create the Input Mask property. You will have to save the table before proceeding. Save the table as **T Purchase Order**. *NOTE: A primary key is not to be designated at this time. When asked if a primary key should be created, click* ***NO****. You will set the primary key later.* Choose **Short Date** for the Input Mask. Click on **Next** twice and then click **Finish**. The Caption should be **PO Date**.

4. The third Field Name is **SupplierNo**. The Data Type should be set to **Text**. Set the Field Size to **5** and enter the Caption as **Supplier Number**. Close the **T Purchase Order** table.

   *Notice that you have already used the Field Name "****SupplierNo.****" It was the primary key in the T Supplier table. When a field name appears in one table that is a primary key in another table, it is called a* ***Foreign Key****. Foreign keys are used to link tables together.*

5. Create a new table.

6. The only field in this table is **PONumber**. The Data Type should be **Number** and the Field Size property should be set to **Long Integer**.

7. Save the table as **T TempPONo**. When asked if a primary key should be created, click **NO**.

8. Open **T TempPONo** by double clicking the table name in the **Database** window. Click on the **Data Sheet** view icon and then set the value of the **PONumber** to **9681**. Close the table.

9. Select the **Queries** tab in the **Database** window and click on **New** and then select **Design View**.

10. Double click on **T TempPONo** from the **Show Table** dialogue window and close the dialogue window.

11. From the menu bar click on the **Query Type** pull-down menu and select **Append Query**.

12. The **Append Query** copies some or all of the records from one table (e.g., the **T TempPONo**) to another table (e.g., the **T Purchase Order**). To begin the prenumbering of the purchase orders with 9682, the number you just entered in the **T TempPONo** table must be appended to the **T Purchase Order** table. To do this, select **T Purchase Order** in the **Table Name** pull-down menu in the **Append** window. Be sure that **Current Database** is selected and click **OK**.

13. In the **Append Query** window click on the first Field name cell and then click on the Field name button for the pull-down menu to select **PONumber**. Now, click on the **Run** icon from the menu bar.

14. A dialog window will appear stating that one row will be appended. Click on **Yes** to append the row. Close and save the query as **Q PONumber.**

15. Open **T Purchase Order** in the Design view and designate **PONumber** as the primary key. Close and save the table. Finally, delete **T TempPONo**.

16. If you wish to quit *Access* at this time, simply close the program and your database will be saved with the name you used to create it.

CREATING RELATIONS

As stated previously, *Access* is a relational database. This implies that associations or relationships are created between common fields (i.e., columns) in two tables to link the data from one table to another. For example, one-to-one (1:1) relationships occur when a record (i.e., row) in a table relates to a record in another table once and only once. One-to-many (1:N) relationships occur when a record in a table relates to several records in another table. Many-to-many (N:N) relationships occur when several records in a table relate to several records in another table.

For example, there should be a one-to-many relationship established between the **Supplier** table and the **Purchase Order** table so that data regarding suppliers does not have to be duplicated on the purchase orders. In this section, you will set up these other tables for the expenditure cycle and create relations among them. The following instructions will aid in setting up a relationship linking the **Purchase Order** table to the **Supplier** table.

Requirements

1. Open your previously created database. Click on the **Relationships** icon, or select **Relationships** from the **Tools** menu.

2. In the **Relationships** window **Add** both the **T Supplier** and **T Purchase Order**. Close the **Show Table** dialogue window.

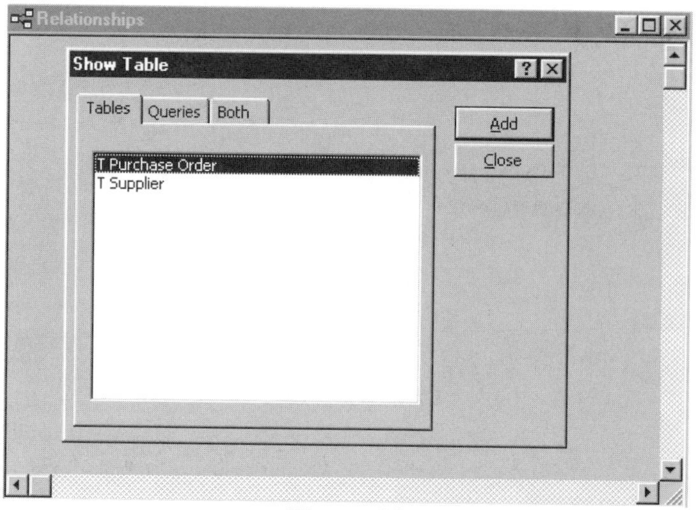

Figure 16

3. Click and drag the **SupplierNo** field in **T Supplier** to the **SupplierNo** field in the **T Purchase Order**.

4. Click the **Enforce Referential Integrity** check box. Referential integrity ensures that records referenced by a foreign key cannot be deleted unless the record containing the foreign key is first removed. Thus, in this case, a supplier cannot be deleted from the database if there is an outstanding purchase order for that supplier.

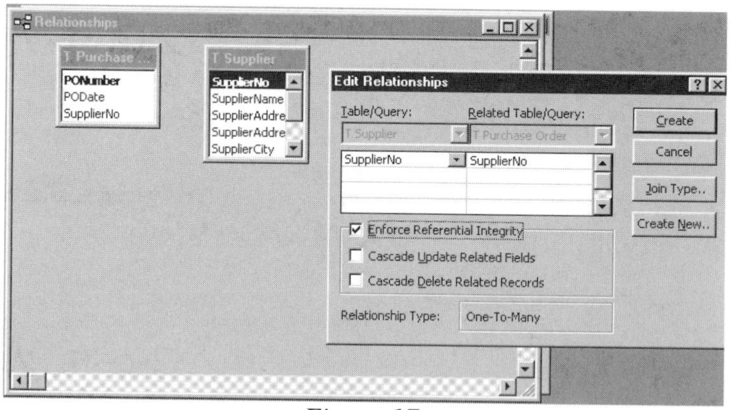

Figure 17

5. Click on the **Create** button.

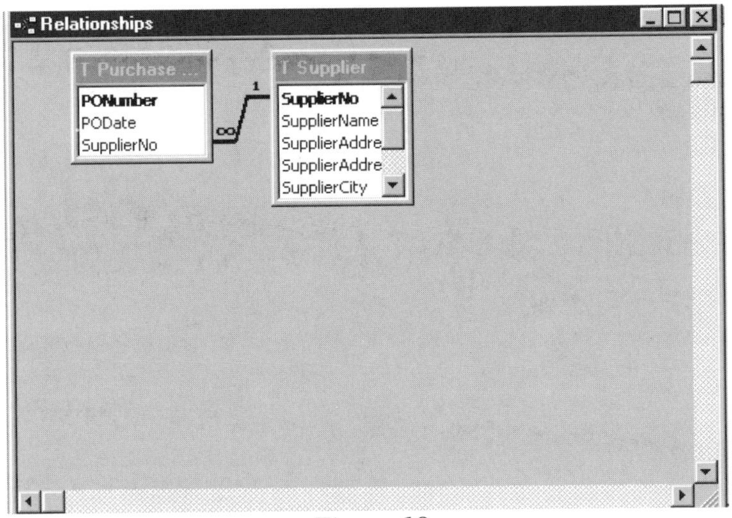

Figure 18

6. Save and close the relationship.

7. If you wish to quit *Access* at this time, simply close the program and your database will be saved with the name you used to create it.

INTEGRATING FORMS WITHIN FORMS

There are times when you may want to show data from tables that are linked with a one-to-many relationship. To do this, we can insert one form within another. That is, we can create a subform within the main form. For example, we might want to insert inventory data into a purchase order form. The following instructions will assist you in doing this.

Requirements

1. Open your *Access* database used for the previous assignments and create a new table.

2. The first Field Name is **InvCode**. Set the Data Type to **Text** and the Field Size to **7.** Enter the Caption as **Inventory Code**. Set this field as the table's primary key. Do not change any other default values for this or other Field Names in the **Field Properties** pane unless instructed to do so.

3. The second Field Name is **InvDescription**. Set Data Type to **Text**, the Field Size to **35**, and enter the Caption as **Description**.

4. The third Field Name is **InvCost**. Set Data Type to **Currency** and enter the Caption as **Cost**.

5. Save the table as **T Inventory** and close the table.

6. Create a new form with the **Form Wizard**.

7. Choose **T Inventory** from the combo box list in the **Form Wizard** dialogue window.

8. Select all of the available fields from **T Inventory** for inclusion in your new form. Click on **Next**. Choose a **Tabular** format and click on **Next**. Now, choose a backdrop for the form and click on **Next**. The form's title should be **F Inventory.** Be sure to select the radio button that allows you to modify the form design. Click on **Finish**.

9. Enlarge the **Form Header** section to create room for the heading. Drag the subheadings in the **Form Header** section lower to allow sufficient room for the form's heading. Click the **Label** *Aa* icon on the **Toolbox** toolbar and then click in the form header area to create a stand-alone label for inclusion in the **Header** window Type the label "**Inventory.**" Set the font size for the label to an appropriate size.

10. Left align the label for **Cost** and drag it and its corresponding control box to the right to make more room for the **Description** field. Shrink the width of the label and the control box since these are more than wide enough for any potential entries. Widen the **Description** control box to allow for longer descriptions.

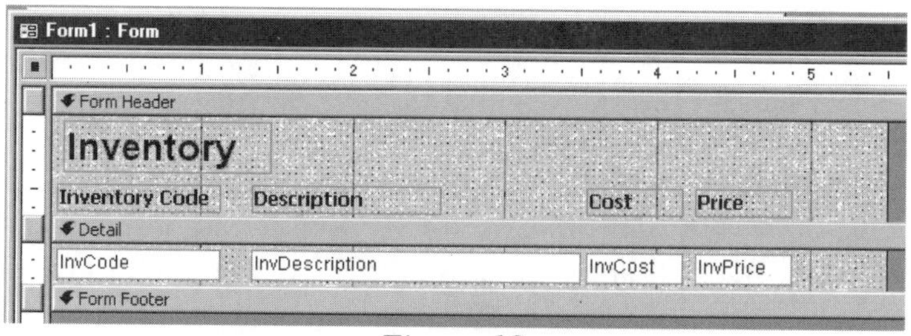

Figure 19

11. Review *Figure 19.* Notice that there is little empty space below the control boxes in the **Detail** section and the **Form Footer**. This is because the **Detail** section represents one record. Therefore, any space that is left in the **Detail** section will be included as space between each record (i.e., space between each line of inventory in our Inventory form).

12. Close and save the form. Open the **Inventory Form** and enter all inventory data from Chateau Americana's Inventory Price List found below. Close the form after all data is entered.

Inventory Code	Description	Cost
CK30110	1 ¾ US Cork	0.25
CK30120	2 US Cork	0.34
CP30130	Crème Caps Wine	0.11
CP30140	Black Caps Wine	0.09

BT30010	750 Green Bottle	0.47
BT30020	750 Brown Bottle	0.44
LB30210	Crème Wine Bottle Labels	0.18
RG10005	Red Grapes	1.10
WG20004	White Grapes	1.05

13. Now you need to create the table that will store the inventory data so that it can be inserted into the **Purchase Order** table. Create a new table.

14. The first Field Name is **PONumber**. Set the field's Data Type to **AutoNumber**. Enter the Caption as **PO #**. Set the Indexed property to **Yes (Duplicates OK)**. Do not change any other default values for this or other Field Names in the **Field Properties** pane unless instructed to do so.

15. Enter **InvCode** in the next field and set the field's Data Type to **Text**. Set Field Size to **7** and enter the Caption as **Inventory Code**. Set the Required property to **Yes**. Set the Indexed property to **Yes (Duplicates OK)**.

16. While holding down the **Control** key, select the **PONumber** and **InvCode** fields by clicking on their row selectors.

17. Click on the **Primary Key** icon. This will allow both fields to be the primary key.

18. Enter **POInvQuantity** in the next field name and set its Data Type to **Number**. Set the Field Size property to **Long Integer** and the Decimal Places property to **0**. Set the Caption property to **Quantity**.

19. Enter **InvCost** in the last field name and set its Data Type to **Currency**. Set the Caption property to **Cost**.

20. Save the table as **T Purchase Order Sub** and close.

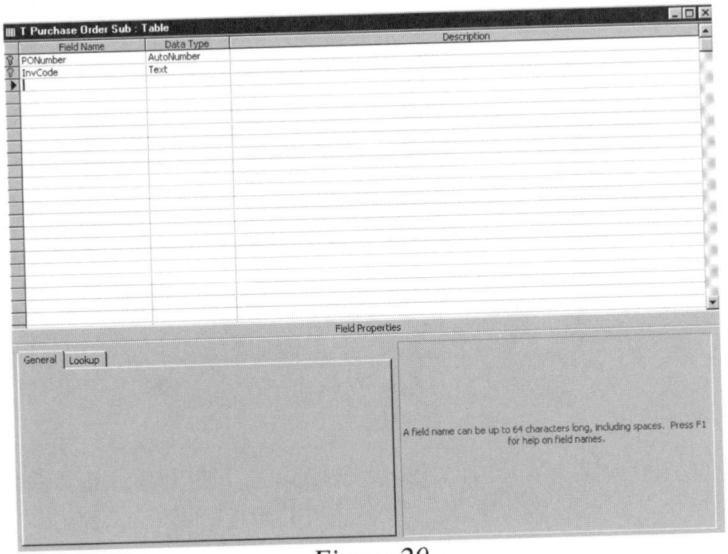

Figure 20

21. Click on the **Relationships** icon again. Choose the menu bar command **Relationships** - select **Show Table** from the pull-down menu. Add **T Inventory** and **T Purchase Order Sub**. Create a link between the two tables that is based on **InvCode**. Be sure to click the **Enforce Referential Integrity** check box. Save the new relationship and close the **Relationships** window.

22. Create a new form by clicking **Forms** and selecting the **New** icon in the **Database** window. Highlight **Form Wizard** and be sure that **T Purchase Order Sub** is selected in the **Tables/Queries** box.

23. Double-click on **POInvQuantity**, **InvCode**, and **InvCost**, respectively. Click on **Next**.

24. Select the **Tabular** format and then choose a style for the form. Delete the title text and click the radio button to allow you to modify the form's design. Next click on **Finish**.

25. Increase the size of the newly created form to 4 ½ to 5 inches.

26. Left align both the **Quantity** header and **Cost** header.

27. Choose the menu bar command **Edit** - **Select Form** (or click in the upper left-hand box just below the form's title bar where the two rulers meet), then choose the menu bar command **View** - **Properties** to open the property sheet for the form.

28. Select the **Record Source** property and click on the **Build** button (it has 3 dots on it). Click **Yes** to open the form's **Query Builder** window. The **Record Source** property specifies the source of the data for a form or a report. It can be a Table name, a Query name, or an SQL statement.

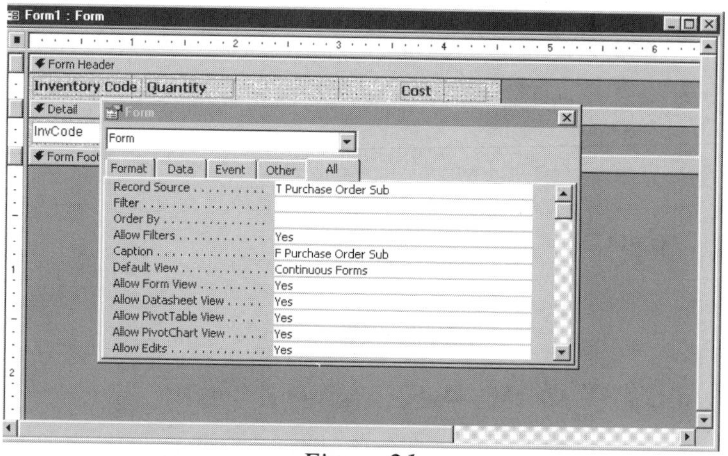

Figure 21

29. Choose the menu command **Query** – **Show Table** (or click the Show Table icon) and add the **T Inventory** table. Close the **Show Table** window.

30. Click and drag the **PONumber** field from **T Purchase Order Sub** to the first field cell in the QBE grid, then set its Sort order to Ascending. See *Figure 22*.

31. Click and drag the **POInvQuantity** field from **T Purchase Order Sub** to the second field cell in the QBE grid. Click and drag the **InvCode** and the **InvCost** fields from **T Purchase Order Sub** to the third and fourth field cells, respectively.

32. Click and drag the **asterisk** row from **T Inventory** to the fifth field cell in the QBE grid. Note that **T Inventory*** appears in the cell. Selecting the **asterisk** captures all rows from that table.

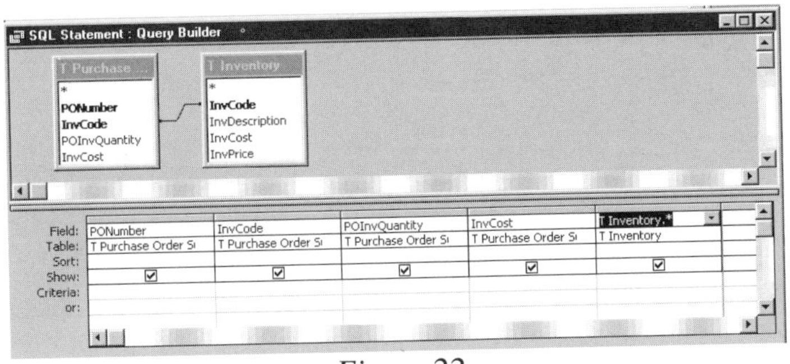

Figure 22

33. Click **Run** . Return to the design view by selecting **File** - **Close** - **Yes**. Close the **Properties** window.

34. Right click on the **InvCode** control box in the **Detail** section and select **Properties** from the pull-down menu. Make sure the **Control Source** property (**Data** tab) is set to **T Purchase Order Sub.InvCode**. If it is not, use the **Control Source** pull-down menu and select it. The **Control Source** property specifies what data is to appear in the control. As stated before, a control can be bound to a table, query, or SQL statement. It can also be the result of an expression (i.e., a combination of field names, controls, constants, functions, operators, etc.).

35. On the form, arrange all controls and their labels (e.g., **Quantity**, **Inventory Code**, and **Cost)** in a horizontal manner, leaving a space to insert **Description** between **Inventory Code** and **Cost**. Shrink the width of the control boxes for **Quantity** and **Cost**.

36. From the menu bar, click on the **View** pull-down menu to select the **Toolbox**. In the **Toolbox** window, click the **Text Box** ab tool and draw a new control in the **Detail** section of the form in between the controls for **Inventory Code** and **Cost**. Delete the textbox label associated with the new control. Click on the **Label** icon and draw a label in the **Form Header** section above the new control. Type "**Description**" in the new label box.

37. Right click on the **Description** control box and select **Properties** from the pull down menu. Click on the **Data** tab and set the **Control Source** property for the new text box to **InvDescription**.

38. In the **Properties** window, for both **InvDescription** and **InvCost,** change the controls as follows:

- Click on the **Data** tab and change the **Enabled** property to **No**. The Enabled property specifies whether the field can receive user input.
- Click on the **Data** tab and change the **Locked** property to **Yes**. The Locked property specifies whether the field can be edited by the user in the Form view.

  Note that setting these two properties in this fashion embeds internal controls in the database. This prevents unauthorized editing of the data.

- Click on the **Other** tab and change the **Tab Stop** property to **No**. The Tab Stop specifies whether the cursor will stop in a particular field when the tab or enter key is hit.
- Click on the **Format** tab and change the **Back Color** property to **12632256** (or choose gray from the color palette). The Back Color property specifies the color in the interior of a control box.
- Click on the **Format** tab and change the **Border Style** property to **Transparent**. The Border Style property specifies the type of border surrounding a control box.

  Note that setting these three properties in this fashion facilitates form design. They signal to the user that no input is intended in these fields.

39. You will have to set the **Control Source** (**Data** tab) for **InvCost** so that the cost for each inventory item will appear. Think about where this data is stored.

40. Close and save the form as **F Purchase Order Sub**.

41. Create a new form using the **Form Wizard** for **T Purchase Order**. Include all of the fields in the form. Accept **Columnar** and select a style. Title the form **F Purchase Order**. Click the radio button that allows you to modify the form's design.

42. Use the mouse to create a sufficient amount of working room (both width and depth) in the form window.

43. Give the form a heading (e.g., **Purchase Order Form**) with similar size and font to headings included in the forms you created for suppliers and inventory.

44. From the **Toolbox** window, click on the **Subform/Subreport** icon. Draw the outline of a subform in the bottom area of the **Detail** section. Cancel the **Subform/Subreport Wizard**.

45. Delete the subform's label.

46. Right-click inside the new object, select **Properties** and select the **Source Object** property to **F Purchase Order Sub**. **PONumber** should automatically appear for **Link Child** and **Link Master** fields (**Data** tab). If not, use the pull-down menu to select it. Close the **Properties** window.

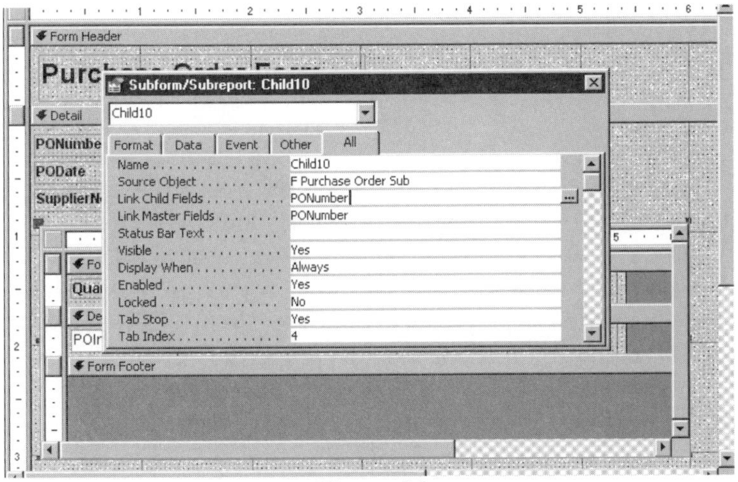

Figure 23

47. Select **Edit - Select Form** from the menu bar and then select the **Record Source** property (**Data** tab) and click on the **Build** button (it has 3 dots on it). Click **Yes** in the dialogue box that appears to open the form's **Query Builder** window.

48. Select **Query - Show Table** from the menu bar. Add **T Supplier** and close the **Show Table** window.

49. Click and drag the **PONumber** field from **T Purchase Order** to the first field cell in the QBE grid and then designate **Sort** as ascending.

50. Click and drag the remaining two fields from **T Purchase Order** to the second and third QBE grid field cells.

51. Click and drag the **SupplierName** field from the **T Supplier** to the fourth QBE grid field cell. Now, select **Query - Run**. Save and close the query to return to the form in the **Design View**. Close the form **Properties** window.

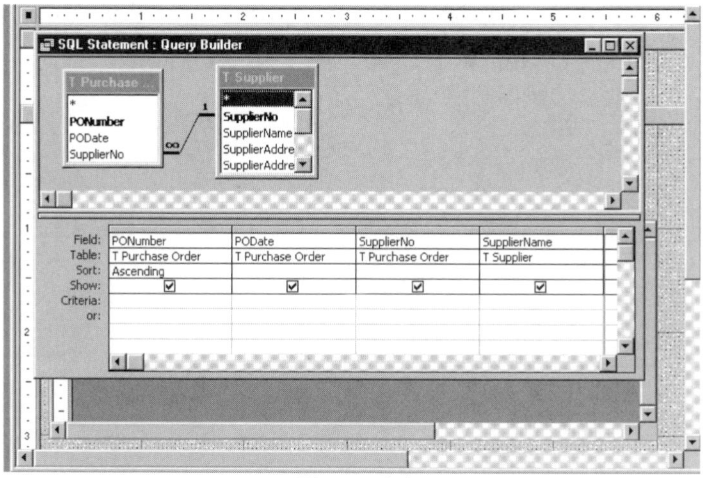

Figure 24

52. Use the **Text Box** tool in the **Toolbox** window to create a new control just to the right of the **Supplier Number** control. Delete the new control's label. Set the **Control Source** property (**Data** tab) to **SupplierName.** Set the **Enabled** property (**Data** tab) to **No**, the **Locked** property (**Data** tab) to **Yes**, and the **Tab Stop** property (**Other** tab) to **No**. Set the **Font Size** (**Format** tab) to 10 and make the **Font Weight** property (**Format** tab) to bold. Set the **Back Color** property (**Format** tab) to **12632256**, and the **Border Style** property (**Format** tab) to **Transparent**. Close the **Properties** window and save the form as **F Purchase Order**.

53. Open the **Purchase Order** form and create Purchase Order No. 9682 for the following transaction:

On December 16, 2003, Franz Bieler (CA Buyer) ordered 18,000 lbs. of white grapes (inventory code: WG20004) at $1.05 per pound from Mendocino Vineyards (Supplier #: P0652).

54. If you wish to quit *Access* at this time, simply close the program and your database will be saved with the name you used to create it.

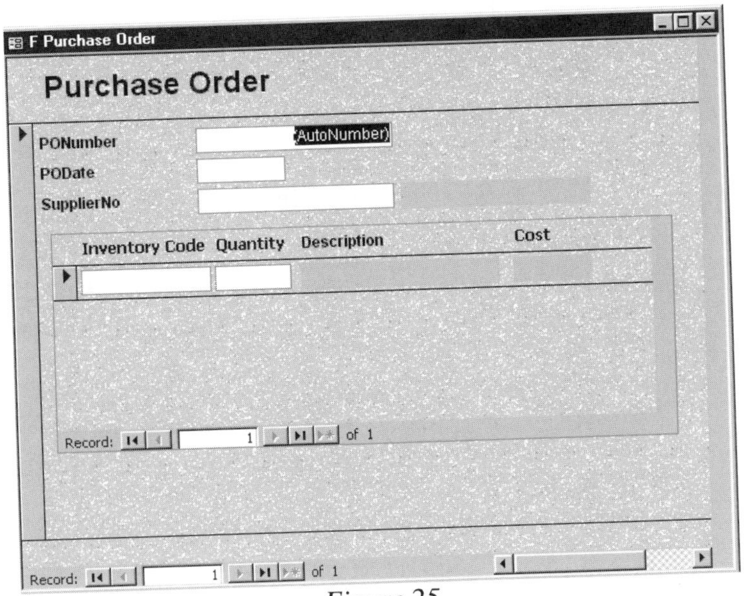

Figure 25

CREATING A QUERY

Recall that queries can be used to ask questions about data or to perform actions on data. As you will now see, they can also be used as the basis for a report. You will need to create a purchase order to send to the supplier to order the inventory required by Chateau Americana. To do this, you will have to build a query that will obtain data from fields in several different tables. In this query, you will create a field that will calculate totals by extending unit prices and quantities ordered and a field that combines several address fields into a single address field.

Requirements

1. Open *Access* database you created and click on the **Queries** tab in the **Database** window, click on the **New** button, then, with **Design View** highlighted in the **New Query** dialogue box, click the **OK** button.

2. Highlight all four previously created tables (T Inventory, T Purchase Order, T Purchase Order Sub, and T Supplier) by clicking on each while holding down the **Shift** key, and click on **Add**. Close the **Show Table** window.

3. Drag and click the fields from the tables listed below to the QBE grid Field cells:

   T Purchase Order fields:
   - **PONumber**
   - **PODate**
   - **SupplierNo**

T Inventory fields:

- **InvCode**
- **InvDescription**
- **InvCost**

T Supplier fields:

- **SupplierName**
- **SupplierAddress1**
- **SupplierAddress2**
- **SupplierCity**
- **SupplierState**
- **SupplierZip**

T Purchase Order Sub field:

- **POInvQuantity**

4. Set the QBE grid **Sort** cells for **PONumber** and **InvCode** from **T Purchase Order** and **InvCode** from **T Inventory** to **Ascending**.

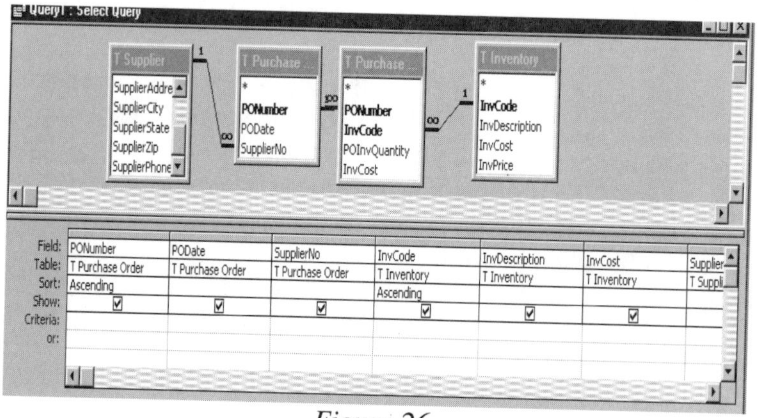

Figure 26

5. It is necessary to concatenate (i.e., link together) the city, state, and zip code fields. This is done by creating an additional field in the next open Field cell in the QBE grid. Click on the next open Field cell and then click on the **Build** icon to bring up the **Expression Builder** window. In the lower left portion of the **Expression Builder** window, double-click on the + symbol next to **Tables** and click on **T Supplier**.

IMPORTANT NOTE: In the following instructions, the symbol ^ represents a space.

6. In the upper portion of the **Expression Builder** window, type **SupplierAddressComp:^**

7. In the middle lower portion of the Expression Builder window, double-click on **SupplierCity**. Notice that when you did this the field name appeared in the upper portion of the window **BUT** some unwanted text also appeared that you will need to remove. Before you do, let’s finish the expression.

8. Type **& “, ^” &** (with quotation marks) then double-click on **SupplierState**, type **& “ ^^ “ &** (with quotation marks) and double-click on **SupplierZip**. Now we will go back and remove the unwanted text. Scroll back to the beginning of the field name. Note that when you double-clicked on **SupplierCity**, *Access* inserted “«Expr»” into the expression just after the field name **SupplierAddressComp**. This must be deleted for the expression to work. Next click **OK**.

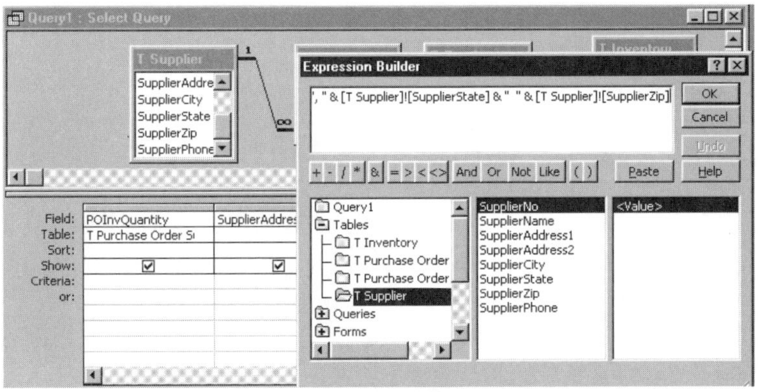

Figure 27

9. The next open QBE grid Field cell will be used to calculate the extension for the cost times the quantity ordered. The Build button can again be utilized to obtain help in entering the text for this field. Enter **Extension: [T Purchase Order Sub]![POInvQuantity]*[T Inventory]![InvCost]**. Next click **OK**.

10. Click on the **Run** button to test the query. The result should include each of the fields listed above as well as the two new fields created in steps 6 through 9. Close and save this query as **Q Purchase Order**.

11. If you wish to quit *Access* at this time, simply close the program and your database will be saved with the name you used to create it.

CREATING A REPORT

The purchase order form you have created is an internal form. Its intent was to provide a convenient, user-friendly form for employees, but it is not in a format that provides all the information needed by suppliers. Therefore, it will be necessary to create a **report** (using *Access* terminology) that can be sent to suppliers when Chateau Americana wants to make a purchase. You will use the query that you just created to build this report.

Requirements

1. Open your *Access* database and click on the **Report** tab in the **Database** window, click on the **New** button, select **Design View**, and select **Q Purchase Order** from the pull down menu. Then click **OK**.

2. Click and drag the right edge of the report to about the 6-inch mark on the top ruler. Click and drag the **Page Footer** and **Page Header** area edges up to reduce the height of each to zero. **NOTE: You will not enter anything into these sections!!!**

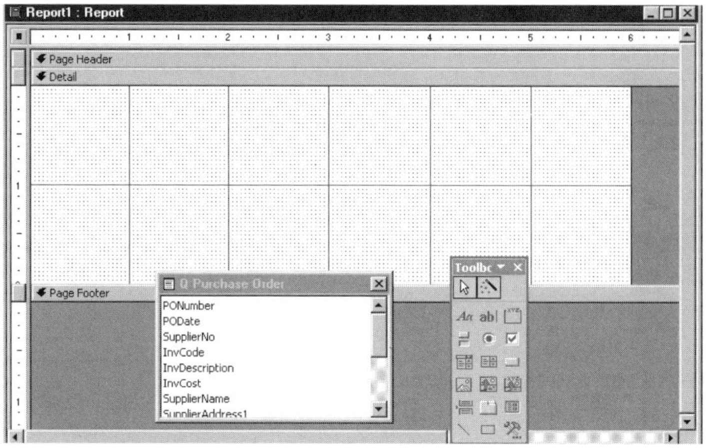

Figure 28

3. Click on the **Sorting and Grouping**  icon from the menu bar and enter **PONumber** in the first Field/Expression cell in the **Sorting and Grouping** dialogue box. Click on the **Group Header** in the **Properties** window and change the property to **Yes**. Do the same for the **Group Footer**. Set the **Keep Together** property to **Whole Group**, then press **Alt-F4** to close the dialogue box.

4. Click on the **Field List**  toolbar button from the main menu, then click and drag the following fields to the **Detail** section.

   - **InvCode**
   - **InvDescription**
   - **InvCost**
   - **POInvQuantity**
   - **Extension**

   Each field will become a control on the report. Close the **Field List** window.

5. Click on the **Inventory Code** label (**NOT** the control box, just the label) and press Ctrl-X. This will cut the label away from the control box. Click on the **PONumber Header** bar, then press Ctrl-V to place the label in that section. Do the same for the remaining labels. Line the labels up horizontally with the control boxes just below their related labels.

6. Enlarge the **Header** section by dragging the **Detail** bar downward. Bring down the labels for the **Detail** section also.

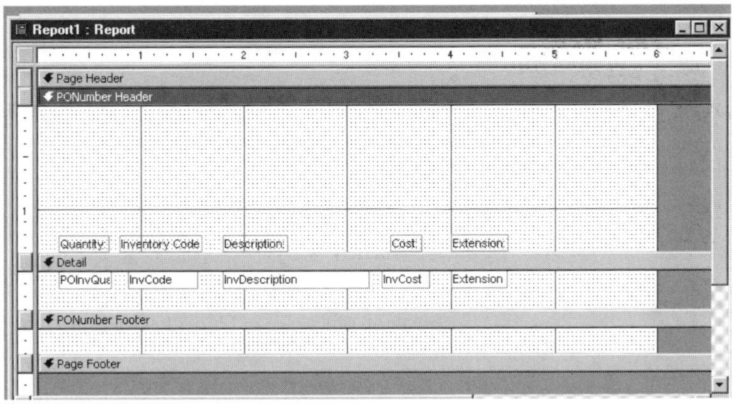

Figure 29

7. Using the **Field List** again, click and drag the following fields to the PONumber Header section:

   - **PONumber**
   - **PODate**
   - **SupplierNo**
   - **SupplierName**
   - **SupplierAddress1**
   - **SupplierAddress2**
   - **SupplierAddressComp**

   Delete the labels for everything but the purchase order number. Arrange the control boxes using good form design principles. Close the **Field List** window.

8. Using the **Label** icon from the **Toolbox** window, create a label for Chateau Americana's name, address and telephone number at the top of the purchase order. Use an appropriate font size so that the supplier will know immediately who the buyer is.

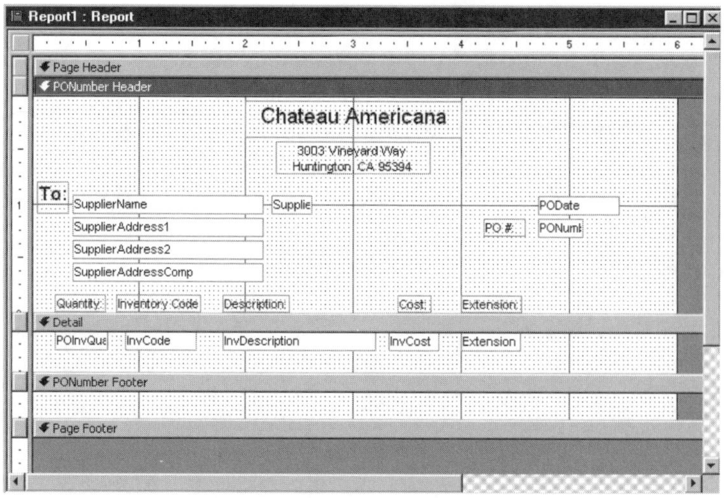

Figure 30

9. A **Control** box must be made to calculate the total of the extension amounts for each line of the purchase order. Use the **Text Box** tool from the **Toolbox** window to create a control in the **PONumber** footer section. Position the control box just below the **Extension** control box in the **Detail** section. Set its **Control Source** property to **=Sum([Extension])** and its **Format** property to **Currency**. Set the attached label **Caption** property to **Total**.

10. Look at the report you have just created by clicking on the **Print Preview** icon from the menu bar. Feel free to change the formatting (e.g., font sizes, bold, etc.) for any field you desire. The key is to utilize good form design principles to enhance the user's understanding of the purchase order.

11. Close and save the report as **R Purchase Order**.

12. You have now completed the *Access* assignment. Simply close the program and your database will be saved with the name you used to create it.

SUMMARY

In the preceding exercises, you have explored some of the power behind a database management system. You have created *Access* tables. You have learned the importance of primary keys and foreign keys. You have created queries to create composite fields and to combine fields from multiple tables into a single form or report. You have designed forms to display the information in a more user-friendly, intuitive manner and you have entered the data into those forms to see how they work. Finally, you have designed a report using the data from multiple tables. But this is just the beginning. There is much more to learn about database systems!

CLIENT ACCEPTANCE:
The Winery At Chateau Americana

LEARNING OBJECTIVES

After completing and discussing this case, you should be able to:

- Understand the types of information used to evaluate a prospective audit client
- Evaluate background information about a company and key members of management
- Perform and evaluate preliminary analytical procedures
- Make and justify a client acceptance decision
- Describe information that should be addressed in an engagement letter

INTRODUCTION

Since its founding in 1980, Chateau Americana (CA) has cultivated a reputation as one of America's finest wineries. The small, family-owned winery has an impressive vineyard whose 125 acres yields a variety of grapes including Cabernet Sauvignon, Cabernet Franc, Chardonnay and Riesling. In the last several years, CA's wines have received accolades at several highly regarded wine competitions which have dramatically increased the demand for its wines. This recent growth, along with the accompanying challenges and opportunities, has caused the winery's management to have doubts as to whether their current accounting firm is prepared to provide the advice and services required by a growing company.

Claire Helton, a partner with your accounting firm (Boston & Greer, LLP) recently met with the winery's president and chief financial officer (CFO) about the company's present and future needs. After several follow-up meetings, the winery's CFO contacted Claire to notify her that CA would like to have your firm submit a proposal to perform the company's financial statement audit. You have been asked by Claire to assist her in the evaluation of CA as a potential audit client and to assist with the preparation of the engagement proposal.

BACKGROUND INFORMATION

CA, owned by the Summerfield family, is a relatively modest winery with an annual production of approximately 385,000 cases of wine. Several years of sales growth have enabled the company to reinvest in its operations while simultaneously reducing its debts. Encouraged by its success and growing acclaim, management is contemplating an initial public offering within the next several years.

The Wine Industry

The domestic wine industry is comprised of almost 1,800 wineries. California is home to more than 800 of these wineries, almost half of the nation's wineries. More impressive still, California wineries account for more than 90 percent of the annual domestic wine production (565 million gallons) and approximately 70 percent of the nation's $19 billion in sales. An understanding of California's wineries is instructive because it is a "snapshot" of the domestic wine industry. The wine industry is highly concentrated with the five largest US winemakers accounting for 55 percent of domestic wine production.

Several of the world's largest winemakers are located in California. Ernest & Julio Gallo, the largest winemaker in the world, is privately owned and is estimated to have annual sales of more than $1.5 billion. The second largest winemaker is Constellation Brands (formerly known as Canandaigua Wine Company) that has annual sales of approximately $1 billion. Although there are several other large California wineries, they are much smaller than Gallo and Constellation with annual sales that are generally less than $200 million. In addition, many small California wineries specialize in the production of particular varieties of grapes and generate much lower sales.

Wine reaches the consumer through a variety of distribution channels. More than 43 percent of wine sales occur through supermarket chains. Specialty shops and mass merchandisers account for 24 percent and 19 percent of sales, respectively. The remainder is accounted for by restaurants, small convenience stores, and other outlets. Internet sales and distribution are relatively small primarily because of financial security concerns and interstate alcohol shipping regulations.

The wine industry appears to have a bright future. Wine consumption is directly related to household income, with higher income families consuming more wine than lower income families. Consumption is highest among adults between the ages of 35 and 64 because of higher disposable income. An aging and prosperous baby boom generation is expected to increase wine consumption and support premium priced wines. Consolidation within the industry is likely to continue as wineries search for economies of scale in production and advertising and interest in product expansion (i.e., grape varieties and brand names) broadens.

Chateau Americana

CA has experienced significant sales growth in recent years and expects to report record sales of almost $22 million for the year ending December 31, 2003. Audited sales for the two prior years totaled $20.2 and $18.2 million, respectively. Over the same three year period, the company's asset base has also grown, increasing by more than 15 percent from $36.4 to $42 million. CA has been a profitable winery for a number of years and expects to report profits of approximately $2 million for the current year. Much of CA's growth has been fueled through the company's policy of reinvestment. To this end, retained earnings have increased approximately $3.7 million over the last three years, while total liabilities have increased $1.9 million. The winery's CFO provided the balance sheets and income statements for the current and two preceding years which are presented at the end of this narrative.

The winery's crown jewel is its 125-acre vineyard which yields a harvest of some fifteen varieties of grapes. Each year the vineyard provides approximately 800 tons of grapes, or one-fourth of the winery's production requirement. The remaining grapes are purchased from other vineyards, most of which are in California. CA is particularly proud of its production process - a blend of Old World techniques and state-of-the-art technology – which produces widely acclaimed red and white wines. The company primarily sells its wines to distributors and retail shops. CA has developed several exclusive distribution agreements which have significantly increased its presence in several large metropolitan areas. The company is seeking similar opportunities in other areas.

The Winery's Management

CA has a management team that is widely respected in the industry. The winery's owners have invested considerable time and energies in hiring individuals whom they believe are competent and trustworthy. Several members of the Summerfield family occupy key management positions. Edward Summerfield is the family's patriarch and president of the company. He has received several entrepreneurship awards and is generally perceived as an astute business person. Taylor Summerfield is vice president of marketing for the company. Prior to assuming this position, she had a successful career in sales and marketing. Taylor is well-educated and earned an MBA from an Ivy League school. Edward's son-in-law, Jacques Dupuis, is vice-president of winery operations. He has an extensive background in viticulture (i.e., grape growing) and vinification (i.e., wine making). Rob Breeden, the company's CFO, is the sole individual to hold a key management position who is not a member of the Summerfield family. He has substantial financial experience and was previously employed in public accounting for nine years and served as controller and CFO for another winery in California. Rob holds undergraduate and graduate degrees in accounting and is a CPA.

Edward Summerfield and other members of management have taken considerable steps to ensure the stability of the winery's management team. To this end, he has an open door policy that encourages a free exchange of ideas and concerns. In addition, Edward has instituted a compensation plan that provides substantial bonuses to all employees, including members of management, who meet performance goals. He believes that his policies and approach to business are the reasons that CA has had very low employee turnover. In fact, Rob Breeden is the newest member of management with just over two years of service to the company. He replaced the former CFO who resigned from the company after more than 15 years. According to Edward, the former CFO resigned because he wanted to spend more time with his wife who was suffering from a serious illness.

Client Background Investigation

Your firm customarily has a background investigation conducted prior to accepting a new audit client. The investigation of CA included the winery's corporate history and the background of each member of management. Two issues arose during the investigation. First, the company's credit history indicates that the company was delinquent on several obligations that were referred to collection agencies six years ago. Recent credit history is much more favorable and no problems of ongoing significance were found. The second issue relates to criminal charges filed against Jacques Dupuis while living in France. According to public records and news sources, Jacques and several other employees were accused of stealing trade secrets from a former employer – a French winery. Although charges were eventually dropped because of insufficient evidence, many in France still believe Jacques was guilty of stealing trade secrets.

Accounting Information System

The winery employs a fully integrated accounting information system (AIS) to collect, store and share data among its employees. The present system has been operational for approximately 14 months. Although employees are generally satisfied with the system, some complain that the transition from the previous system occurred too quickly and without adequate planning and training. Although the company has been computerized for more than 10 years, its former system was a combination of manual and computerized processes. Consequently, the new system represents a significant change in the company's AIS.

Management believes the new system is the best on the market. After having been through a similar AIS conversion process at his former employer, Rob Breeden insisted that the company investigate the prospects of developing an integrated AIS using database technology. Following his detailed evaluation of the potential for in-house development of the system, Rob advised Edward that the system could be developed by the company's employees. Internal memos obtained from the company indicate that Edward deferred to Rob's judgment in making the decision to proceed with the in-house development process.

The current system is based on *Access,* a relational database. The AIS modules include purchasing and accounts payable, sales and accounts receivable, production and inventory, payroll, and the general ledger. Each of these modules provides data that are critical to the company's continued growth and success. Internal memos indicate that the company has experienced some employee turnover because of continuing problems with the accounts payable and accounts receivable modules. In fact, there are rumors that the former CFO resigned over disagreements with Edward about the need for a new AIS.

Communications with the Predecessor Auditor

As required by auditing standards, your firm asked for and received permission from management to contact the company's former auditor. Several phone calls were required before you were able to speak with the former partner-in-charge of the CA audit, Harry Lawson. At first, Harry was hesitant to talk with you about his firm's past relationship with CA. He said he needed to speak with Rob Breeden before you and he could have any substantive conversation.

You met with Harry at his office a few days later to learn more about his firm's relationship with the winery's management and recent audits. Harry was very complementary of the Summerfield family, describing Edward as a man of great integrity and business savvy. He stated that he was very impressed by the company's strong professional environment and complete lack of nepotism. Harry did express concerns about the winery's new CFO. He felt that Rob was too eager to "make his mark" on the company as evidenced by the implementation of the company's new AIS. According to Harry, Rob believed the winery's old AIS was limiting CA's future because of its inability to provide accurate data in a timely manner and was insistent that a new system be implemented. Several of the winery's internal memos reviewed by you indicated that Rob was the real force behind the new system.

You asked Harry if there were any disagreements with management about either accounting principles or his firm's audit procedures. He quickly mentioned that his firm had always enjoyed a very good relationship with CA until Rob became CFO. When you asked him to explain further, Harry said that Rob is very knowledgeable, but also more aggressive than CA's former CFO. He specifically mentioned that last year's audit team noted policy changes related to Accounts Receivable (A/R) and Accounts Payable (A/P). With respect to A/R, the company instituted more aggressive collection procedures and reduced the Allowance for Bad Debts by more than $100,000 from the previous year. The company also implemented a practice of paying vendors who offer discounts within that discount period, but simultaneously delayed payments to vendors who offer no discounts by 10 to 15 days beyond the indicated terms. Notwithstanding these changes, Harry said that he was unaware of any significant negative reaction by customers or vendors.

Finally, you asked Harry to explain his understanding of why CA had decided to change audit firms. After a brief silence, he said that Edward and Rob had told him that they believed the company needed a "fresh perspective" and was concerned that his firm would not be able to provide the services required as their company continued its growth.

Financial Statements

Financial statements for the current and preceding two years were provided by Rob Breeden and are included at the end of this narrative. Harry Lawson's firm issued an unqualified audit opinion on the company's financial statements for each of the preceding two years.

REQUIREMENTS

Client acceptance is a challenging process that requires considerable professional judgment. Although such decisions are typically made by highly experienced auditors, you have so impressed the managers and partners in your office that you have been asked to assist with the client acceptance procedures for Chateau Americana. Before you perform the remaining audit procedures, you should identify four to six procedures auditors may perform as part of the client acceptance process. Are any of the procedures identified by you required by generally accepted auditing standards?

Now you are ready to assist the engagement partner, Claire Helton, by completing audit procedures 3 through 6 in the following audit program. Document your work on the audit schedules that follow Chateau Americana's financial statements. You should assume that audit schedules CA-104 and CA-105 were properly prepared and have already been included with the audit documentation.

The Winery at Chateau Americana
Audit Program for Client Acceptance

For the Year Ended December 31, 2003

Reference: *CA-100*
Prepared by: *CH*
Date: *11/5/03*
Reviewed by:

Audit Procedures	Initial	Date	A/S Ref.
1. Obtain an overview of the client's operations by interviewing client personnel and touring the facilities.	*CH*	*11/4/03*	*CA-104*
2. Obtain permission from the potential client to communicate with the predecessor auditor. Contact the predecessor and request relevant information regarding the client.	*CH*	*11/5/03*	*CA-105*
3. Identify and discuss financial and non-financial factors that are relevant to the decision to accept the potential client.			*CA-106*
4. Perform preliminary analytical procedures using the financial statements provided by the client. Calculate ratios for comparison to the industry averages provided and identify relationships or areas that may be of concern during the audit.			*CA-107* *CA-108*
5. Based on the information obtained do you recommend that the firm accept or reject the potential client? Prepare a memo that clearly outlines your recommendation and the basis for your decision.			*CA-109*
6. Identify matters that should be included in the engagement letter for this client. You may wish to refer to SAS No. 83, "Establishing an Understanding With the Client."			*CA-110*

The Winery at Chateau Americana, Inc.
Balance Sheets as of December 31, 2003 – 2001
(In Thousands)

ASSETS

	(Projected) 2003	2002	2001
CURRENT ASSETS			
Cash	$ 3,005	$ 2,992	$ 3,281
Accounts receivable (net of allowance)	5,241	4,816	3,703
Investments	3,095	2,081	2,294
Production inventories	11,578	10,407	9,107
Finished goods inventories	4,015	3,902	3,567
Prepaid expenses	142	85	69
Total Current Assets	27,076	$ 24,283	$ 22,021
PROPERTY, PLANT & EQUIPMENT	30,230	28,135	27,612
Less accumulated depreciation	15,277	14,096	13,185
Net Property, Plant & Equipment	14,953	14,039	14,427
TOTAL ASSETS	$ 42,029	$ 38,322	$ 36,448

LIABILITIES AND SHAREHOLDERS' EQUITY

	(Projected) 2003	2002	2001
CURRENT LIABILITIES			
Accounts payable	$ 4,988	$ 3,683	$ 2,221
Accrued expenses	599	569	640
Notes payable	813	654	891
Current portion of long term debt	410	525	464
Payroll taxes withheld and payable	100	95	96
Federal income tax payable	172	157	134
Total Current Liabilities	7,082	5,683	4,446
LONG TERM DEBT	7,229	6,918	7,983
TOTAL LIABILITIES	14,311	12,601	12,429
SHAREHOLDERS' EQUITY			
Common stock (No par value, 5,000,000 shares authorized, 45,000 shares issued)	90	90	90
Additional paid-in capital	3,567	3,567	3,567
Retained earnings	24,061	22,064	20,362
Total Shareholders' Equity	27,718	25,721	24,019
TOTAL LIABILITIES AND SHAREHOLDERS' EQUITY	$ 42,029	$ 38,322	$ 36,448

The Winery at Chateau Americana, Inc.
Statements of Income for Years Ended December 31, 2003 – 2001
(In Thousands)

	(Projected) 2003	2002	2001
Sales	$ 21,945	$ 20,189	$ 18,170
Cost of goods sold	11,543	10,525	9,777
Gross profit	10,402	9,664	8,393
Selling, general and administrative expenses	7,017	6,824	6,218
Operating income	3,386	2,840	2,175
Interest expense	360	211	257
Provision for income taxes	1,028	927	483
Net income	$ 1,997	$ 1,702	$ 1,435

Selected Industry Ratios

	2003	2002
Current Ratio	4.9	4.7
Accounts Receivable Turnover	4.42	4.30
Average Days to Collect Accounts Receivable	82.58	84.88
Inventory Turnover	0.67	0.80
Days in Inventory	545	456
Assets to Equity	1.99	2.14
Debt to Equity Ratio	0.49	0.46
Times Interest Earned	6.91	7.29
Return on Assets	5.56 %	7.61 %
Return on Equity	5.92 %	10.76 %

The Winery at Chateau Americana
Evaluation of Financial and Non-financial Factors

For the Year Ended December 31, 2003

Reference: CA-106
Prepared by: ____________
Date: ____________
Reviewed by: ____________

Comments:

The Winery at Chateau Americana
Preliminary Analytical Procedures

For the Year Ended December 31, 2003

Reference:	CA-107
Prepared by:	
Date:	
Reviewed by:	

Ratio	Industry Ratios 2003	Industry Ratios 2002	Chateau Americana 2003	Comments
Current Ratio	4.9	4.7		
Accounts Receivable Turnover	4.42	4.30		
Average Days to Collect A/R	81.45	84.88		
Inventory Turnover	0.67	0.80		
Days in Inventory	545	456		
Assets to Equity	1.99	2.14		
Debt to Equity Ratio	0.49	0.46		
Times Interest Earned	4.91	4.29		
Return on Assets	5.56%	7.61%		
Return on Equity	5.92%	10.76%		

The Winery at Chateau Americana
Preliminary Analytical Procedures

For the Year Ended December 31, 2003

Reference: CA-108
Prepared by: ____________
Date: ____________
Reviewed by: ____________

Summary comments:

The Winery at Chateau Americana
Client Acceptance Recommendation
For the Year Ended December 31, 2003

Reference: CA-109
Prepared by:
Date:
Reviewed by:

Comments:

The Winery at Chateau Americana
Establishing an Understanding with the Client
For the Year Ended December 31, 2003

Reference: CA-110
Prepared by: ____________
Date: ____________
Reviewed by: ____________

Comments:

UNDERSTANDING THE BUSINESS ENVIRONMENT:
The Winery At Chateau Americana

LEARNING OBJECTIVES

After completing and discussing this case, you should be able to:

- Describe and document information related to a client's business and industry, operations, management and governance, objectives and strategies, and performance measurement
- Describe sources of business risks
- Describe the relationship between business risk and the risk of material misstatements in the financial statements
- Describe the types of information that should be used in assessing the risk of material misstatements in the financial statements

INTRODUCTION

Chateau Americana (CA) recently hired your accounting firm to perform an audit of its financial statements for the year ended December 31, 2003. Your partner, Claire Helton, approached you several days ago with a request for help in planning this year's audit engagement. She asked for assistance in three specific areas: understanding the winery's business environment, assessing business risks, and identifying and assessing factors relevant to the risk of material misstatements in CA's financial statements. As you work to develop an understanding of the business environment, Claire asked that you specifically consider factors related to business operations, management and corporate governance, business objectives and strategies, and performance measurement.

Claire invited you to accompany her on a recent visit to the winery during which she interviewed CA's president Edward Summerfield, vice-president of marketing Taylor Summerfield, and chief financial officer Rob Breeden. The following transcripts were taken from those interviews. At the end of the transcripts, you will also find excerpts from various trade publications which will help you learn more about the wine industry.

INTERVIEW TRANSCRIPTS

Claire: Edward, thank you for meeting with us this morning. We're here to learn more about the winery's history and your vision of the company's future.

Edward: Well Claire, we're thrilled to have you and the rest of your team working with us. I believe Chateau Americana has an amazing future. Many fine people have worked hard to make this company great and we've endured our share of bumps along the way, but I think most of us would agree that we've learned a great deal over the years and have a stronger company as a consequence.

Let me give you a bit of background about us. After spending more than 20 years working for other companies in the wine industry, I decided to start my own company. Although my family was a bit skeptical at first, they were and continue to be supportive. The winery has become the typical family business with a good deal of family involvement. My daughter is vice president of marketing, my son-in-law is vice president of winery operations, and several of my grandchildren have worked for us during their summer breaks. In all, we have approximately 250 permanent employees and we hire an additional 30 to 40 seasonal employees for harvest. Many of our employees have been with us for a number of years and we have been fortunate to have very little employee turnover.

Our current production is approximately 385,000 cases with capacity for an additional 80,000 cases. Our intention is to grow our business to a sustained level between 410,000 and 450,000 cases. We expect to achieve this level within the next three to five years. Our wines are sold in more than 20 states and we have exclusive distribution agreements with several small wine distributors in a few states. We have a sales force of highly motivated and experienced individuals. We plan to add several new sales positions in the coming months.

The wine business is highly competitive and because we're one of almost 1,800 wineries, we have to remain vigilant if we want to continue to thrive. Our geographic location assists us in staying abreast of industry trends. Almost half of all domestic wineries are in California, so there's a concentration of talent here that's nowhere else in the U.S.

Claire: I've read about the trend toward consolidation in the industry. How will this trend affect your company?

Edward: Well, that's a great question. As I mentioned a minute ago, this is a family business and we have no interest in being taken over by a bigger winery. My family and I have had a number of discussions about this and we all agree that this company is our family's future.

I'm certain that we will need to be vigilant as we move forward, and I believe that our people are committed to being as efficient and innovative as possible while maintaining our winery's commitment to its small business values.

Claire: What kinds of innovations have been made recently?

Edward: We have adopted new technologies in our winemaking process and even more recently in our accounting information system. I understand that you plan to talk with Rob later this morning. I would suggest you speak to him about the details.

However, I can give you my perspective on our new accounting information system. When we first started our company, we were very small and primarily relied on a paper trail to document our business. We had numerous journals and ledgers and were constantly relying on information that was outdated. Over the last ten years, we've become much more reliant on technology and until about 18 months ago we were using a combination of software programs to maintain our records. I became convinced several years ago that we needed to move to a more integrated system that would grow with us and provide more current information. Rob was instrumental in helping us make the transition to the new system.

Claire: How have your employees reacted to the new system? Have you had any turnover related to the system change?

Edward: Like any change, some employees have been unhappy with the new system, but they'll become accustomed to it. We've had some turnover in accounting, but I don't know the details. You'll have to ask Rob about that.

Claire: Okay, I have questions on two additional matters before we meet with Rob. First, how would you describe the management group's operating style and philosophy? Second, could you describe how the board of directors operates?

Edward: Well, as I've mentioned before, this is a family company. All of us place a great deal of value on integrity and hard work. I, along with the rest of management, support open communications and encourage employees to approach any member of management with suggestions and concerns. Since we started our business in 1980, we have been focused on producing excellent wines and establishing a solid reputation. I believe that we've stayed true to our mission and I feel strongly that we have employees that are committed to the same values.

Our board of directors is comprised of three employees and four non-employees. I serve as chairman of the board. The other employee board members are my daughter Taylor and Rob Breeden, our CFO. The four non-employee board members are my wife Charlotte, Bill Jameson, and Susan Martinez, and Terrence Dillard. Bill and Susan are local business owners and have a great deal of experience with family-owned businesses. Terrence is an attorney with whom I have a longstanding personal relationship. Like me, my wife worked in the wine industry before we started Chateau Americana. I wanted our company to benefit from her work experience, so she agreed to serve on our board.

Claire: How often does the board meet and generally how long are the meetings?

Edward: The length of the meetings varies quite a bit, but a typical meeting lasts for two to three hours. We generally meet four times a year, but we can meet as often as our operations necessitate.

Claire: Do you have either an audit committee or a compensation committee?

Edward: No. Our company is so small that no one on the board has ever felt it necessary to establish such committees. Everyone is on the same page regarding our company and its future, so we always discuss and resolve any differences that may arise during our meetings.

Claire: Those are all of my questions for now. Thanks very much for taking the time to meet with us. We'll let you know if we have other questions.

♦♦

After meeting with Edward, you met with Taylor Summerfield, the company's vice president of marketing.

Claire: Taylor, it's great to see you again. We wanted to meet with you this morning so that we could learn about the winery's marketing strategy and how the company is positioning itself in the industry.

Taylor: The wine industry is very competitive. Most consumers choose wine based on just three factors: price, brand, or variety. In addition, consumers tend to buy wines only for special occasions. Domestic consumers have a long way to go before they purchase and consume wines in the same patterns as Europeans.

In the past, we've relied on a product differentiation strategy. That is, we have not competed on price, but have focused our energies and resources on appealing to a certain set of wine drinkers. For instance, several of our wines have won highly coveted awards which we have tried to leverage into targeted advertising campaigns aimed at consumers who are willing to spend $10 to $30 for a good bottle of wine. We've found that many of these consumers are baby boomers.

Claire: How are other demographic groups addressed by your marketing strategy?

Taylor: Although baby boomers purchase a significant percentage of our wines, we are making inroads with younger consumers. There are a significant number of individuals between the ages of 35 and 64 who have sufficient disposable income and the desire to purchase better table wines. We are currently discussing some new strategies targeted at that segment of the population. We have discussed the possibility of sponsoring or co-sponsoring certain events such as arts festivals, golf tournaments, and various charity functions.

Claire: What is your advertising budget?

Taylor: Approximately $750,000.

Claire: Is this sufficient?

Taylor: I would like to devote more of our resources to advertising and marketing, but I'm also aware of some of our other needs. My father and I meet frequently about the company's marketing strategy and we both agree that we need to increase the advertising budget. I expect that we will increase our budget by 10 to 20 percent in the next couple of years.

Claire: Turning to your customer base, do you have any *key* customers?

Taylor: We've specifically tried to avoid over reliance on a single customer or a small number of customers. However, we have developed close relationships with several reasonably large distributors. We monitor sales and collections activity with these customers to limit our exposure. I should tell you that no single customer accounts for more than five percent of our annual sales.

Claire: One last question if I may. How large is your sales force?

Taylor: Currently, we have 20 sales people. We intend to add several sales positions in the near future to help with our projected sales growth. Our goal is to increase sales by eight to ten percent per year.

Claire: Is that a realistic goal?

Taylor: I think so. Our sales growth has averaged approximately nine percent over the last several years. I feel confident that a bigger sales force will allow us to easily increase our sales.

Claire: Great, thanks for meeting with us. We'll be in touch if we have any other questions.

♦♦

Following the meeting with Taylor, you made your way to Rob Breeden's office. Rob is the company's chief financial officer.

Claire: Rob, thank you for meeting with us this afternoon. We wanted to talk about several issues. Let's start with the company's accounting department. Can you describe the personnel and the general operations of the department?

Rob: Sure, we have a great group of folks in accounting. With the exception of two individuals who left within the last several months we've had very little turnover. We only use full-time employees in the department. Each employee reports directly to me and has very clearly defined responsibilities.

Edward is very concerned about employee training and so everyone is encouraged to maintain their education. In fact, the company reimburses employees for the cost of courses taken at the local university. We've been very pleased at the employee response to the policy. I believe it helps us retain our people.

Claire: Next, can you tell us about the new accounting information system. Can you give us a brief overview of the system and explain why you chose it?

Rob: The system is the result of an intense in-house development process. During my tenure with my former employer we developed a similar system using database technology. Here we based our system on Access. The software is really quite powerful and it allowed us to develop all of the modules that we need to have updated and accurate information.

In addition, the new system will easily accommodate our needs for the foreseeable future. Integration was also important to us as our previous system was not well integrated. With this system, all of our functional areas are linked so that employees have access to the same updated information. The integration has dramatically improved our operations in areas such as purchasing, shipping, and cash management.

Claire: I understand there has been some employee turnover as a consequence of frustrations with the new system.

Rob: We've had a few employees to leave in recent months, but I'm not sure that I would agree with the contention that they left because of frustration with the system. We have made every effort to train our people and to address their concerns, but I recognize that some individuals may still not be happy with changes that I've made.

Claire: You mentioned cash management – I noticed the company generally maintains a healthy cash balance.

Rob: Yes, we've really improved our cash management in the last 12 to 18 months. There are several reasons for the improvement. First, we've instituted a new disbursements policy that allows us to take advantage of any early payment discounts. This policy alone has saved us quite a bit of money. We continually monitor our cash collections and credit granting practices to avoid excessive write-offs. In fact, one of my concerns when I started working with the winery was the company's potential exposure to several large customers. Since my arrival, we've dramatically cut our reliance on certain customers. Finally, our new AIS has enabled us to monitor our cash position more closely than ever before.

Claire: So, I take it that you're comfortable with the reliability of the financial reports that are generated?

Rob: Absolutely. I was less comfortable with the old system because of the lack of integration. In addition, I've encouraged Edward and the Board to be more active in reviewing our monthly financials. My sense is that they were less involved in the financial aspect of the business prior to my arrival because of their relationship with the former CFO.

Claire: Have they become more involved?

Rob: Yes, Grant and I meet regularly to review the financial statements and I make a presentation to the board at every meeting.

Claire: How is the company financed?

Rob: Like many similar companies, the winery is financed through a combination of the owners' personal wealth and debt. The Summerfield family invested in the company many years ago and they have been rewarded handsomely. The company does have a modest amount of long-term debt, but we are reducing that debt as our operations allow. We plan to eliminate most of the outstanding long-term debt within the next three to five years.

Claire: Does the company have ready access to a line of credit?

Rob: Yes. Edward has developed very strong relationships with several local banks. We currently have a line of credit at Bank of Huntington.

Claire: With respect to the company's equity - are there any non-family stockholders?

Rob: No. Although we've discussed plans about a future IPO, Edward and the family have been reluctant to issue shares to anyone outside of the family. Their view is that non-family ownership may complicate operations in an unnecessary way.

Claire: Do you agree with them?

Rob: Yes. I don't see any value in diluting the family's ownership of the company given our current financial position.

Claire: Are there any related party transactions?

Rob: None to speak of really. Edward personally owns some of the equipment that we use in the winery, but there are no other significant transactions. We pay him approximately $9,000 each month.

Claire: Okay, we'll need to get a copy of that lease agreement. Let's move on to compensation matters. Give us an overview of the company's compensation philosophy.

Rob: Edward is a self-made man. He expects employees to work hard and believes the company should pay them well. Given our status as a family-owned business, employees are viewed as more than labor.

Claire: Are there any incentive compensation plans?

Rob: Our salespeople are paid a base salary plus a commission. All other employees receive annual bonuses based on the company's overall performance.

Claire: Does management participate in this annual bonus plan?

Rob: Yes. Everyone has the potential to receive a bonus.

Claire: What is the typical bonus?

Rob: The average bonus is approximately 10 percent of an employee's annual salary, but we've had bonuses as high as 30 percent.

Claire: What basis is used to calculate the bonuses?

Rob: Our bonus plan emphasizes operating efficiency and effectiveness. We consider factors such as employee performance evaluations, production efficiencies and innovations, sales, and profits.

Claire: So, you would say that there is a strong link between performance and compensation.

Rob: Yes, this is not a company that tolerates lazy employees or lackluster performance.

♦♦

You returned to the office following your meeting with Rob to find that Claire had asked one of the firm's assistants to gather information to help in your understanding of the wine industry. The assistant prepared the following summary observations based on her readings of various trade publications.

- The wine industry spent slightly more than $100 million on marketing activities in the U.S. in 2000.
- U.S. wine consumers are more brand-oriented than consumers in other countries.
- There has been an increase in non-traditional wine marketing including direct mail, offbeat advertising and such Internet sites as Wine.com.
- The U.S. wine market is characterized by a large number of wineries producing a wide variety of products, most with a small market share.
- In the fragmented wine market, the middle tier of medium-sized wine producers is expected to fall prey to merger and acquisition activity over the next few years. Smaller niche producers will need to specialize if they are to survive.
- Supermarkets dominate off-premises sales of wine. Their distribution strategy focuses on improved merchandising, stocking larger bottle sizes and strong price promotions.
- Significant demand for wines during the late 1990s led to rising prices, resulting in faster growth in sales value than in sales volume.
- Wine consumption is directly related to income. High income families are much more likely to consume wine than lower income families.

- Prosperous baby boomers are expected to increase their wine consumption in the future, especially of premium wines.
- The trend towards consolidation is expected to continue as companies search for strategies to benefit from economies of scale in production and distribution.

REQUIREMENTS

Claire Helton, the partner in charge of the Chateau Americana audit engagement, has asked that you complete select audit procedures relevant to understanding the company's business environment. Use the audit schedules that follow the audit program to document your work for each audit procedure.

The Winery at Chateau Americana
Audit Program for Understanding the Business Environment
For the Year Ended December 31, 2003

Reference: *UB-200*
Prepared by: ______
Date: ______
Reviewed by: ______

Audit Procedures	Initial	Date	A/S Ref.
1. Prepare a memo that assesses Chateau Americana on each of the following criteria: a. business and industry, b. operations, c. management and corporate governance system, d. objectives and strategies, and e. performance measurement system.			*UB-201*
2. Document your assessment of Chateau Americana's control environment.			*UB-202* *UB-203*
3. Identify and discuss three to five factors affecting Chateau Americana's business risk. For each of the factors, indicate the business objective at risk.			*UB-204*
4. Explain the relationship between business risk and the risk of material misstatements in the financial statements. Based on your knowledge of Chateau American, what accounts are likely to have a lower risk of material misstatement and what accounts are likely to have higher risk of material misstatement?			*UB-205*

The Winery at Chateau Americana
Evaluation of Business Environment

For the Year Ended December 31, 2003

Reference: UB-201
Prepared by: ____________
Date: ____________
Reviewed by: ____________

Business and industry:

Operations:

Management and corporate governance system:

Objectives and strategies:

Performance measurement system:

The Winery at Chateau Americana
Assessment of Control Environment

For the Year Ended December 31, 2003

Reference:	UB-202
Prepared by:	
Date:	
Reviewed by:	

Integrity and ethical values:

Commitment to competence:

Board of directors or audit committee participation:

Management's philosophy and operating style:

The Winery at Chateau Americana
Assessment of Control Environment

For the Year Ended December 31, 2003

Reference:	UB-203
Prepared by:	
Date:	
Reviewed by:	

Organizational structure:

Assignment of authority and responsibility:

Human resource policies and practices:

Overall Assessment: Summarize your overall assessment of Chateau Americana's control environment by selecting from among the following statements:

_____ The overall control environment is weak.
_____ The overall control environment is moderately weak.
_____ The overall control environment is neither weak nor strong.
_____ The overall control environment is moderately strong.
_____ The overall control environment is strong.

The Winery at Chateau Americana
Business Risk Factors and At-risk Objectives

For the Year Ended December 31, 2003

Reference:	*UB-204*
Prepared by:	
Date:	
Reviewed by:	

Comments:

The Winery at Chateau Americana
Evaluation of Potential Misstatements

For the Year Ended December 31, 2003

Reference: UB-205
Prepared by:
Date:
Reviewed by:

Comments:

IDENTIFICATION OF AUDIT TESTS FOR THE EXPENDITURE CYCLE (ACQUISITIONS AND CASH DISBURSEMENTS): The Winery at Chateau Americana

LEARNING OBJECTIVES

After completing and discussing this case, you should be able to:

- Recognize common business documents used with purchases and cash disbursements
- Recognize common control activities used to process purchases and cash disbursements
- Identify control activities that reduce the likelihood of material misstatements
- Link control activities to management assertions
- Design tests of controls for control activities related to purchases and cash disbursements
- Design substantive tests of transactions to detect material misstatements for non-payroll accounts in the expenditure cycle
- Design analytical tests to detect potential material misstatements for non-payroll accounts in the expenditure cycle
- Design substantive tests of balances to detect material misstatements for accounts payable
- Link tests of controls, substantive tests of transactions, analytical tests, and substantive tests of balances to management assertions related to purchases, cash payments, and accounts payable
- Identify reportable conditions and material weaknesses for non-payroll expenditure cycle accounts to discuss with management and the audit committee

INTRODUCTION

Chateau Americana (CA) has an annual production of approximately 385,000 cases of wine. Production of the 385,000 cases of wine requires roughly 3,200 tons of grapes. One-fourth of the needed grapes are harvested from CA's 125-acre vineyard, the remaining grapes are predominantly purchased from California vineyards. Other purchases associated with the production of wine include oak barrels, bottles, cork, neck wrappers, and labels. CA also has non-payroll administrative, marketing, and maintenance expenditures associated with its wine operations. Marketing expenditures such as priority distribution, special promotions, and print advertising have substantially increased in the past year to improve CA's market penetration.

BACKGROUND INFORMATION ABOUT THE AUDIT

CA has the following general ledger accounts related to purchasing and cash disbursement activities:

- Inventory – Production
- Prepaid Expenses
- Accounts Payable
- Accrued Expenses
- Cost of Goods Sold
- Occupancy Expense
- Marketing Expense
- Communications Expense
- Professional Services Expense
- Supplies Expense
- Data Processing Expense
- Travel and Entertainment Expense
- Insurance Expense
- Dues and Subscriptions Expense
- Tax Expense
- Maintenance Expense
- Automobile Expense
- Lease Expense
- Other Operating Expense
- Miscellaneous Expense

In accordance with professional standards, Mikel Frucella, audit manager, reviewed CA's control environment, risk assessment policies, and monitoring system and has assessed them as strong. Julia Granger, staff auditor, reviewed CA's information system and control activities related to purchases and cash disbursements and prepared the enclosed flowcharts (referenced in the top right hand corner as *E-110, E-111,*and *E-112*). Mikel has decided there is no need to document the company's policies nor perform tests of controls for purchase returns and allowances as the number and size of purchase returns and allowances is relatively small.

As the audit senior, you have been assigned responsibility for (1) identifying internal control activities that assure that non-payroll purchase and cash disbursement transactions are properly stated in all material respects, (2) developing tests of controls that test the design and operating effectiveness of identified internal control activities, and (3) identifying substantive tests to detect material misstatements related to non-payroll expenditure cycle accounts. You have conducted some preliminary discussions with client personnel and noted the following

- Purchase returns and allowances transactions are recorded in the purchases journal
- Purchase discounts are recorded in the cash disbursements journal
- Adjustments to expenditure cycle accounts are recorded in the general journal and require preparation of a prenumbered adjustment memo

REQUIREMENTS

Complete steps 5 through 8 in the Expenditure Cycle Planning Audit Program (audit schedule *E-100*) and document your work on audit schedules *E-100, E-120, E-121, E-130, E-140, E-141, E-150, E-151, E-160, E-161, E-170,* and *E-171*. Julia Granger has already completed steps 1 through 4 and has documented the results of her work on audit schedules *E-100, E-110, E-111,* and *E-112*. Assume that the client performs the control activities identified in the flowcharts.

The Winery at Chateau Americana
Expenditure Cycle Planning Audit Program

For the Year Ended: December 31, 2003

Reference: *E-100*
Prepared by: *JG*
Date: *11/12/03*
Reviewed by:

Audit Procedures	Initial	Date	A/S Ref.
1. Obtain and study a copy of the client's policies and procedures manuals related to purchases and cash disbursements.	*JG*	*11/12/03*	*N/A*
2. Discuss with and observe client personnel performing control activities related to purchases and cash disbursements.	*JG*	*11/12/03*	*N/A*
3. Perform a document walk-through of the client's polices and procedures related to purchases and cash disbursements.	*JG*	*11/12/03*	*N/A*
4. Obtain or prepare a flowchart for purchases and cash disbursements showing control activities, document flows, and records.	*JG*	*11/12/03*	*E-110* *E-111* *E-112*
5. Use the control activities matrix to list client control activities that reduce the likelihood of material misstatements for management assertions related to purchases and cash disbursements.			*E-120* *E-121*
6. Based on the previous audit procedures, list potential internal control deficiencies on the internal control deficiencies schedule.			*E-130*
7. Use the planning audit test matrices to list potential tests of controls related to purchases and cash disbursements.			*E-140* *E-141*
8. Use the planning audit test matrices to identify potential			
a. Substantive tests of transactions,			*E-150* *E-151*
b. Analytical tests, and			*E-160* *E-161*
c. Tests of balances related to non-payroll expenditure cycle accounts.			*E-170* *E-171*

The Winery at Chateau Americana
Expenditure Cycle - Purchases Flowchart

For the Year Ended December 31, 2003

Reference: *E-110*
Prepared by: *JG*
Date: *11/12/03*
Reviewed by: ____________

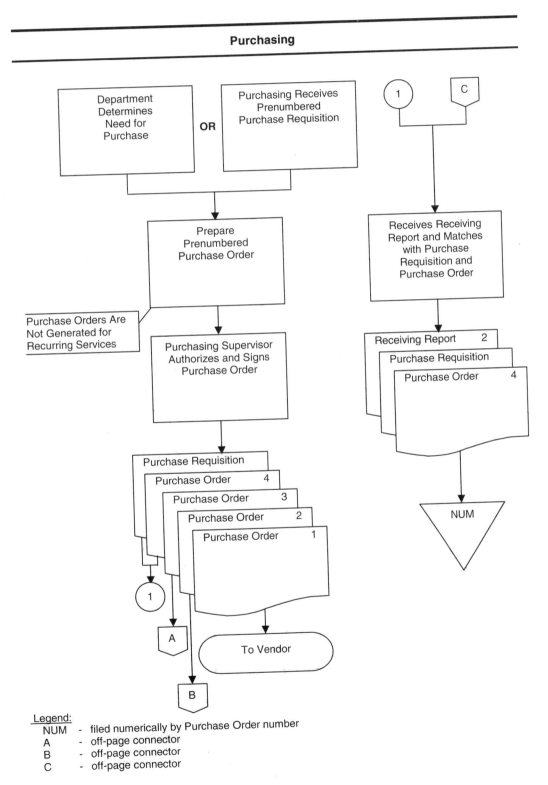

Purchasing

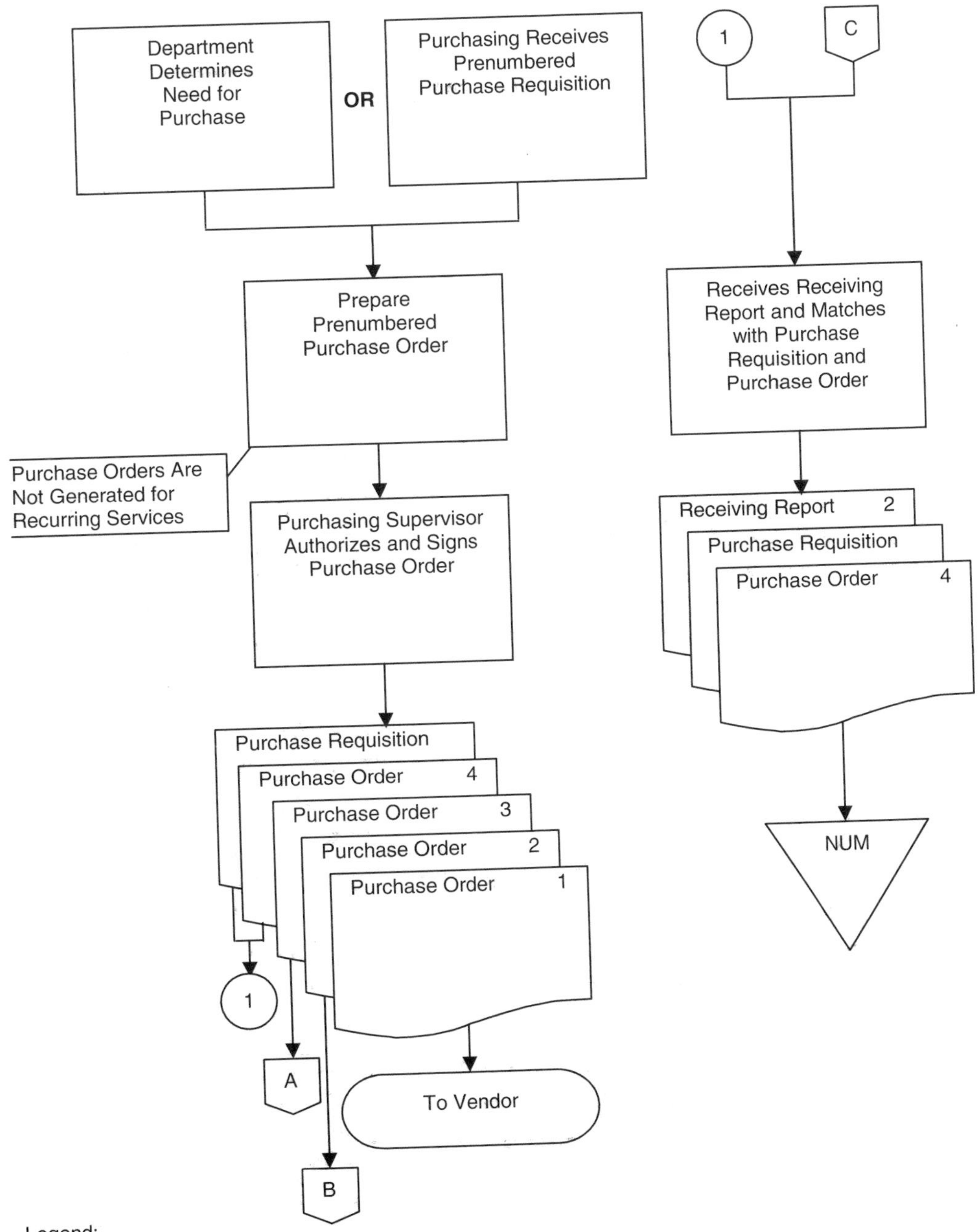

Legend:
NUM - filed numerically by Purchase Order number
A - off-page connector
B - off-page connector
C - off-page connector

The Winery at Chateau Americana
Expenditure Cycle - Purchases Flowchart

For the Year Ended December 31, 2003

Reference:	E-111
Prepared by:	JG
Date:	11/12/03
Reviewed by:	

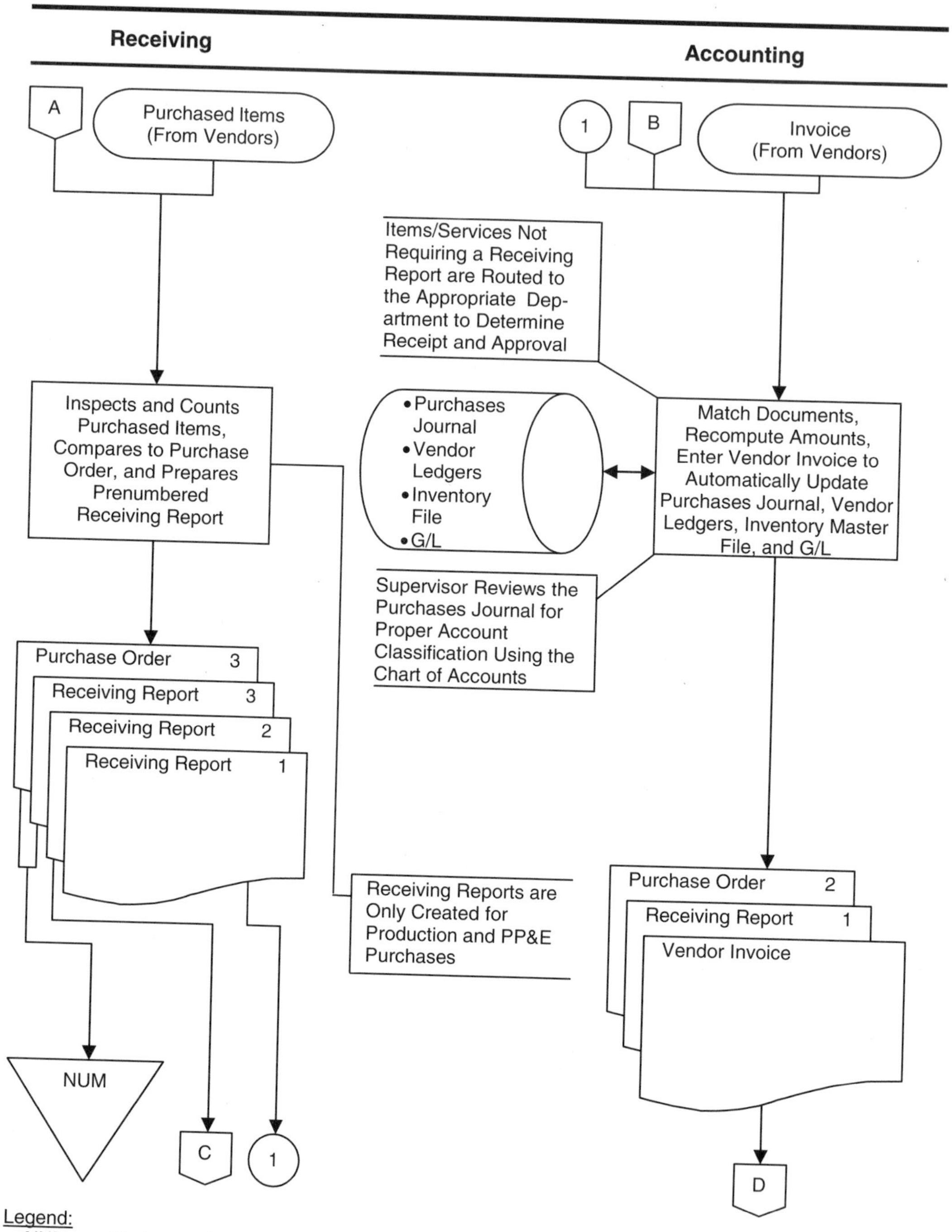

Legend:
NUM - filed numerically by Receiving Report number
A - off-page connector
B - off-page connector
C - off-page connector
D - off-page connector

The Winery at Chateau Americana
Expenditure Cycle - Cash Disbursement Flowchart

For the Year Ended December 31, 2003

Reference: *E-112*
Prepared by: *JG*
Date: *11/12/03*
Reviewed by: ______

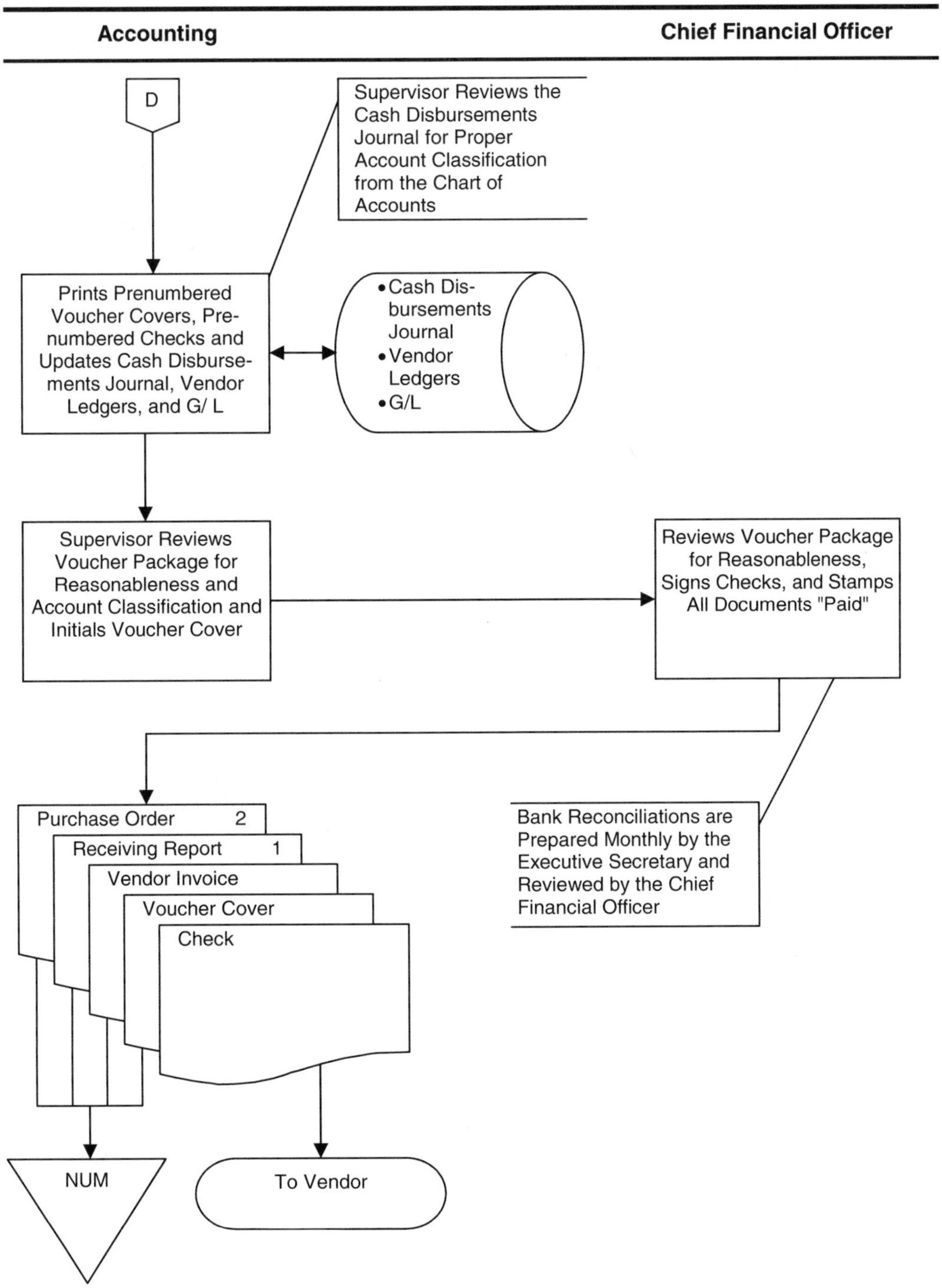

Legend:
NUM – filed numerically by Voucher number
D – off-page connector

The Winery at Chateau Americana
Expenditure Cycle – Purchases Control Activities Matrix
For the Year Ended December 31, 2003

Reference: *E-120*
Prepared by: ____
Date: ____
Reviewed by: ____

Control Activities	Existence	Rights and Obligations	Valuation	Presentation and Disclosure	Completeness
1) Purchasing supervisor reviews and signs all purchase orders.	*X*	*X*			
Identify the management assertion(s) each control activity affects with an "X."					

The Winery at Chateau Americana
Expenditure Cycle – Cash Disbursements Control Activities Matrix
For the Year Ended December 31, 2003

Reference: E-121
Prepared by: ________
Date: ________
Reviewed by: ________

Control Activities	Existence	Rights and Obligations	Valuation	Presentation and Disclosure	Completeness

Identify the management assertion(s) each control activity affects with an "X."

The Winery at Chateau Americana
Expenditure Cycle – Internal Control Deficiencies

For the Year Ended December 31, 2003

Reference: *E-130*
Prepared by: ______
Date: ______
Reviewed by: ______

Internal Control Deficiencies	Client Personnel Discussed With	RC	MW
1) The client does not internally account for all used receiving reports.		*Yes*	*No*

Legend:
RC – Reportable Condition (Yes or No)
MW – Material Weakness (Yes or No)

The Winery at Chateau Americana
Expenditure Cycle - Tests of Controls Planning Matrix

For the Year Ended December 31, 2003

Reference: *E-140*
Prepared by: ____________
Date: ____________
Reviewed by: ____________

	Purchases					Cash Disbursements					Accounts Payable				
Tests of Controls	Existence	Rights/Obligations	Valuation	Presentation/Disclosure	Completeness	Existence	Rights/Obligations	Valuation	Presentation/Disclosure	Completeness	Existence	Rights/Obligations	Valuation	Presentation/Disclosure	Completeness
TC1) Inquire and observe the purchasing supervisor reviewing and signing purchase orders.	*W*										*W*	*W*			

Indicate whether the test provides Strong (S), Moderate (M), or Weak (W) evidence for the specific management assertion.

The Winery at Chateau Americana
Expenditure Cycle - Tests of Controls Planning Matrix

For the Year Ended December 31, 2003

Reference: E-141
Prepared by: ____________
Date: ____________
Reviewed by: ____________

	Purchases					Cash Disbursements					Accounts Payable				
Tests of Controls	Existence	Rights/Obligations	Valuation	Presentation/Disclosure	Completeness	Existence	Rights/Obligations	Valuation	Presentation/Disclosure	Completeness	Existence	Rights/Obligations	Valuation	Presentation/Disclosure	Completeness

Indicate whether the test provides Strong (S), Moderate (M), or Weak (W) evidence for the specific management assertion.

The Winery at Chateau Americana
Expenditure Cycle - Substantive Tests of Transactions
Planning Matrix
For the Year Ended December 31, 2003

Reference: *E-150*
Prepared by: ____________
Date: ____________
Reviewed by: ____________

	Purchases					Cash Disbursements					Accounts Payable				
Substantive Tests of Transactions	Existence	Rights/Obligations	Valuation	Presentation/Disclosure	Completeness	Existence	Rights/Obligations	Valuation	Presentation/Disclosure	Completeness	Existence	Rights/Obligations	Valuation	Presentation/Disclosure	Completeness
TT1) Vouch purchase transactions recorded in the purchases journal to supporting documents.	*M*		*M*	*M*							*M*		*M*	*M*	

Indicate whether the test provides Strong (S), Moderate (M), or Weak (W) evidence for the specific management assertion.

The Winery at Chateau Americana
Expenditure Cycle - Substantive Tests of Transactions
Planning Matrix
For the Year Ended December 31, 2003

Reference: E-151
Prepared by: ____________
Date: ____________
Reviewed by: ____________

	Purchases					Cash Disbursements					Accounts Payable				
Substantive Tests of Transactions	Existence	Rights/Obligations	Valuation	Presentation/Disclosure	Completeness	Existence	Rights/Obligations	Valuation	Presentation/Disclosure	Completeness	Existence	Rights/Obligations	Valuation	Presentation/Disclosure	Completeness

Indicate whether the test provides Strong (S), Moderate (M), or Weak (W) evidence for the specific management assertion.

The Winery at Chateau Americana
Expenditure Cycle – Analytical Tests Planning Matrix

For the Year Ended December 31, 2003

Reference: *E-160*
Prepared by: ______
Date: ______
Reviewed by: ______

	Purchases					Cash Disbursements					Accounts Payable				
Analytical Tests	Existence	Rights/Obligations	Valuation	Presentation/Disclosure	Completeness	Existence	Rights/Obligations	Valuation	Presentation/Disclosure	Completeness	Existence	Rights/Obligations	Valuation	Presentation/Disclosure	Completeness
AT1) Scan the year-end vendor ledgers for unusual, related party or debit balances and perform follow-up procedures for each one identified.	M		M	M				M	M	M	M		M	M	

Indicate whether the test provides Strong (S), Moderate (M), or Weak (W) evidence for the specific management assertion.

The Winery at Chateau Americana
Expenditure Cycle - Analytical Tests Planning Matrix

For the Year Ended December 31, 2003

Reference: *E-161*
Prepared by: ____________
Date: ____________
Reviewed by: ____________

Analytical Tests	Purchases					Cash Disbursements					Accounts Payable				
	Existence	Rights/Obligations	Valuation	Presentation/Disclosure	Completeness	Existence	Rights/Obligations	Valuation	Presentation/Disclosure	Completeness	Existence	Rights/Obligations	Valuation	Presentation/Disclosure	Completeness

Indicate whether the test provides Strong (S), Moderate (M), or Weak (W) evidence for the specific management assertion.

The Winery at Chateau Americana
Expenditure Cycle - Tests of Balances Planning Matrix

For the Year Ended December 31, 2003

Reference: *E-170*
Prepared by: ____________
Date: ____________
Reviewed by: ____________

	Purchases					Cash Disbursements					Accounts Payable				
Tests of Balances	Existence	Rights/Obligations	Valuation	Presentation/Disclosure	Completeness	Existence	Rights/Obligations	Valuation	Presentation/Disclosure	Completeness	Existence	Rights/Obligations	Valuation	Presentation/Disclosure	Completeness
TB1) Obtain the last five receiving reports issued before year-end and determine if they were properly included in the purchases journal and year-end vendor ledgers.			W		M								W		M

Indicate whether the test provides Strong (S), Moderate (M), or Weak (W) evidence for the specific management assertion.

The Winery at Chateau Americana
Expenditure Cycle - Tests of Balances Planning Matrix

For the Year Ended December 31, 2003

Reference: E-171
Prepared by: ____________
Date: ____________
Reviewed by: ____________

Tests of Balances	Purchases					Cash Disbursements					Accounts Payable				
	Existence	Rights/Obligations	Valuation	Presentation/Disclosure	Completeness	Existence	Rights/Obligations	Valuation	Presentation/Disclosure	Completeness	Existence	Rights/Obligations	Valuation	Presentation/Disclosure	Completeness

Indicate whether the test provides Strong (S), Moderate (M), or Weak (W) evidence for the specific management assertion.

SELECTION OF AUDIT TESTS AND RISK ASSESSMENT FOR THE EXPENDITURE CYCLE (ACQUISITIONS AND CASH DISBURSEMENTS): The Winery at Chateau Americana

LEARNING OBJECTIVES

After completing and discussing this case, you should be able to:

- Select planned tests of controls, substantive tests of transactions, analytical tests, and tests of balances for non-payroll expenditure cycle accounts
- Assess planned control risk for the non-payroll expenditure cycle based on planned tests of controls
- Assess planned detection risk for the non-payroll expenditure cycle based on planned substantive tests

INTRODUCTION

Chateau Americana (CA) has an annual production of approximately 385,000 cases of wine. Production of the 385,000 cases of wine requires roughly 3,200 tons of grapes. One-fourth of the needed grapes are harvested from CA's 125-acre vineyard, the remaining grapes are predominantly purchased from California vineyards. Other purchases associated with the production of wine include oak barrels, bottles, cork, neck wrappers, and labels. CA also has non-payroll administrative, marketing, and maintenance expenditures associated with its wine operations. Marketing expenditures such as priority distribution, special promotions, and print advertising have substantially increased in the past year to improve CA's market penetration.

BACKGROUND INFORMATION ABOUT THE AUDIT

CA has the following general ledger accounts related to purchasing and cash disbursement activities:

- Inventory – Production
- Prepaid Expenses
- Accounts Payable
- Accrued Expenses
- Cost of Goods Sold
- Travel and Entertainment Expense
- Insurance Expense
- Dues and Subscriptions Expense
- Tax Expense

- Occupancy Expense
- Marketing Expense
- Communications Expense
- Professional Services Expense
- Supplies Expense
- Data Processing Expense
- Maintenance Expense
- Automobile Expense
- Lease Expense
- Other Operating Expense
- Miscellaneous Expense

In accordance with professional standards, Mikel Frucella, audit manager, reviewed CA's control environment, risk assessment policies, and monitoring system and has assessed them as strong. Additionally, Mikel determined that tolerable misstatement should be $40,000 for the non-payroll expenditure cycle and that acceptable audit risk should be low. Julia Granger, staff auditor, assessed inherent risk related to purchases, non-payroll cash payments, and accounts payable and prepared the enclosed audit risk matrix (referenced in the top right hand corner as *E-180* and *E-181*). As the audit senior, you have been assigned responsibility for selecting audit procedures to perform for the expenditure cycle that will achieve the desired acceptable audit risk at the lowest possible cost.

REQUIREMENTS

This assignment cannot be completed until the previous CA audit planning assignment is completed. Review the materials in the previous assignment plus the materials in this assignment. Complete audit steps 3 and 4 in the Expenditure Cycle Planning Audit Program – Risk Assessment and Selection of Audit Tests (audit schedule *E-101*) and document your work in audit schedules *E-101, E-140, E-141, E-150, E-151, E-160, E-161, E-170, E-171, E-180, E-182,* and *E-183*. Julia Granger has already completed steps 1 and 2 and has documented the results of her work in audit schedules *E-101, E-180,* and *E-181*.

Reference:	*E-101*
Prepared by:	*JG*
Date:	*11/13/03*
Reviewed by:	

The Winery at Chateau Americana
Expenditure Cycle Planning Audit Program –
Risk Assessment and Selection of Audit Tests
Year Ended: December 31, 2003

Audit Procedures	Initial	Date	A/S Ref.
1. Complete the acceptable audit risk section of the expenditure cycle "Planning Audit Risk Matrix" by obtaining the acceptable audit risk from the general planning audit schedules.	*JG*	*11/13/03*	*E-180*
2. Form an initial assessment of inherent risk related to non-payroll expenditure cycle accounts and complete the initial inherent risk assessment section of the "Planning Audit Risk Matrix."	*JG*	*11/13/03*	*E-180* *E-181*
3. Select audit tests to perform by circling the procedure number on the audit tests planning matrices (note: audit tests should be selected such that the combination of inherent risk, control risk, and detection risk for each management assertion related to non-payroll expenditure cycle accounts is reduced to the appropriate level).			*E-140* *E-141* *E-150* *E-151* *E-160* *E-161* *E-170* *E-171*
4. Based on the procedures selected in audit step 3, complete the planned control risk and detection risk sections of the expenditure cycle "Planning Audit Risk Matrix."			*E-180* *E-182* *E-183*

The Winery at Chateau Americana
Expenditure Cycle - Planning Audit Risk Matrix
For the Year Ended December 31, 2003

Reference: *E-180*
Prepared by: *JG*
Date: *11/13/03*
Reviewed by:

Tolerable Misstatement: *$40,000, G6*	Reference	Existence*	Rights /Obligations	Valuation	Presentation/Disclosure	Completeness**
Acceptable Audit Risk	*G-10*	*L*	*L*	*L*	*L*	*L*
Initial Inherent Risk – Purchases	*E-181*	*M*		*M*	*M*	*H*
Initial Inherent Risk – Cash Payments		*M*		*M*	*L*	*M*
Initial Inherent Risk – Accounts Payable		*L*	*M*	*L*	*L*	*H*
Planned Control Risk – Purchases	*E-182*					
Planned Control Risk – Cash Payments						
Planned Control Risk – Accounts Payable						
Planned Detection Risk – Purchases	*E-183*					
Planned Detection Risk – Cash Payments						
Planned Detection Risk – Accounts Payable						

Planned Inherent Risk should be assessed as:
High (H) unless the combination of inherent risk factors present justify a lower assessment.
Moderate (M) if the combination of inherent risk factors present justify this assessment.
Low (L) if the combination of inherent risk factors present justify this assessment.
Factors justifying a lower inherent risk assessment are:
High management integrity, Low motivation to materially misstate for external parties, Repeat engagement, No material prior year misstatements, No related party transactions, Routine transactions, Limited judgement required to correctly record transactions, Low susceptibility to defalcation, Stable business environment.

Planned Control Risk should be assessed as:
Low (L) if control activity(ies) reduces the likelihood of a material misstatement to a negligible level and persuasive tests of controls are planned.
Moderate (M) if control activity(ies) reduces the likelihood of a material misstatement to a negligible level and moderately persuasive tests of controls are planned or control activity(ies) reduces the likelihood of a material misstatement to a moderate level and persuasive tests of controls are planned.
High (H) if control activity(ies) does not reduce the likelihood of a material misstatement to a reasonable level or no tests of controls are planned.

Planned Detection Risk should be assessed as:
Low (L) if persuasive substantive tests are planned.
Moderate (M) if moderately persuasive substantive tests are planned.
High (H) if minimal substantive tests are planned.

Note: * completeness for cash payments, ** existence for cash payments

The Winery at Chateau Americana
Expenditure Cycle - Comments Planned Inherent Risk Assessment
For the Year Ended December 31, 2003

Reference: *E-181*
Prepared by: *JG*
Date: *11/13/03*
Reviewed by: ________

Comments:

The inherent risk assessment for the existence, valuation, and presentation and disclosure assertions for purchases is set at a moderate level even though no misstatements were identified in prior year audit schedules because of the high volume and variable nature of purchased items and this is a first time engagement.

The inherent risk assessment for the completeness assertion for purchases is set at a high level even though no misstatements were identified in prior year audit schedules because of the external incentives for management to understate this account and this is a first time engagement.

The inherent risk assessment for the existence, valuation, and completeness assertion for cash payments is set at a moderate level even though no misstatements were identified in prior year audit schedules because of the high volume of transactions and this is a first time engagement.

The inherent risk assessment for the presentation and disclosure for cash payments is set at a low level as no misstatements were identified in prior year audit schedules and the recording of cash payments is routine and straight forward.

The inherent risk assessment for the existence, valuation, and presentation and disclosure for accounts payable is set at a low level as no misstatements were identified in prior year audit schedules and the recording of accounts payable transactions is routine and straight forward.

The inherent risk assessment for the rights and obligations for accounts payable is set at a moderate level even though no misstatements were identified in prior year audit schedules because of the motivation for employees to purchase items for their own personal use and this is a first time engagement.

The inherent risk assessment for the completeness for accounts payable is set at a high level even though not misstatements were identified in prior year audit schedules due to the external incentive for management to understate this account and this is a first time engagement.

The Winery at Chateau Americana
Expenditure Cycle - Comments Planned Control Risk Assessment
For the Year Ended December 31, 2003

Reference:	E-182
Prepared by:	
Date:	
Reviewed by:	

Comments:

The Winery at Chateau Americana
Expenditure Cycle - Comments Planned Detection Risk Assessment
For the Year Ended December 31, 2003

Reference: E-183
Prepared by: ___
Date: ___
Reviewed by: ___

Comments:

PERFORMANCE OF AUDIT TESTS FOR THE REVENUE CYCLE (SALES AND CASH COLLECTIONS): The Winery At Chateau Americana

LEARNING OBJECTIVES

After completing and discussing this case, you should be able to:

- Recognize common documents and records used with sales and cash collections
- Recognize common control activities used to process sales and cash collection transactions
- Link client control activities, tests of controls, substantive tests of transactions, and tests of balances to management assertions for sales, cash collections, and accounts receivable
- Link client control activities, tests of controls, substantive tests of transactions, and tests of balances to risk assessments for sales, cash collections, and accounts receivable
- Perform tests of controls, substantive tests of transactions, and tests of balances for revenue cycle accounts
- Evaluate the results of tests of controls, substantive tests of transactions, and tests of balances revenue cycle accounts using a non-statistical approach

INTRODUCTION

Chateau Americana (CA) produces and sells premium wines targeted to upscale wine drinkers with retail prices ranging from $10 to $35 per bottle of wine. This year CA sold approximately 385,000 cases of wines. The direct sale and distribution of wine to end consumers is generally not permitted by state regulations. Therefore, CA relies on a network of distributors to sell its wines to consumers. CA currently has agreements with distributors to sell its wines in over 20 state jurisdictions. Most agreements are with small to midsize distributors with a few agreements with large distributors. At the moment, CA does not have any sales agreements with large supermarket chains. No distributor accounts for more than five percent of CA's total sales. Last year, CA had net sales of approximately $22 million.

BACKGROUND INFORMATION ABOUT THE AUDIT

CA has the following general ledger accounts related to sales and cash collection activities

- Sales
- Sales Discounts
- Sales Returns and Allowances
- Bad Debt Expense
- Accounts Receivable
- Allowance for Bad Debts

Julia Granger, audit staff, reviewed CA's policies and procedures related to sales and cash collection activities and prepared the enclosed flowcharts (referenced in the top right hand corner as *R-110, R-111, R-112,*and *R-113*) and planned control risk matrix (audit schedule *R-180*). As a result of this process, Julia developed the enclosed audit program (audit schedules *R-101, R-102, R-103, R-104*). The audit program was approved by Mikel Frucella, audit manager, and Claire Helton, audit partner. The two staff auditors assigned to this engagement are Julia Granger and you. Together, you and Julia are responsible for performing the tests of transactions and test of balances outlined in the revenue cycle audit program (audit schedules *R-101, R-102, R-103,* and *R-104*).

Julia Grainger has already selected the audit samples for the tests of transactions and tests of balances and completed audit procedures 2 through 13 and 15 through 17. Her work is documented on various audit schedules provided in this case.

REQUIREMENTS

You have been assigned responsibility for completing audit steps 1a-c, 14a-b, and 18 listed on audit program *R-101, R-103,* and *R-104.* You will want to review the flowcharts on audit schedules *R-110, R-111, R-112,* and *R-113* to become familiar with the accounting documents and records used with sales and cash collections. Assume you have tested 25 of the 30 sample items selected for audit steps 1a-c. Also assume you have tested 15 of the 20 sample items selected for audit steps 14a-b. No deviations or misstatements were observed for these sample items. The accounting documents and records related to the remaining five sample items for audit steps 1a-c and 14a-b are provided behind the audit schedules. The audit firm has a policy of using the same audit sample for planned tests of controls and substantive tests of transactions (dual-purpose tests) whenever possible to maximize audit efficiency. Thus, the results of the test-of-controls aspect of audit steps 1a-c should be documented on audit schedule *R-410*, whereas the substantive test aspect should be documented on audit schedule *R-440.* The results of the test of balances should be documented on audit schedule *R-520.* Adjusting entries should be proposed on schedule *R-210* for any observed misstatements. You should assume that there was no systematic pattern or intent to commit a fraud based on a review and discussion with client personnel concerning observed deviations and misstatements. Finally, you may want to review the audit schedules already completed by Julia Grainger to have an idea of how each audit step is to be documented.

The Winery at Chateau Americana
Revenue Cycle Audit Program

For the Year Ended December 31, 2003

Reference: *R-101*
Prepared by: *JG*
Date: *2/18/04*
Reviewed by: ______

Audit Procedures	Initial	Date	A/S Ref.
1. Select a sample of 30 transactions recorded in the sales register throughout the year and perform the following:	JG	2/16/04	R-310
a. Examine purchase orders, shipping documents, and sales invoices for authenticity and reasonableness.			R-410 R-440
b. Determine if the sales register amounts were correct based on the sales invoice and shipping document.			R-410 R-440
c. Determine if the sales amounts were posted to the correct customer's accounts receivable master file.			R-410 R-440
2. Reconcile sales recorded in the sales register to sales and accounts receivable recorded in the general ledger for the month of November.	JG	2/17/04	R-420
3. Scan the monthly sales registers for large, unusual, or related party transactions and perform follow-up procedures for each one identified.	JG	2/17/04	R-430
4. Select a sample of 30 shipping documents issued throughout the year and perform the following:	JG	2/16/04	R-311
a. Obtain the related sales invoice and customer purchase order and determine if shipping document was properly accounted for in the sales register.	JG	2/17/04	R-411 R-440
5. Inquire and observe the office receptionist open mail in the presence of one other CA employee.	JG	2/18/04	R-400
6. Inquire and observe the office receptionist prepare a cash summary in the presence of one other CA employee.	JG	2/18/04	R-400

The Winery at Chateau Americana
Revenue Cycle Audit Program

For the Year Ended December 31, 2003

Reference: *R-102*
Prepared by: *JG*
Date: *2/19/04*
Reviewed by:

Audit Procedures	Initial	Date	A/S Ref.
7. Select a sample of 30 transactions recorded in the cash receipts journal throughout the year and perform the following:	*JG*	*2/16/04*	*R-312*
a. Examine validated bank deposit slip and cash receipt summary for authenticity and reasonableness.	*JG*	*2/18/04*	*R-412* *R-441*
b. Determine if the cash receipts journal amounts were correct based on the validated deposit slip and cash receipt summary.	*JG*	*2/18/04*	*R-412* *R-441*
c. Determine if the cash collection amounts were posted to the correct customer's accounts receivable master file.	*JG*	*2/18/04*	*R-412* *R-441*
8. Reconcile cash receipts recorded in the cash receipts journal to cash and accounts receivable recorded in the general ledger for the month of March.	*JG*	*2/18/04*	*R-421*
9. Scan the monthly cash receipts journal for large, unusual, or related party transactions and perform follow-up procedures for each one identified.	*JG*	*2/18/04*	*R-431*
10. Select a sample of 30 cash summaries prepared throughout the year and perform the following:	*JG*	*2/16/04*	*R-313*
a. Obtain the related validated deposit slip and determine if cash collection was properly accounted for in the cash receipts journal.	*JG*	*2/19/04*	*R-413* *R-441*
11. Scan the general journal for the write-off of specific customer accounts and examine credit memo and other supporting documents for customer write-offs greater than $1,000.	*JG*	*2/19/04*	*R-432*
12. Obtain a lead schedule for revenue cycle accounts and perform the following:	*JG*	*2/16/04*	*R-200*
a. Agree the prior year balances to prior year audit schedules.	*JG*	*2/16/04*	*R-200*
b. Agree current year balances to the general ledger.	*JG*	*2/16/04*	*R-200*

The Winery at Chateau Americana
Revenue Cycle Audit Program

For the Year Ended December 31, 2003

Reference:	R-103
Prepared by:	JG
Date:	2/20/04
Reviewed by:	

Audit Procedures	Initial	Date	A/S Ref.
13. Obtain an aged trial balance printout of year-end customer accounts receivable balances and perform the following:	JG	1/02/04	N/A
a. Foot the year-end aged trial balance and agree amount to the general ledger and lead schedule.	JG	2/16/04	R-200
b. Scan the year-end aged trial balance for unusual, related party or credit balances and perform follow-up procedures for each one identified.	JG	2/19/04	R-511
c. Test the aging of the aged accounts receivable trial balance by examining supporting sales documents for five customers.	JG	2/20/04	R-500
d. Inquire of the office manager concerning large old outstanding receivable balances.	JG	2/20/04	R-501
e. Obtain the last 5 bill of ladings issued before year-end and determine if they were properly included in the year-end customer ledgers and aged trial balance printout.	JG	2/20/04	R-502
f. Obtain the first 5 bill of ladings issued after year-end and determine if they were properly excluded from the year-end customer ledgers and aged trial balance printout.	JG	2/20/04	R-502
14. Select a sample of the 20 largest customer balances from the aged trial balance and perform the following:	JG	1/02/04	R-314
a. Confirm the balances directly with the customers using positive confirmations.			R-520
b. Examine documentation supporting subsequent cash collections for positive confirmations not returned.		N/A	R-520
15. Perform the following analytical procedures:			
a. Compare accounts receivable turnover to prior year results.	JG	2/20/04	R-510
b. Compare the percent aging of accounts receivable to prior year results.	JG	2/20/04	R-510
b. Compare the allowance for bad debts as a percent of accounts receivable to prior year results.	JG	2/20/04	R-510

The Winery at Chateau Americana
Revenue Cycle Audit Program

For the Year Ended December 31, 2003

Reference:	R-104
Prepared by:	JG
Date:	3/05/04
Reviewed by:	

Audit Procedures	Initial	Date	A/S Ref.
16. Review board of directors' meeting minutes for indication of the factoring or pledging of accounts receivable.	JG	3/05/04	R-503
17. Inquire of management concerning the:			
a) Factoring or pledging of receivables.	JG	3/05/04	R-503
b) Existence of related party and/or noncurrent receivables.	JG	3/05/04	R-503
18. Conclude as to the fair presentation of revenue cycle accounts in all material respects.			R-200

The Winery at Chateau Americana
Revenue Cycle - Sales Flowchart

For the Year Ended December 31, 2003

Reference: R-110
Prepared by: JG
Date: 11/14/03
Reviewed by: ______

Sales Department

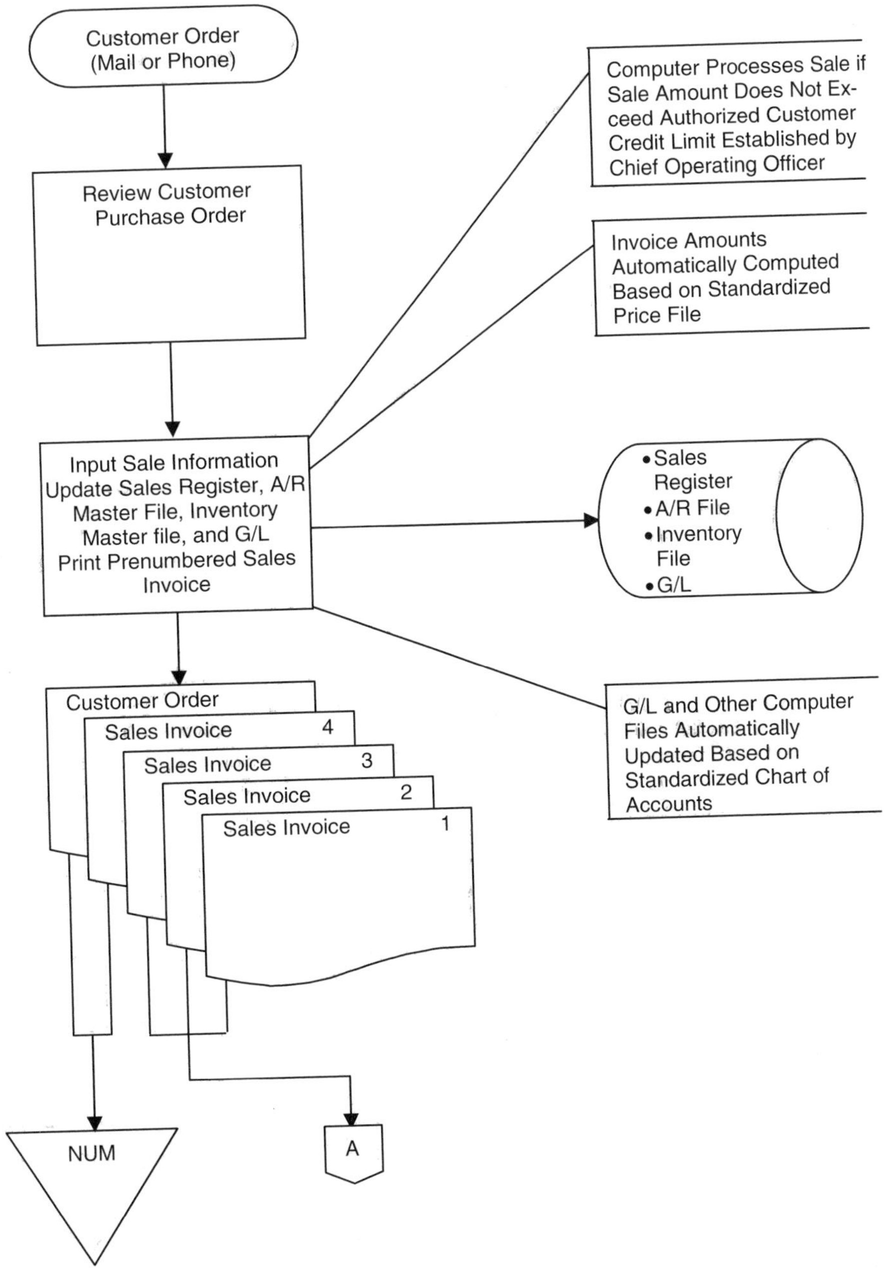

Legend:
NUM - filed numerically by Sales Invoice number
A - off-page connector

The Winery at Chateau Americana
Revenue Cycle - Sales Flowchart

For the Year Ended December 31, 2003

Reference: *R-111*
Prepared by: *JG*
Date: *11/14/03*
Reviewed by:

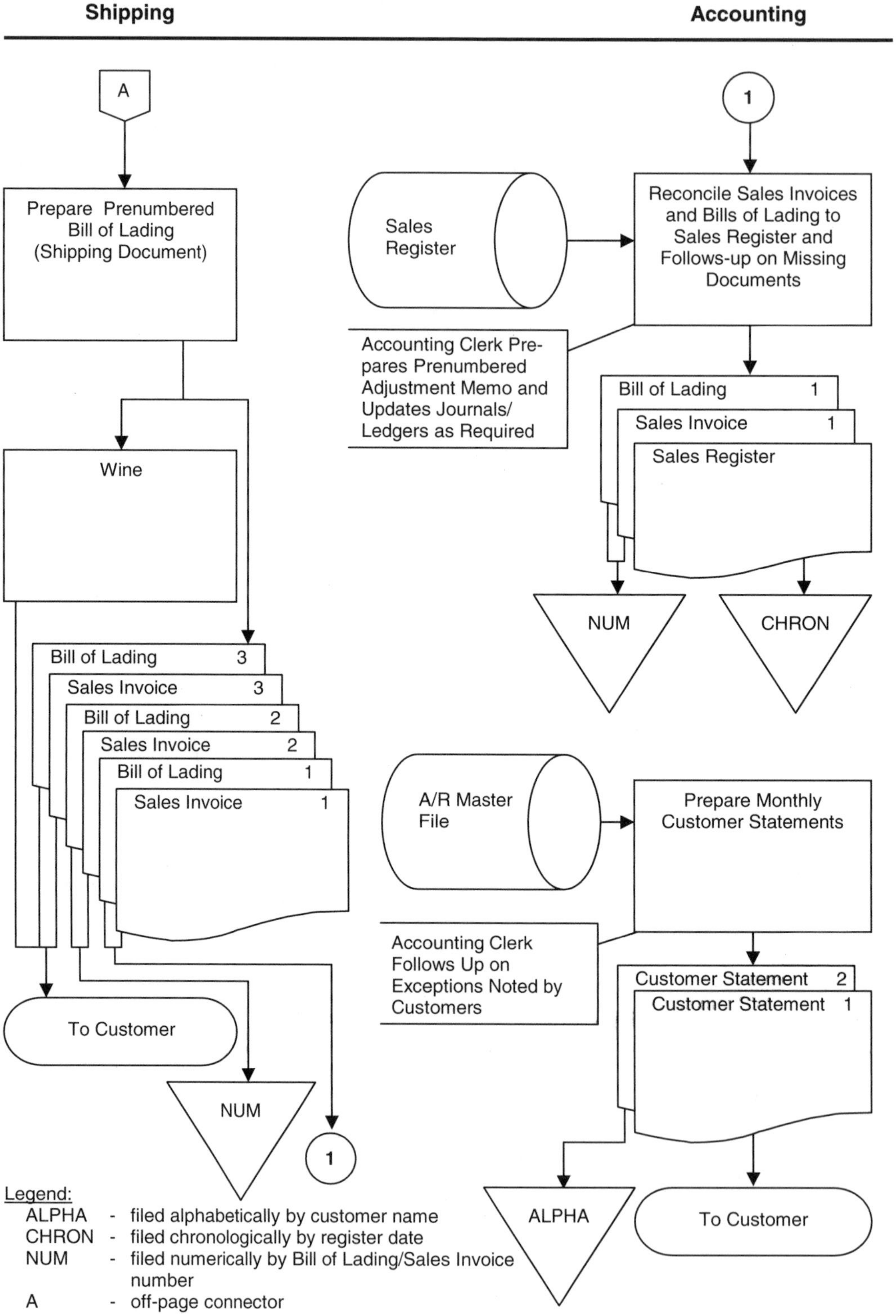

Legend:
- ALPHA - filed alphabetically by customer name
- CHRON - filed chronologically by register date
- NUM - filed numerically by Bill of Lading/Sales Invoice number
- A - off-page connector

The Winery at Chateau Americana
Revenue Cycle - Cash Receipts Flowchart

For the Year Ended December 31, 2003

Reference: *R-112*
Prepared by: *JG*
Date: *11/14/03*
Reviewed by: ______

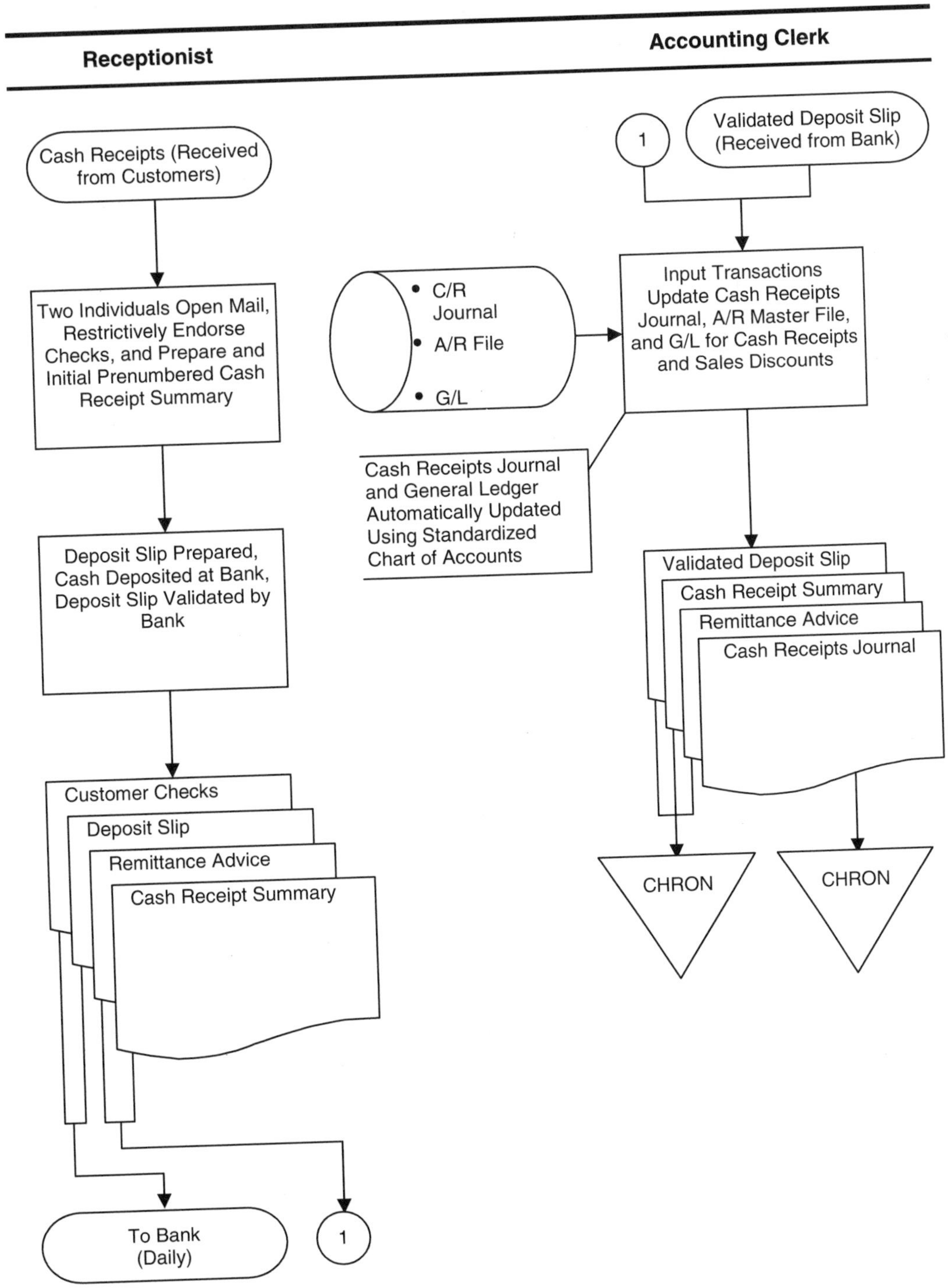

Legend:
CHRON - filed chronologically by summary/journal date.

The Winery at Chateau Americana
Revenue Cycle - Cash Receipts Flowchart

For the Year Ended December 31, 2003

Reference:	*R-113*
Prepared by:	*JG*
Date:	*11/14/03*
Reviewed by:	

Office Manager

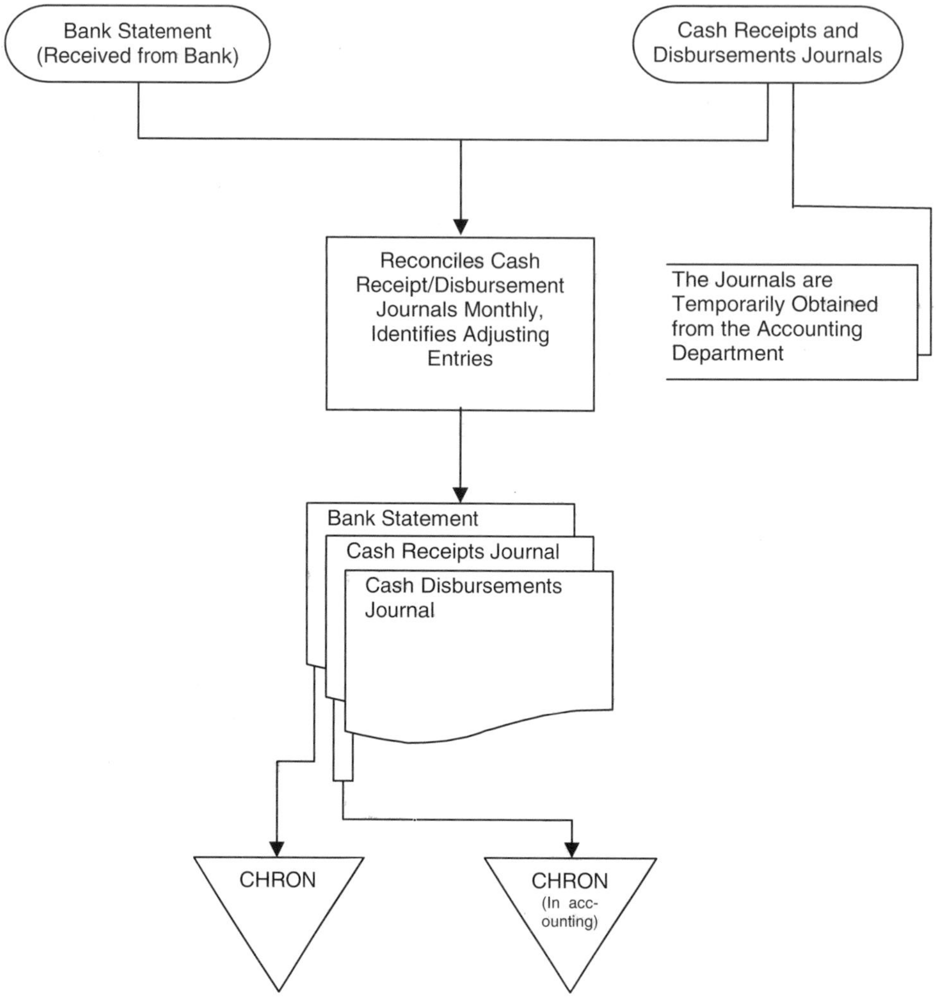

Legend:
CHRON - filed chronologically by statement/journal date.

The Winery at Chateau Americana
Revenue Cycle - Planned Audit Risk Matrix

Year Ended December 31, 2003

Reference: *R-180*
Prepared by: *JG*
Date: *11/14/03*
Reviewed by:

Tolerable Misstatement: *$40,000, G6*	**Reference**	**Existence***	**Rights /Obligations**	**Valuation**	**Presentation/Disclosure**	**Completeness****
Acceptable Audit Risk	*G5*	*L*	*L*	*L*	*L*	*L*
Initial Inherent Risk – Sales		*M*		*M*	*L*	*H*
Initial Inherent Risk – Cash Collections		*H*		*H*	*L*	*H*
Initial Inherent Risk – Accounts Receivables		*M*	*L*	*M*	*L*	*L*
Planned Control Risk – Sales		*M*		*M*	*H*	*M*
Planned Control Risk – Cash Collections		*M*		*M*	*H*	*M*
Planned Detection Risk – Sales		*M*		*M*	*M*	*M*
Planned Detection Risk – Cash Collections		*M*		*M*	*M*	*M*
Planned Detection Risk – Accounts Receivable		*M*	*M*	*M*	*M*	*M*

Planned Inherent Risk should be assessed as:
- High (H) unless the combination of inherent risk factors present justify a lower assessment.
- Medium (M) if the combination of inherent risk factors present justify this assessment.
- Low (L) if the combination of inherent risk factors present justify this assessment.

Factors justifying a lower inherent risk assessment are:
High management integrity, Low motivation to materially misstate for external parties, Repeat engagement, No material prior year misstatements, No related party transactions, Routine transactions, Limited judgement required to correctly record transactions, Low susceptibility to defalcation, Stable business environment.

Planned Control Risk should be assessed as:
- Low (L) if control activity(ies) reduces the likelihood of a material misstatement to a negligible level and persuasive tests of controls are planned.
- Medium (M) if control activity(ies) reduces the likelihood of a material misstatement to a negligible level and moderately persuasive tests of controls are planned or control activity(ies) reduces the likelihood of a material misstatement to a moderate level and persuasive tests of controls are planned.
- High (H) if control activity(ies) does not reduce the likelihood of a material misstatement to a reasonable level or no tests of controls are planned.

Planned Detection Risk should be assessed as:
- Low (L) if persuasive substantive tests are planned.
- Medium (M) if moderately persuasive substantive tests are planned.
- High (H) if minimal substantive tests are planned.

Note: * completeness for cash collections, ** existence for cash collections

The Winery at Chateau Americana
Revenue Cycle - Lead Schedule

For the Year Ended December 31, 2003

Reference:	*R-200*
Prepared by:	*JG*
Date:	*2/16/04*
Reviewed by:	

Account	Audited Balance 12/31/02	Unaudited Balance 12/31/03	Adjustments Debit	Adjustments Credit	Adjusted Balance 12/31/03
Accounts Receivable	*$ 4,913,697* ✔	*$ 5,347,094* *f, GL*			
Allowance for Bad Debts	*$97,460* ✔	*$106,375* *GL*			
Net Sales	*$ 20,189,194* ✔	*$ 21,945,422* *GL*			
Bad Debt Expense	*$9,957* ✔	*$10,974* *GL*			

Conclusion:

Tickmark Legend

✔ - *Agreed to prior year audit schedules without exception (audit step 12a).*
GL - *Agreed to 12/31/2003 general ledger without exception (audit step 12b).*
f - *Agreed to the footed balance of the 12/31/2003 accounts receivable customer ledgers and 12/31/2003 aged accounts receivable trial balance without exception (audit step 13a).*

The Winery at Chateau Americana
Revenue Cycle - Proposed Adjusting Entry Schedule

For the Year Ended December 31, 2003

Reference: *R-210*
Prepared by: *JG*
Date: *2/20/04*
Reviewed by:

Account	Debit	Credit
dr. Bad debt expense	*$13,488*	
cr. Accounts receivable		*$13,488*
Explanation: *To eliminate the uncollectible receivable balance of $13,488 from accounts receivable while still maintaining an allowance for bad debts balance of 2% of A/R (see R-501).*		
Explanation:		
Explanation:		
Explanation:		

The Winery at Chateau Americana
Tests of Transactions Sample Plan -
Revenue Cycle Sales Transactions
For the Year Ended December 31, 2003

Reference:	*R-310*
Prepared by:	*JG*
Date:	*2/16/04*
Reviewed by:	

Sampling Frame	Beg. Doc. # or Page #	End. Doc. # or Page #	Sample Size
Lines recorded in the sales register during the year	*Page 1 (Line 1)*	*Page 166 (Line 1,992)*	*30*

Sample Selection Method:

The sample was selected by using the "=randbetween(1,1992)" Microsoft Excel spreadsheet function. Line numbers drawn twice were discarded and a new line number was selected using the Excel "randbetween" function.

Sample: *Line number starting with line 1 on page 1 to line 1,992 on page 166*

Sample Item	Sample Ref.	Sample Item	Sample Ref.	Sample Item	Sample Ref.	Sample Item	Sample Ref.
1	*4*	*16*	*904*				
2	*43*	*17*	*908*				
3	*111*	*18*	*945*				
4	*148*	*19*	*960*				
5	*154*	*20*	*1077*				
6	*276*	*21*	*1241*				
7	*311*	*22*	*1284*				
8	*348*	*23*	*1381*				
9	*435*	*24*	*1561*				
10	*444*	*25*	*1633*				
11	*459*	*26*	*1756*				
12	*560*	*27*	*1757*				
13	*657*	*28*	*1821*				
14	*716*	*29*	*1906*				
15	*767*	*30*	*1985*				

The Winery at Chateau Americana
Tests of Transactions Sample Plan -
Revenue Cycle Sales Transactions
For the Year Ended December 31, 2003

Reference: *R-311*
Prepared by: *JG*
Date: *2/16/04*
Reviewed by: ________

Sampling Frame	Beg. Doc. # or Page #	End. Doc. # or Page #	Sample Size
Bill of ladings (shipping documents) issued during the year	*134617*	*136608*	*30*

Sample selection method:

The sample items were selected by using the "=randbetween (134617,136608)" Microsoft Excel spreadsheet function. Bill of ladings drawn twice were discarded and a new random number was selected using the Excel "randbetween" function.

Sample: *Bill of Lading Number*

Sample Item	Sample Ref.	Sample Item	Sample Ref.	Sample Item	Sample Ref.	Sample Item	Sample Ref.
1	*134628*	*16*	*135449*				
2	*134657*	*17*	*135467*				
3	*134687*	*18*	*135675*				
4	*134711*	*19*	*135785*				
5	*134776*	*20*	*135980*				
6	*134846*	*21*	*136245*				
7	*134942*	*22*	*136260*				
8	*134949*	*23*	*136266*				
9	*134950*	*24*	*136356*				
10	*135111*	*25*	*136378*				
11	*135114*	*26*	*136421*				
12	*135251*	*27*	*136425*				
13	*135329*	*28*	*136528*				
14	*135358*	*29*	*136637*				
15	*135382*	*30*	*136728*				

The Winery at Chateau Americana
Tests of Transactions Sample Plan -
Revenue Cycle Cash Receipts
For the Year Ended December 31, 2003

Reference: *R-312*
Prepared by: *JG*
Date: *2/16/04*
Reviewed by:

Sampling Frame	Beg. Doc. # or Page #	End. Doc. # or Page #	Sample Size
Lines recorded in the cash receipt journal during the year	*Page 1 (Line 1)*	*Page 178 (Line 2,133)*	*30*

Sample Selection Method:

The sample was selected by using the "=randbetween(1,2133)" Microsoft Excel spreadsheet function. Line numbers drawn twice were discarded and a new line number was selected using the Excel "randbetween" function.

Sample: *Line number starting with line 1 on page 1 to line 2,133 on page 178*

Sample Item	Sample Ref.	Sample Item	Sample Ref.	Sample Item	Sample Ref.	Sample Item	Sample Ref.
1	*69*	*16*	*1152*				
2	*86*	*17*	*1157*				
3	*98*	*18*	*1226*				
4	*364*	*19*	*1351*				
5	*387*	*20*	*1387*				
6	*526*	*21*	*1424*				
7	*563*	*22*	*1435*				
8	*622*	*23*	*1458*				
9	*827*	*24*	*1466*				
10	*831*	*25*	*1545*				
11	*859*	*26*	*1679*				
12	*900*	*27*	*1755*				
13	*985*	*28*	*1758*				
14	*1000*	*29*	*1920*				
15	*1048*	*30*	*2091*				

The Winery at Chateau Americana
Nonstatistical Tests of Transactions Sample Plan - Revenue Cycle Cash Receipt Transactions
For the Year Ended December 31, 2003

Reference: *R-313*
Prepared by: *JG*
Date: *2/16/04*
Reviewed by: ____________

Sampling Frame	Beg. Doc. # or Page #	End. Doc. # or Page #	Sample Size
Cash receipt summaries prepared during the year	*5468*	*5719*	*30*

Sample selection method:

The sample items were selected by using the "=randbetween(5468,6179)" Microsoft Excel spreadsheet function. Cash summary sheets drawn twice were discarded and a new random number was selected using the Excel "randbetween" function.

Sample: *Cash Receipt Summary Sheet Number*

Sample Item	Sample Ref.	Sample Item	Sample Ref.	Sample Item	Sample Ref.	Sample Item	Sample Ref.
1	*5473*	*16*	*5593*				
2	*5483*	*17*	*5616*				
3	*5484*	*18*	*5618*				
4	*5487*	*19*	*5619*				
5	*5494*	*20*	*5624*				
6	*5515*	*21*	*5646*				
7	*5519*	*22*	*5653*				
8	*5520*	*23*	*5663*				
9	*5525*	*24*	*5666*				
10	*5534*	*25*	*5671*				
11	*5535*	*26*	*5675*				
12	*5538*	*27*	*5692*				
13	*5552*	*28*	*5695*				
14	*5558*	*29*	*5712*				
15	*5569*	*30*	*5714*				

The Winery at Chateau Americana
Nonstatistical Tests of Transactions Sample Plan -
Revenue Cycle Sales Transactions
For the Year Ended December 31, 2003

Reference: *R-314*
Prepared by: *JG*
Date: *1/02/04*
Reviewed by:

Sampling Frame	Beg. Doc. # or Page #	End. Doc. # or Page #	Sample Size
Lines recorded on the aged accounts receivable trial balance	*Page 1 (Line 1)*	*Page 2 (Line 81)*	*20*

Sample Selection Method:

The sample was selected by taking the 20 customers with the largest outstanding balances at year-end.

Sample: Customer *line number starting with line 1 on page 1 to line 81 on page 2*

Sample Item	Sample Ref.	Sample Item	Sample Ref.	Sample Item	Sample Ref.	Sample Item	Sample Ref.
1	*0501*	*16*	*3502*				
2	*0502*	*17*	*3801*				
3	*0504*	*18*	*3803*				
4	*0701*	*19*	*4301*				
5	*0901*	*20*	*4601*				
6	*0902*						
7	*1001*						
8	*1301*						
9	*2001*						
10	*2101*						
11	*2201*						
12	*3001*						
13	*3201*						
14	*3302*						
15	*3501*						

The Winery at Chateau Americana
Tests of Transactions -
Revenue Cycle Cash Receipt Transactions
For the Year Ended December 31, 2003

Reference: *R-400*
Prepared by: *JG*
Date: *2/18/04*
Reviewed by: ________

Procedure:

Observations and inquires were made of the office receptionist regarding the handling of cash receipt mail and preparation of cash summary sheets. Consistent with established company policy, cash receipt envelopes are always opened by the office receptionist in the presence of one other company employee and the cash receipt is immediately recorded on a cash summary sheet.

Exceptions/Misstatements Identified:

No exceptions or misstatements were noted as a result of performing audit procedures 5 and 6.

Follow-up procedures performed:

No follow-up procedures are necessary.

The Winery at Chateau Americana
Nonstatistical Tests of Controls Evaluation -
Revenue Cycle Sales Transactions
For the Year Ended December 31, 2003

Reference: *R-410*
Prepared by: ______
Date: ______
Reviewed by: ______

Sampling Frame: *Lines recorded in the sales register during the year*

Attribute	RCL	Sample Size	SDR	TDR	ASR
Purchase order, shipping document, and sales invoice look authentic and reasonable.	*M*	*30*		*5%*	
Sales register amount is correct based on sales invoice and shipping document.	*M*	*30*		*5%*	
Sales invoice is posted to correct customers accounts receivable master file.	*M*	*30*		*5%*	

Conclusion:

Legend:
ASR - Allowance for Sampling Risk (TDR-SDR)
RCL - Risk of Assessing Control Risk Too Low (L – Low or M – Moderate)
SDR - Sample Deviation Rate
TDR - Tolerable Deviation Rate

The Winery at Chateau Americana
Nonstatistical Tests of Controls Evaluation -
Revenue Cycle Sales Transactions
For the Year Ended December 31, 2003

Reference: *R-411*
Prepared by: *JG*
Date: *2/17/04*
Reviewed by:

Sampling Frame: *Bill of ladings (shipping documents) issued during the year*

Attribute	RCL	Sample Size	SDR	TDR	ASR
Bill of lading is properly accounted for in sales register.	*M*	*30*	*0%*	*5%*	*5%*

Conclusion:

The results of audit procedure 4a support a reduced control risk assessment for the completeness and valuation of sales as no deviations from company policy were noted. Therefore, no changes to the planned audit program are required.

Legend:
ASR - Allowance for Sampling Risk (TDR-SDR)
RCL - Risk of Assessing Control Risk Too Low (L – Low or M – Moderate)
SDR - Sample Deviation Rate
TDR - Tolerable Deviation Rate

The Winery at Chateau Americana
Nonstatistical Tests of Controls Evaluation - Revenue Cycle Cash Receipts
For the Year Ended December 31, 2003

Reference: *R-412*
Prepared by: *JG*
Date: *2/18/04*
Reviewed by:

Sampling Frame: *Lines recorded in the cash receipt journal during the year*

Attribute	RCL	Sample Size	SDR	TDR	ASR
Validated bank deposit slip and cash summary sheet look authentic and reasonable.	*M*	*30*	*0%*	*5%*	*5%*
Cash receipt journal amount is correct based on deposit slip and cash summary sheet.	*M*	*30*	*0%*	*5%*	*5%*
Cash collection amount is posted to correct customers accounts receivable master file.	*M*	*30*	*0%*	*5%*	*5%*

Conclusion:

The results of audit procedures 7a, b, and c support a reduced control risk assessment for the existence and valuation of cash receipts as no deviations from company policy were noted. Therefore, no changes to the planned audit program are required.

Legend:
ASR - Allowance for Sampling Risk (TDR-SDR)
RCL - Risk of Assessing Control Risk Too Low (L – Low or M – Moderate)
SDR - Sample Deviation Rate
TDR - Tolerable Deviation Rate

The Winery at Chateau Americana
Nonstatistical Tests of Controls Evaluation -
Revenue Cycle Cash Receipts
For the Year Ended December 31, 2003

Reference: *R-413*
Prepared by: *JG*
Date: *2/19/04*
Reviewed by: ______

Sampling Frame: Cash summary sheets prepared *during the year*

Attribute	RCL	Sample Size	SDR	TDR	ASR
Cash summary sheet is properly accounted for in cash receipt journal.	*M*	*30*	*0%*	*5%*	*5%*

Follow-up procedures performed:

The results of audit procedure 10a support a reduced control risk assessment for the completeness and valuation of cash receipts as no deviations from company policy were noted. Therefore, no changes to the planned audit program are required.

Legend:
ASR - Allowance for Sampling Risk (TDR-SDR)
RCL - Risk of Assessing Control Risk Too Low (L – Low or M – Moderate)
SDR - Sample Deviation Rate
TDR - Tolerable Deviation Rate

The Winery at Chateau Americana
Tests of Transactions -
Revenue Cycle Sales Transactions
For the Year Ended December 31, 2003

Reference: *R-420*
Prepared by: *JG*
Date: *2/17/04*
Reviewed by:

Procedure:

Sales recorded in the sales register were reconciled to sales and accounts receivable recorded in the general ledger for the month of November.

Exceptions/Misstatements Identified:

No exceptions or misstatements were noted as a result of performing audit procedure 2.

Follow-up procedures performed:

No follow-up procedures are necessary.

The Winery at Chateau Americana
Tests of Transactions -
Revenue Cycle Cash Receipt Transactions
For the Year Ended December 31, 2003

Reference:	*R-421*
Prepared by:	*JG*
Date:	*2/18/04*
Reviewed by:	

Procedure:

Cash receipts recorded in the cash receipts journal were reconciled to cash and accounts receivable recorded in the general ledger for the month of March.

Exceptions/Misstatements Identified:

No exceptions or misstatements were noted as a result of performing audit procedure 8.

Follow-up procedures performed:

No follow-up procedures are necessary.

The Winery at Chateau Americana
Unusual Transactions - Revenue Cycle
Sales Register
For the Year Ended December 31, 2003

Reference: *R-430*
Prepared by: *JG*
Date: *2/17/04*
Reviewed by:

Date	Account Description or Customer of Unusual Transactions Identified	Ref.	Account IDs	Amount
	No unusual transactions identified.			

Follow-up procedures performed:

No follow-up procedures are necessary.

Reference:	R-431
Prepared by:	JG
Date:	2/18/04
Reviewed by:	

The Winery at Chateau Americana
Unusual Transactions - Revenue Cycle
Cash Receipts Journal
For the Year Ended December 31, 2003

Date	Account Description or Payer of Unusual Transactions Identified	Ref.	Account IDs	Amount
	No unusual transactions identified.			

Conclusion/Follow-up procedures performed:

No follow-up procedures are necessary.

The Winery at Chateau Americana
Unusual Transactions - Revenue Cycle
General Journal - Customer Write-offs
For the Year Ended December 31, 2003

Reference: *R-432*
Prepared by: *JG*
Date: *2/19/04*
Reviewed by:

Date	Account Description or Customer of Unusual Transactions Identified	Ref.	Account IDs	Amount
	No unusual transactions identified.			

Follow-up procedures performed:

No follow-up procedures are necessary.

The Winery at Chateau Americana
Nonstatistical Substantive Tests Evaluation -
Revenue Cycle Sales Transactions
For the Year Ended December 31, 2003

Reference: *R-440*
Prepared by: ______
Date: ______
Reviewed by: ______

Misstatements:	Recorded Amount	Audited Amount	Misstatement Amount
Total sample misstatement			

Projected misstatement:		
Total sample misstatement		
Dollar value of sample	÷	*$727,107*
Percentage sample dollar misstatement	=	
Dollar value of population per register	×	*$21,945,490*
Projected population dollar misstatement	=	

Allowance for sampling risk		
Tolerable misstatement		*$40,000*
Projected population dollar misstatement	–	
Recorded adjustments	+	
Allowance for sampling risk	=	

Conclusions:

The Winery at Chateau Americana
Nonstatistical Substantive Tests Evaluation -
Revenue Cycle Cash Receipts Transactions
For the Year Ended December 31, 2003

Reference: *R-441*
Prepared by: *JG*
Date: *2/19/04*
Reviewed by:

Misstatements:	**Recorded Amount**	**Audited Amount**	**Misstatement Amount**
No missatements were identified as a			
result of performing audit procedures			
7a-c and 10.			
Total sample misstatement			*$0*

Projected misstatement:		
Total sample misstatement		*$0*
Dollar value of sample	÷	*$ 662,470*
Percentage sample dollar misstatement	=	*$0*
Dollar value of population per journal	×	*$25,233,126*
Projected population dollar misstatement	=	*$0*

Allowance for sampling risk		
Tolerable misstatement		*$40,000*
Projected population dollar misstatement	–	*$0*
Recorded adjustments	+	*$0*
Allowance for sampling risk	=	*$40,000*

Conclusions:

The results of audit procedures 7a-c and 10 support the completeness, existence, valution, and presentation and disclosure of cash receipts in all material respects. Therefore, no changes to the planned audit program are required.

The Winery at Chateau Americana
Tests of Balances – Revenue Cycle
Accounts Receivable
For the Year Ended December 31, 2003

Reference: *R-500*
Prepared by: *JG*
Date: *2/20/04*
Reviewed by:

Procedure:

The proper aging of the aged accounts receivable trial balance was verified by examining the supporting sales invoices for the following five customers: Blue Ridge Beverage Company, Johnson Brothers Company, Premier Wine and Spirits, Southern Wine and Spirits, Young's Market Company.

Exceptions/Misstatements Identified:

No exceptions or misstatements were noted as a result of performing audit procedure 13c.

Follow-up procedures performed:

No follow-up procedures are necessary.

The Winery at Chateau Americana
Inquires – Revenue Cycle
Accounts Receivable
For the Year Ended December 31, 2003

Reference: *R-501*
Prepared by: *JG*
Date: *2/20/04*
Reviewed by:

Inquires of: *Office Manager*

Question:	**Response:**
The collectibility of the Fine Wine and Spirits, Inc. receivable balance of $13,488 was discussed with the office manager as it was over a year old.	*Per the office manager, CA has stopped selling to Fine Wine and Spirits because of the lack of payment and has referred the balance to a collection agency. The office manager does not believe the company will collect on this balance.*
The collectibility of the Desert Beverage Company receivable balance of $6,221 was discussed with the office manager as it was almost a year old.	*Per the office manager, CA had negotiated at year-end a payment plan of $1,037 over the next six months starting in January. A review of the January and February 2004 cash receipts reveals that two payments totaling $2,074 were received From Desert Beverage Co. This balance appears collectible.*

Follow-up procedures performed:

No other receivable balances listed on the aged trial balance were identified as unusually large and old. Therefore, no change to the planned audit program is necessary. Based on the discussions with the office manager and analytic procedures performed related to the collection of receivables (see R-510). The following adjusting entry is proposed (see R-210):

dr. Bad debt expense	*$13,488*	
cr. Accounts receivable		*$13,488*

This entry will eliminate the uncollectible receivable balance of $13,488 from accounts receivable account while still maintaining an allowance for bad debts balance at 2% of accounts receivable.

The Winery at Chateau Americana
Tests of Balances – Revenue Cycle
Accounts Receivable
For the Year Ended December 31, 2003

Reference: *R-502*
Prepared by: *JG*
Date: *2/20/04*
Reviewed by: ____________

Procedure:

The last bill of lading issued before December 31, 2003 was 136608. The sales invoices and purchase orders supporting the last five bill of ladings issued before year-end and first five bill of ladings issued after year-end were examined and traced to proper inclusion/exclusion in/from the December 31, 2003 accounts receivable customer ledgers.

Exceptions/Misstatements Identified:

No exceptions or misstatements were noted as a result of performing audit procedures 13e and f.

Follow-up procedures performed:

No follow-up procedures are necessary.

The Winery at Chateau Americana
Tests of Balances – Revenue Cycle
Accounts Receivable
For the Year Ended December 31, 2003

Reference:	*R-503*
Prepared by:	*JG*
Date:	*3/1/04*
Reviewed by:	

Procedure:

The board of directors' meeting minutes issued from 1/1/2003 through 3/1/2004 were reviewed for indication of the factoring or pledging of accounts receivable. Additionally, inquiries were made of the chief financial officer concerning the factoring or pledging of receivables and/or the existence of related party/noncurrent receivables.

Exceptions/Misstatements Identified:

No exceptions or misstatements were noted as a result of performing audit procedures 16, 17a, and 17b.

Follow-up procedures performed:

No follow-up procedures are necessary.

The Winery at Chateau Americana
Ratio Analysis - Revenue Cycle

For the Year Ended December 31, 2003

Reference: R-510
Prepared by: JG
Date: 2/20/04
Reviewed by: ______

Ratio Description	2003 Ratio Amount	2002 Ratio Amount	Conclusion/Follow-up Procedures Performed
Accounts Receivable Turnover	4.36	4.74	Per the office manager the turnover and aging of receivables has worsened slightly as the company started offering more favorable credit terms to select
Percent of Receivables: 0 to 60 days old 61 to 120 days old 121 to 180 days old greater than 181 days old	 42.6% 34.9% 15.9% 6.6%	 46.8% 34.2% 14.3% 4.7%	customers to encourage higher sales volume. The office manager believes that the allowance for bad debts of $200,000 is sufficient to cover any uncollectible balances.
Allowance for Bad Debts as Percent of Accounts Receivable	2.0%	2.0%	Based on the review of the A/R aged trial balance (see R-501), past history, and current economic conditions the allowance percent of 2% of A/R is reasonable.

The Winery at Chateau Americana
Unusual Transactions - Revenue Cycle Printout of Aged Accounts Receivable Trial Balance
For the Year Ended December 31, 2003

Reference: *R-511*
Prepared by: *JG*
Date: *2/19/04*
Reviewed by:

Date	Account Description or Customer of Unusual Transactions Identified	Ref.	Account IDs	Amount
	No unusual transactions identified.			

Follow-up procedures performed:

No follow-up procedures are necessary.

The Winery at Chateau Americana
Nonstatistical Tests of Balance Evaluation –
Revenue Cycle Accounts Receivable
For the Year Ended December 31, 2003

Reference: R-520
Prepared by: __________
Date: __________
Reviewed by: __________

Misstatements:	**Recorded Amount**	**Audited Amount**	**Misstatement Amount**
Total Sample Misstatement			
Projected Misstatement:			
Total Sample Misstatement			
Dollar Value of Sample		÷	$1,785,704
Percentage Sample Dollar Misstatement		=	
Dollar Value of Population per G/L		×	$5,240,719
Projected Dollar Misstatement for Accounts Receivable		=	
Allowance for Sampling Risk			
Tolerable Misstatement			$40,000
Projected Dollar Misstatement for Accounts Receivable		−	
Recorded Adjustments		+	
Allowance for Sampling Risk		=	

Conclusions:

The Winery at Chateau Americana
Chart of Accounts

Account Description	Account Number	Account Description	Account Number
General Checking Account	111000	Sales	410000
Payroll Checking Account	112000	Sales Discounts	420000
Money Market Account	113000	Sales Returns and Allowances	430000
Savings Account	114000	Gains/Loss Marketable Securities	452000
Petty Cash	119000	Dividend Income	491000
Accounts Receivable	121000	Interest Income	492000
Allowance for Bad Debts	129000	Cost of Goods Sold	510000
Inventory- Production	141000	Wages and Salary Expense	601000
Inventory - Finished Goods	145000	Sales Commission Expense	601500
Prepaid Expenses	150000	FICA Tax Expense	602100
Land and Buildings	160000	Medicare Tax Expense	602200
Equipment	170000	FUTA Tax Expense	602300
Accumulated Depreciation	180000	SUTA Tax Expense	602400
Investments	191000	Utilities Expense	611000
Accounts Payable	210000	Irrigation & Waste Disposal Expense	611300
Federal Income Tax Withheld	222100	Landscaping Expense	612000
FICA Withheld	222200	Advertising Expense	621000
Medicare Withheld	222300	Marketing Expense	623000
FICA Payable - Employer	223100	Festivals & Competitions Expense	624000
Medicare Payable - Employer	223200	Telephone Expense	631000
Unemployment Taxes Payable	223300	Internet & Computer Expense	632000
Federal Income Taxes Payable	235000	Postage Expense	633000
Property Taxes Payable	236000	Legal & Accounting Fees	641000
Mortgages Payable	240000	Office Supplies Expense	651000
Notes Payables	261000	Data Processing Expense	660000
Common Stock	310000	Depreciation Expense	670000
Paid in Capital Excess Par - Common	311000	Travel and Entertainment Expense	680000
Dividends - Common	312000	Other Insurance Expense	691000
Retained Earnings	390000	Medical Insurance Expense	692000
		Workmen's Compensation Insurance	693000
		Other Employee Benefit Expense	699000
		Dues and Subscription Expense	700000
		Federal Income Tax Expense	711000
		Property Tax Expense	712000
		Repairs and Maintenance Expense	721000
		Automobile Expense	731000
		Lease Expense	740000
		Bad Dept Expense	791000
		Miscellaneous Expense	792000
		Interest Expense	793000

The Winery at Chateau Americana
Sales Register for Audit Procedure 1*
For the Period From January 1, 2003 to December 31, 2003

Date	G.L. Account ID - Account Description	Customer ID	Invoice No.	Debit Amount	Credit Amount
01/10/03	121000 - Accounts Receivable	0501	13713	16,186.80	
(43)	410000 - Sales				16,186.80
03/19/03	121000 - Accounts Receivable	3301	14081	8,373.60	
(348)	410000 - Sales				8,373.60
06/12/03	121000 - Accounts Receivable	0901	14386	11,986.80	
(716)	410000 - Sales				11,986.80
11/20/03	121000 - Accounts Receivable	1301	15303	11,444.40	
(1633)	410000 - Sales				11,444.40
12/11/03	121000 - Accounts Receivable	3802	15491	10,220.40	
(1821)	410000 - Sales				10,220.40

*Abstracted from the Sales Register using exact format of the actual Sales Register. Note that the number in parenthesis under the transaction date is not normally included in the Sales Register. This number is provided as it represents the line number of the transaction in the Sales Register.

Purchase Order

Bock Wines and Vines
Pier 19, The Embarcadero
San Francisco, CA 94111

Phone: (415) 834-9675

Date: 01/06/2003
Shipment Date: 01/11/2003
P.O. #: 9340
Terms: Net 60
Shipped: US Express
FOB: Shipping Point

To:
Chateau Americana
3003 Vineyard Way
Huntington, CA 95394

Ship To:
Bock Wines and Vines
Pier 19, The Embarcadero
San Francisco, CA 94111

Item CD.	Quantity	Size	Description	BPC	Unit Cost	Extended Cost
R130061	336	0.750	Cabernet Sauvignon	012	$ 6.50	$ 2,184.00
R130056	336	0.750	Merlot	012	6.00	2,016.00
W120080	1344	0.750	Chardonnay	012	7.00	9,408.00
W120019	168	0.750	Chenin Blanc	012	5.25	882.00
W120015	168	0.750	Riesling	012	4.85	814.80
W120016	168	0.750	Sauvignon Blanc	012	5.25	882.00
					Total Cost	$16,186.80

Sue Ravens — Authorized by
01/07/03 — Date

CREDIT SALES INVOICE

Chateau Americana, Inc.
3003 Vineyard Way
Huntington, CA 95394
(707)368-8485
CA-NC-67

Invoice Number: 13713
Invoice Date: 01/10/03
Credit Terms: Net 60

Sold To:
Bock Wines and Vines
Pier 19, The Embarcadero
San Francisco, CA 94111

Ship To:
Bock Wines and Vines
Pier 19, The Embarcadero
San Francisco, CA 94111

Salesperson	Customer P.O. Number	Customer Number	ABC Number
WAB	9340	0501	CA07891

Product	Description	Size	Quantity	Cost	Extended
R130061	Cabernet Sauvignon	0.750	336	$ 6.50	$ 2,184.00
R130056	Merlot	0.750	336	6.00	2,016.00
W120080	Chardonnay	0.750	1344	7.00	9,408.00
W120019	Chenin Blanc	0.750	168	5.25	882.00
W120015	Riesling	0.750	168	4.85	814.80
W120016	Sauvignon Blanc	0.750	168	5.25	882.00

Grand Total Bottles: 2,520
Grand Total Cost: $ 16,186.80
Total Cases: 210
Comments:

Date 01/10/03
Invoice Number 13713
Customer Number 0501

Distribution: Copy 1 - Accounting; Copy 2 - Shipping; Copy 3 - Customer; Copy 4 - Sales

Uniform Bill of Lading

Date 01/10/03

Ship From
Name: *Chateau Americana, Inc.*
Address: *3003 Vineyard Way*
City/State/Zip: *Huntington, CA 95394*
SID No.: *122448*

Bill of Lading Number: 134659

Ship To
Name: *Bock Wines and Vines*
Address: *Pier 19, The Embarcadero*
City/State/Zip: *San Francisco, CA 94111*
CID No.: *244888*

Carrier Name: *US Express*
Trailer Number: *KLDF 897*
Serial Number: *000123123*

Special Instructions:

Freight Charge Terms: (Freight charges are prepaid unless marked otherwise)
Prepaid: ☐ Collect: ☐ 3rd Party: ☐
☐ **(check box):** Master bill of lading with attached underlying bills of lading.

Customer Order Information

Description of Items	Quantity	Weight	Pallet/Slip (circle one)		Additional Shipper Information
Wine	*210*	*7,140*	(Y)	N	
			Y	N	
			Y	N	
			Y	N	
Grand Total	*210*	*7,140*			

Where the rate is dependent on value, shippers are required to state specifically in writing the agreed or declared value of the property as follows: "The agreed or declared value of the property is specifically stated by the shipper to be not exceeding ____________ per ____________________.

COD Amount: $ *N/A*
Free Terms:
☐ **Collect**
☐ Prepaid
☐ **Customer check acceptable**

Note: Liability limitation for loss or damage in this shipment may be applicable. See 49 USC §14706(c)(1)(A)&(B)

Received, subject to individually determined rates or contracts that have been agreed upon in writing between the carrier and shipper, if applicable, otherwise to the rates, classifications and rules that have been established by the carrier and are available to the shipper, on request, and to all applicable state and federal regulations.

The carrier shall not make delivery of this shipment without payment of and all other lawful charges.

Shipper Signature *Jerry Richards*

Shipper Signature/Date
This is to certify that the above named materials are properly classified, packaged, marked and labeled, and are in proper condition for transportation according to the applicable regulations of the DOT.
Jerry Richards 01/10/03

Trailer Loaded:
☐ **By shipper**
☐ **By Driver**

Carrier Signature/Pickup Date
Carrier acknowledges receipt of packages and required placards. Carrier certifies emergency response information was made available and/or carrier has the DOT emergency response guidebook or equivalent documentation in the vehicle. **Property described above is received in good order, except as noted.**
Frank Loren 01/10/03

Distribution: Copy 1 - Accounting; Copy 2 - Shipping; Copy 3- Customer

Purchase Order

Blue Ridge Wholesale Wine Co Inc
4933 Brookshire Boulevard
Charlotte, NC 28216
704-393-1618

P.O. # **392876**

Order Date: 3/12/03
Shipment Date: 3/19/03

Terms: Net 60
Shipped: EA Shipping
FOB: Shipping Point

To
Chateau Americana
3003 Vineyard Way
Huntington, CA 95394

Ship To
Blue Ridge Wholesale Wine Co Inc
4933 Brookshire Boulevard
Charlotte, NC 28216

Item #	Cases	Size	Description	BPC	Unit Price	Extend Price
R130061	12	0.750	Cabernet Sauvignon	012	$ 78.00	$ 936.00
R130056	9	0.750	Merlot	012	72.00	648.00
R130072	6	0.750	Shiraz	012	75.00	450.00
W120080	54	0.750	Chardonnay	012	84.00	4,536.00
W120019	6	0.750	Chenin Blanc	012	63.00	378.00
W120015	18	0.750	Riesling	012	58.20	1,047.60
W120016	6	0.750	Sauvignon Blanc	012	63.00	378.00
Total Cases	111				Total Price	$ 8,373.60

BiancaTelfair — Authorization
3/12/03 — Date

Comments:

CREDIT SALES INVOICE

Invoice Number: 14081
Invoice Date: 03/19/03
Credit Terms: Net 60

Chateau Americana, Inc.
3003 Vineyard Way
Huntington, CA 95394
(707)368-8485
CA-NC-67

Sold To:
Blue Ridge Whs Wine Co Inc
4933 Brookshire Boulevard
Charlotte, NC 28216

Ship To:
Blue Ridge Whs Wine Co Inc
4933 Brookshire Boulevard
Charlotte, NC 28216

Salesperson	Customer P.O. Number	Customer Number	ABC Number
MMM	392876	3301	NC45963

Product	Description	Size	Quantity	Cost	Extended
R130061	Cabernet Sauvignon	0.750	144	$ 6.50	$ 936.00
R130056	Merlot	0.750	108	6.00	648.00
R130072	Shiraz	0.750	72	6.25	450.00
W120080	Chardonnay	0.750	648	7.00	4,536.00
W120019	Chenin Blanc	0.750	72	5.25	378.00
W120015	Riesling	0.750	216	4.85	1,047.60
W120016	Sauvignon Blanc	0.750	72	5.25	378.00

Grand Total Bottles: 1,332 Grand Total Cost: $ 8,373.60

Total Cases: 111
Comments:

Date 03/19/03
Invoice Number 14081
Customer Number 3301

Distribution: Copy 1 - Accounting; Copy 2 - Shipping; Copy 3 - Customer; Copy 4 - Sales

Uniform Bill of Lading

Date 03/19/03

Ship From
Name: Chateau Americana, Inc.
Address: 3003 Vineyard Way
City/State/Zip: Huntington, CA 95394
SID No.: 122448

Bill of Lading Number: 134964

Carrier Name: EA Shipping
Trailer Number: 7777 SOU
Serial Number: 022323444

Ship To
Name: Blue Ridge Whs Wine Co Inc
Address: 4933 Brookshire Boulevard
City/State/Zip: Charlotte, NC 28216
CID No.: 883229

Special Instructions:

Freight Charge Terms: (Freight charges are prepaid unless marked otherwise)
Prepaid: ☐ Collect: ☐ 3rd Party: ☐

☐ **(check box):** Master bill of lading with attached underlying bills of lading.

Customer Order Information

Description of Items	Quantity	Weight	Pallet/Slip (circle one)		Additional Shipper Information
Wine	111	3,774	(Y)	N	
			Y	N	
			Y	N	
			Y	N	
Grand Total	111	3.774			

Where the rate is dependent on value, shippers are required to state specifically in writing the agreed or declared value of the property as follows: "The agreed or declared value of the property is specifically stated by the shipper to be not exceeding ____________ per ____________.

COD Amount: $ N/A
Free Terms:
☐ **Collect**
☐ Prepaid
☐ **Customer check acceptable**

Note: Liability limitation for loss or damage in this shipment may be applicable. See 49 USC §14706(c)(1)(A)&(B)

Received, subject to individually determined rates or contracts that have been agreed upon in writing between the carrier and shipper, if applicable, otherwise to the rates, classifications and rules that have been established by the carrier and are available to the shipper, on request, and to all applicable state and federal regulations.

The carrier shall not make delivery of this shipment without payment of and all other lawful charges.

Shipper Signature *Jerry Richards*

Shipper Signature/Date
This is to certify that the above named materials are properly classified, packaged, marked and labeled, and are in proper condition for transportation according to the applicable regulations of the DOT.
Jerry Richards 03/19/03

Trailer Loaded:
☐ **By shipper**
☐ **By Driver**

Carrier Signature/Pickup Date
Carrier acknowledges receipt of packages and required placards. Carrier certifies emergency response information was made available and/or carrier has the DOT emergency response guidebook or equivalent documentation in the vehicle. **Property described above is received in good order, except as noted.**
Basi Abbas 03/19/03

Distribution: Copy 1 - Accounting; Copy 2 - Shipping; Copy 3- Customer

Purchase Order

Bill to
Market Wine, Inc.
3750 Hacienda Boulevard
Fort Lauderdale, FL 33314

Phone: 954-587-5019

PO #: 100224
Date: 6/05/03 **Date Required:** 6/13/03
Terms: Net 60
FOB: Shipping Point
Shipped: Best Method

Vendor
Chateau Americana
3003 Vineyard Way
Huntington, CA 95394

Ship To
Market Wine, Inc.
3750 Hacienda Boulevard
Fort Lauderdale, FL 33314

Item #	Size	Quantity	Description	BPC	Unit Cost	Total Cost
R130064	0.750	216	Cabernet Franc	012	$ 7.00	$ 1,512.00
R130061	0.750	216	Cabernet Sauvignon	012	6.50	1,404.00
R130056	0.750	108	Merlot	012	6.00	648.00
R130072	0.750	108	Shiraz	012	6.25	675.00
W120080	0.750	816	Chardonnay	012	7.00	5,712.00
W120019	0.750	144	Chenin Blanc	012	5.25	756.00
W120015	0.750	108	Riesling	012	4.85	523.80
W120016	0.750	144	Sauvignon Blanc	012	5.25	756.00
					Total Amount	$ 11,986.80

Message

Authorization
Signature: *Samantha Kiersted*
Date: 06/05/03

CREDIT SALES INVOICE

Invoice Number: 14386

Chateau Americana, Inc.
3003 Vineyard Way
Huntington, CA 95394
(707)368-8485
CA-NC-67

Invoice Date: 6/12/03
Credit Terms: Net 60

Sold To:
Market Wine, Inc.
3750 Hacienda Boulevard
Fort Lauderdale, FL 33314

Ship To:
Market Wine, Inc.
3750 Hacienda Boulevard
Fort Lauderdale, FL 33314

Salesperson	Customer P.O. Number	Customer Number	ABC Number
MMM	100224	0901	FLS11132

Product	Description	Size	Quantity	Cost	Extended
R130064	Cabernet Franc	0.750	216	$ 7.00	$ 1,512.00
R130061	Cabernet Sauvignon	0.750	216	6.50	1,404.00
R130056	Merlot	0.750	108	6.00	648.00
R130072	Shiraz	0.750	108	6.25	675.00
W120080	Chardonnay	0.750	816	7.00	5,712.00
W120019	Chenin Blanc	0.750	144	5.25	756.00
W120015	Riesling	0.750	108	4.85	523.80
W120016	Sauvignon Blanc	0.750	144	5.25	756.00

Grand Total Bottles: 1,860 Grand Total Cost: $ 11,986.80

Total Cases: 155
Comments:

Date 6/12/03
Invoice Number 14386
Customer Number 0901

Distribution: Copy 1 - Accounting; Copy 2 - Shipping; Copy 3 - Customer; Copy 4 - Sales

Uniform Bill of Lading

Date 06/12/03

Ship From
Name: *Chateau Americana, Inc.*
Address: *3003 Vineyard Way*
City/State/Zip: *Huntington, CA 95394*
SID No.: *122448*

Bill of Lading Number: 135332

Carrier Name: *Crossway Deliveries*
Trailer Number: *ABC 3210*
Serial Number: *000456789*

Ship To
Name: *Market Wine, Inc.*
Address: *3750 Hacienda Boulevard*
City/State/Zip: *Fort Lauderdale, FL 33314*
CID No.: *456987*

Special Instructions:

Freight Charge Terms: (Freight charges are prepaid unless marked otherwise)
Prepaid: ☐ Collect: ☐ 3rd Party: ☐
☐ **(check box):** Master bill of lading with attached underlying bills of lading.

Customer Order Information

Description of Items	Quantity	Weight	Pallet/Slip (circle one)		Additional Shipper Information
Wine	*155*	*5,270*	(Y)	N	
			Y	N	
			Y	N	
			Y	N	
Grand Total	*155*	*5,270*			

Where the rate is dependent on value, shippers are required to state specifically in writing the agreed or declared value of the property as follows: "The agreed or declared value of the property is specifically stated by the shipper to be not exceeding ____________ per ____________________.

COD Amount: $ N/A
Free Terms:
☐ **Collect**
☐ Prepaid
☐ **Customer check acceptable**

Note: Liability limitation for loss or damage in this shipment may be applicable. See 49 USC §14706©(1)(A)&(B)

Received, subject to individually determined rates or contracts that have been agreed upon in writing between the carrier and shipper, if applicable, otherwise to the rates, classifications and rules that have been established by the carrier and are available to the shipper, on request, and to all applicable state and federal regulations.

The carrier shall not make delivery of this shipment without payment of and all other lawful charges.

Shipper Signature *Jerry Richards*

Shipper Signature/Date
This is to certify that the above named materials are properly classified, packaged, marked and labeled, and are in proper condition for transportation according to the applicable regulations of the DOT.
Jerry Richards 06/12/03

Trailer Loaded:
☐ **By shipper**
☐ **By Driver**

Carrier Signature/Pickup Date
Carrier acknowledges receipt of packages and required placards. Carrier certifies emergency response information was made available and/or carrier has the DOT emergency response guidebook or equivalent documentation in the vehicle. **Property described above is received in good order, except as noted.**
Santos Padilla 6/12/03

Distribution: Copy 1 - Accounting; Copy 2 - Shipping; Copy 3- Customer

Pacific Wine & Spirits Co
2701 South Western Avenue
Chicago, IL 60608
Phone: 773-247-8000

Purchase Order

To:
Chateau Americana
3003 Vineyard Way
Huntington, CA 95394

Ship To:
Pacific Wine & Spirits Co
2701 South Western Avenue
Chicago, IL 60608

Date	P.O. No.	Terms	F.O.B. Point	Ship Via
11/14/03	455698	Net 60	Shipping Point	Best Method

Item #	Cases	Size	Description	BPC	Unit Cost	Total Cost
R130064	24	0.750	Cabernet Franc	012	$ 84.00	$ 2,016.00
R130061	24	0.750	Cabernet Sauvignon	012	78.00	1,872.00
R130056	12	0.750	Merlot	012	72.00	864.00
R130072	6	0.750	Shiraz	012	75.00	450.00
W120080	48	0.750	Chardonnay	012	84.00	4,032.00
W120019	12	0.750	Chenin Blanc	012	63.00	756.00
W120015	12	0.750	Riesling	012	58.20	698.40
W120016	12	0.750	Sauvignon Blanc	012	63.00	756.00
Total	150				Total	$ 11,444.40

Cresent Belcher — Authorized by
11/14/03 — Date

Comments:

CREDIT SALES INVOICE

Invoice Number: 15303
Invoice Date: 11/20/03
Credit Terms: Net 60

Chateau Americana, Inc.
3003 Vineyard Way
Huntington, CA 95394
(707)368-8485
CA-NC-67

Sold To:
Pacific Wine & Spirits Co
2701 South Western Avenue
Chicago, IL 60608

Ship To:
Pacific Wine & Spirits Co
2701 South Western Avenue
Chicago, IL 60608

Salesperson	Customer P.O. Number	Customer Number	ABC Number
CEZ	455698	1301	IS48489

Product	Description	Size	Quantity	Cost	Extended
R130064	Cabernet Franc	0.750	288	$ 7.00	$ 2,016.00
R130061	Cabernet Sauvignon	0.750	288	6.50	1,872.00
R130056	Merlot	0.750	144	6.00	864.00
R130072	Shiraz	0.750	72	6.25	450.00
W120080	Chardonnay	0.750	576	7.00	4,032.00
W120019	Chenin Blanc	0.750	144	5.25	756.00
W120015	Riesling	0.750	144	4.85	698.40
W120016	Sauvignon Blanc	0.750	144	5.25	756.00

Grand Total Bottles: 1,800
Grand Total Cost: $ 11,444.40

Total Cases: 150
Comments:

Date 11/20/03
Invoice Number 15303
Customer Number 1301

Distribution: Copy 1 - Accounting; Copy 2 - Shipping; Copy 3 - Customer; Copy 4 - Sales

Uniform Bill of Lading

Date 11/20/03

Bill of Lading Number: 136249

Ship From
Name: Chateau Americana, Inc.
Address: 3003 Vineyard Way
City/State/Zip: Huntington, CA 95394
SID No.: 122448

Carrier Name: Crossway Deliveries
Trailer Number: DDR 7192
Serial Number: 000123123

Ship To
Name: Pacific Wine & Spirits Co
Address: 2701 South Western Avenue
City/State/Zip: Chicago, IL 60608
CID No.: 617493
Special Instructions:

Freight Charge Terms: (Freight charges are prepaid unless marked otherwise)
Prepaid: ☐ Collect: ☐ 3rd Party: ☐
(check box): Master bill of lading with attached underlying bills of lading.

Customer Order Information

Description of Items	Quantity	Weight	Pallet/Slip (circle one)		Additional Shipper Information
Wine	150	5,100	(Y)	N	
			Y	N	
			Y	N	
			Y	N	
Grand Total	150	5,100			

Where the rate is dependent on value, shippers are required to state specifically in writing the agreed or declared value of the property as follows: "The agreed or declared value of the property is specifically stated by the shipper to be not exceeding ____________ per ____________

COD Amount: $ N/A
Free Terms:
☐ Collect
☐ Prepaid
☐ Customer check acceptable

Note: Liability limitation for loss or damage in this shipment may be applicable. See 49 USC §14706 (c) (1) (A) & (B)

Received, subject to individually determined rates or contracts that have been agreed upon in writing between the carrier and shipper, if applicable, otherwise to the rates, classifications and rules that have been established by the carrier and are available to the shipper, on request, and to all applicable state and federal regulations.

The carrier shall not make delivery of this shipment without payment of and all other lawful charges.

Shipper Signature *Jerry Richards*

Shipper Signature/Date
This is to certify that the above named materials are properly classified, packaged, marked and labeled, and are in proper condition for transportation according to the applicable regulations of the DOT.
Jerry Richards 11/20/03

Trailer Loaded:
☐ By shipper
☐ By Driver

Carrier Signature/Pickup Date
Carrier acknowledges receipt of packages and required placards. Carrier certifies emergency response information was made available and/or carrier has the DOT emergency response guidebook or equivalent documentation in the vehicle. **Property described above is received in good order, except as noted.**
Rich Venditti 11/20/03

Distribution: Copy 1 - Accounting; Copy 2 - Shipping; Copy 3- Customer

Purchase Order

P.O. No.: **198885**
Date: 12/03/03

To:
Chateau Americana
3003 Vineyard Way
Huntington, CA 95394

Ship To:
Phila Wine Company
940 South 9th Street
Philadelphia, PA 19147
Phone: 215-733-0655

Ship Via	F.O.B. Point	Terms
Best Method	Shipping Point	Net 60

Item #	Quantity	Size	Description	BPC	Unit Cost	Total Cost
R130064	168	0.750	Cabernet Franc		7.00	1,176.00
R130061	252	0.750	Cabernet Sauvignon		6.50	1,638.00
R130056	72	0.750	Merlot		6.00	432.00
W120080	732	0.750	Chardonnay		7.00	5,124.00
W120015	144	0.750	Riesling		4.85	698.40
W120016	144	0.750	Sauvignon Blanc		5.25	756.00
S140000	36	0.750	Sparkling Brut		11.00	396.00
Total	1548				Total	$ 10,220.40

Georgia Morock — Authorized by
12/03/03 — Date

Comments:

CREDIT SALES INVOICE

Invoice Number: 15491
Invoice Date: 12/11/03
Credit Terms: Net 60

Chateau Americana, Inc.
3003 Vineyard Way
Huntington, CA 95394
(707)368-8485
CA-NC-67

Sold To:
Phila Wine Company
940 South 9th Street
Philadelphia, PA 19147

Ship To:
Phila Wine Company
940 South 9th Street
Philadelphia, PA 19147

Salesperson	Customer P.O. Number	Customer Number	ABC Number
FEW	198885	3802	PA009821

Product	Description	Size	Quantity	Cost	Extended
R130064	Cabernet Franc	0.750	168	$ 7.00	$ 1,176.00
R130061	Cabernet Sauvignon	0.750	252	6.50	1,638.00
R130056	Merlot	0.750	72	6.00	432.00
W120080	Chardonnay	0.750	732	7.00	5,124.00
W120015	Riesling	0.750	144	4.85	698.40
W120016	Sauvignon Blanc	0.750	144	5.25	756.00
S140000	Sparkling Brut	0.750	36	11.00	396.00

Grand Total Bottles: 1,548
Grand Total Cost: $ 10,220.40
Total Cases: 129
Comments:

Date 12/11/03
Invoice Number 15491
Customer Number 3802

Distribution: Copy 1 - Accounting; Copy 2 - Shipping; Copy 3 - Customer; Copy 4 - Sales

Uniform Bill of Lading

Date 12/11/03

Ship From
Name: *Chateau Americana, Inc.*
Address: *3003 Vineyard Way*
City/State/Zip: *Huntington, CA 95394*
SID No.: *122448*

Bill of Lading Number: 136437

Ship To
Name: *Phila Wine Company*
Address: *940 South 9th Street*
City/State/Zip: *Philadelphia,PA 19147*
CID No.: *463728*

Carrier Name: *Crossway Deliveries*
Trailer Number: *CEF 5824*
Serial Number: *000360087*

Special Instructions:

Freight Charge Terms: (Freight charges are prepaid unless marked otherwise)
Prepaid: ☐ Collect: ☐ 3rd Party: ☐
☐ **(check box):** Master bill of lading with attached underlying bills of lading.

Customer Order Information

Description of Items	Quantity	Weight	Pallet/Slip (circle one)		Additional Shipper Information
Wine	*129*	*4,386*	(Y)	N	
			Y	N	
			Y	N	
			Y	N	
Grand Total	*129*	*4,386*			

Where the rate is dependent on value, shippers are required to state specifically in writing the agreed or declared value of the property as follows: "The agreed or declared value of the property is specifically stated by the shipper to be not exceeding ________ per ________.

COD Amount: $ N/A
Free Terms:
☐ Collect
☐ Prepaid
☐ Customer check acceptable

Note: Liability limitation for loss or damage in this shipment may be applicable. See 49 USC §14706(c)(1)(A)&(B)

Received, subject to individually determined rates or contracts that have been agreed upon in writing between the carrier and shipper, if applicable, otherwise to the rates, classifications and rules that have been established by the carrier and are available to the shipper, on request, and to all applicable state and federal regulations.

The carrier shall not make delivery of this shipment without payment of and all other lawful charges.

Shipper Signature *Jerry Richards*

Shipper Signature/Date
This is to certify that the above named materials are properly classified, packaged, marked and labeled, and are in proper condition for transportation according to the applicable regulations of the DOT.
Jerry Richards 12/11/03

Trailer Loaded:
☐ By shipper
☐ By Driver

Carrier Signature/Pickup Date
Carrier acknowledges receipt of packages and required placards. Carrier certifies emergency response information was made available and/or carrier has the DOT emergency response guidebook or equivalent documentation in the vehicle. **Property described above is received in good order, except as noted.**
Tom Greer 12/11/03

Distribution: Copy 1 - Accounting; Copy 2 - Shipping; Copy 3- Customer

The Winery at Chateau Americana
Accounts Receivable Aged Trial Balance for Audit Procedure 14*
As of December 31, 2003

Customer	Customer ID	Total Balance	Days Old			
			0 - 60	61 - 120	121 - 180	Over 180
Atlanta Wholesale Wine	1001	$151,696.20	$151,696.20			
Bock Wines and Vines	0501	$210,198.20	$171,946.40	$38,251.80		
Bolliger, Inc.	0701	$163,570.80	$163,570.80			
Pinnacle Wine Company	3201	$184,610.40	$135,978.00	$48,632.40		
Vintage Wine Company	0502	$255,169.80	$207,893.40	$47,276.40		

*Abstracted from the Accounts Receivable Aged Trial Balance using exact format of the actual Accounts Receivable Aged Trial Balance.

Chateau Americana, Inc.
3003 Vineyard Way, Huntington, CA 95394
(707)368-8485

January 2, 2004

Atlanta Wholesale Wine
275 Spring Street Southwest
Atlanta, Ga 30303

Ladies and Gentlemen:

In connection with an audit of the financial statements of Chateau Americana, Inc. as of December 31, 2003, and for the year then ended, our independent auditors wish to determine whether our records of your indebtedness to us agree with your records. According to our records, your indebtedness to us on December 31, 2003 included the following invoice(s):

Invoice Number	Invoice Date	Amount
15172	11/05/03	$ 21,890.40
15275	11/17/03	22,683.60
15331	11/24/03	27,246.60
15438	12/05/03	24,078.60
15534	12/16/03	28,659.00
15644	12/29/03	27,138.00
Total		$151,696.20

This is neither a request for payment, nor an indication of your total indebtedness to us.

Please confirm whether the information about your indebtedness to us presented above agrees with your records by completing and signing the information below and returning this letter directly to our independent auditors, Boston & Greer, LLP, 1000 Ridge Street, Sacramento, CA, 95814. An addressed envelope is enclosed for your convenience.

Sincerely,

Rob Breeden

Robert Breeden
Chief Financial Officer, Chateau Americana, Inc.

- - - - - - - - - - - - - - - - - - - -

Dear Boston & Greer, LLP:

The above information regarding our indebtedness to Chateau Americana, Inc.

____ Agrees with our records.
_X_ Does not agree with our records as described below

Exception(s):

Did not receive the shipment related to invoice # 15644 until January 1, 2004. Our indebtedness to Chateau American was $124,558.20 as of December 31, 2004.

Name and Title (please print): Blake Conroe, Accounts Payable Clerk

Signature: *Black Conroe* Date: 1/7/04

CREDIT SALES INVOICE

Chateau Americana, Inc.
3003 Vineyard Way
Huntington, CA 95394
(707)368-8485
CA-NC-67

Invoice Number: 15644
Invoice Date: 12/29/03
Credit Terms: Net 60

Sold To:
Atlanta Wholesale Wine
275 Spring Street Southwest
Atlanta, GA 30303

Ship To:
Atlanta Wholesale Wine
275 Spring Street Southwest
Atlanta, GA 30303

Salesperson	Customer P.O. Number	Customer Number	ABC Number
MMM	11332	1001	GA3141

Product	Description	Size	Quantity	Cost	Extended
R130064	Cabernet Franc		204	$7.00	$ 1,428.00
R130061	Cabernet Sauvignon		204	6.50	1,326.00
R130056	Merlot		144	6.00	864.00
R130072	Shiraz		144	6.25	900.00
W120080	Chardonnay		1824	7.00	12,768.00
W120019	Chenin Blanc		396	5.25	2,079.00
W120015	Riesling		300	4.85	1,455.00
W120016	Sauvignon Blanc		600	5.25	3,150.00
S140000	Sparkling Brut		288	11.00	3,168.00

Grand Total Bottles: 4,104
Grand Total Cost: $ 27,138.00
Total Cases: 342
Comments:
Rush delivery

Date 12/29/03
Invoice Number 15644
Customer Number 1001

Distribution: Copy 1 - Accounting; Copy 2 - Shipping; Copy 3 - Customer; Copy 4 - Sales

Purchase Order

Atlanta Wholesale Wine
275 Spring Street Southwest
Atlanta, GA 30303
404-522-3358

P.O. No.: **11332**

To:
Chateau Americana
3003 Vineyard Way
Huntington, CA 95394

Ship To:
Atlanta Wholesale Wine
275 Spring Street Southwest
Atlanta, GA 30303

Date	Terms	F.O.B. Point	Ship Via
12/24/03	Net 60	Shipping Point	Best Method

Item #	Cases	Size	Description	Unit Cost	Total Cost
R130064	17	750ML	Cabernet Franc	$ 84.00	$ 1,428.00
R130061	17	750ML	Cabernet Sauvignon	78.00	1,326.00
R130056	12	750ML	Merlot	72.00	864.00
R130072	12	750ML	Shiraz	75.00	900.00
W120080	152	750ML	Chardonnay	84.00	12,768.00
W120019	33	750ML	Chenin Blanc	63.00	2,079.00
W120015	25	750ML	Riesling	58.20	1,455.00
W120016	50	750ML	Sauvignon Blanc	63.00	3,150.00
S140000	24	750ML	Sparkling Brut	132.00	3,168.00
				Total	$ 27,138.00

Jean Kalicki — Authorized by
12/24/03 — Date

Comments:

Date 12/29/03

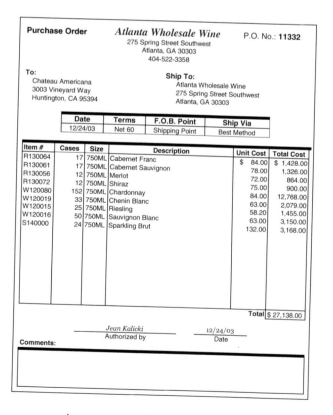

Uniform Bill of Lading

Ship From
Name: *Chateau Americana, Inc.*
Address: *3003 Vineyard Way*
City/State/Zip: *Huntington, CA 95394*
SID No.: *122448*

Bill of Lading Number: 136590

Ship To
Name: Atlanta Wholesale Wine
Address: 275 Spring Street Southwest
City/State/Zip: Atlanta, GA 30303
CID No.: *002996*

Carrier Name: *EA Shipping*
Trailer Number: *4578 CAL*
Serial Number: *000111789*

Special Instructions:

Freight Charge Terms: (Freight charges are prepaid unless marked otherwise)
Prepaid: ☐ Collect: ☐ 3rd Party: ☐
☐ **(check box):** Master bill of lading with attached underlying bills of lading.

Customer Order Information

Description of Items	Quantity	Weight	Pallet/Slip (circle one)		Additional Shipper Information
Wine	*342*	*11,628*	(Y)	N	
			Y	N	
			Y	N	
			Y	N	
Grand Total	*342*	*11,628*			

Where the rate is dependent on value, shippers are required to state specifically in writing the agreed or declared value of the property as follows: "The agreed or declared value of the property is specifically stated by the shipper to be not exceeding ______ per ______.

COD Amount: $ *N/A*
Free Terms:
☐ **Collect**
☐ Prepaid
☐ **Customer check acceptable**

Note: Liability limitation for loss or damage in this shipment may be applicable. See 49 USC §14706 (c) (1) (A) & (B)

Received, subject to individually determined rates or contracts that have been agreed upon in writing between the carrier and shipper, if applicable, otherwise to the rates, classifications and rules that have been established by the carrier and are available to the shipper, on request, and to all applicable state and federal regulations.

The carrier shall not make delivery of this shipment without payment of and all other lawful charges.

Shipper Signature *Jerry Richards*

Shipper Signature/Date
This is to certify that the above named materials are properly classified, packaged, marked and labeled, and are in proper condition for transportation according to the applicable regulations of the DOT.
Jerry Richards 12/29/03

Trailer Loaded:
☐ **By shipper**
☐ **By Driver**

Carrier Signature/Pickup Date
Carrier acknowledges receipt of packages and required placards. Carrier certifies emergency response information was made available and/or carrier has the DOT emergency response guidebook or equivalent documentation in the vehicle. **Property described above is received in good order, except as noted.**
Sam Souza 12/29/03

Distribution: Copy 1 - Accounting; Copy 2 - Shipping; Copy 3- Customer

Chateau Americana, Inc.
3003 Vineyard Way, Huntington, CA 95394
(707)368-8485

January 2, 2004

Bock Wines and Vines
Pier 19, The Embarcadero
San Francisco, CA 94111

Ladies and Gentlemen:

In connection with an audit of the financial statements of Chateau Americana, Inc. as of December 31, 2003, and for the year then ended, our independent auditors wish to determine whether our records of your indebtedness to us agree with your records. According to our records, your indebtedness to us on December 31, 2003 included the following invoice(s):

	Invoice Number	Invoice Date	Amount
	14944	10/09/03	$ 18,501.00
	15072	10/24/03	19,750.80
	15158	11/03/03	19,337.60
	15252	11/14/03	20,206.80
	15335	11/24/03	23,826.00
	15406	12/01/03	22,042.80
	15465	12/08/03	24,682.80
	15551	12/18/03	30,303.60
	15619	12/26/03	31,546.80
Total			$210,198.20

This is neither a request for payment, nor an indication of your total indebtedness to us.

Please confirm whether the information about your indebtedness to us presented above agrees with your records by completing and signing the information below and returning this letter directly to our independent auditors, Boston & Greer, LLP, 1000 Ridge Street, Sacramento, CA, 95814. An addressed envelope is enclosed for your convenience.

Sincerely,

Rob Breeden

Robert Breeden
Chief Financial Officer, Chateau Americana, Inc.

- -

Dear Boston & Greer, LLP:

The above information regarding our indebtedness to Chateau Americana, Inc.

____ Agrees with our records.
_X_ Does not agree with our records as described below

Exception(s):

Mailed check on 12/30/2003 for $18,501.00 (check number 25386), our outstanding balance was $191,697.20 on 12/31/2003.

Name and Title (please print): Diana Meiburg, Controller

Signature: *Diana Meiburg* Date: 1/9/2004

Grand Total Bottles: 2,640 Grand Total Cost: $ 18,501.00

Total Cases: 220

Comments:
Rush delivery

Date	10/09/03
Invoice Number	14944
Customer Number	0501

Distribution: Copy 1 - Accounting; Copy 2 - Shipping; Copy 3 - Customer

---

Bank of Huntington **Customer Receipt**

All items credited subject to verification, collection, and conditions of the Rules and Regulations of this Bank and as otherwise provided by law. Payments are accepted when credit is applied to outstanding balances and not upon issuance of this receipt. Transactions received after the Bank's posted cut-off time or Saturday, Sunday, and Bank Holidays, are dated and considered received as of the next business day.

Please retain this receipt until you receive your account statement.

00406 018 057167 01-03-03 16:52 DEP BUS
640665135 000000000739601109 $131,677.20

86-15-2007C 06-2001

Cash Receipt Summary # 5719

Chateau Americana
3003 Vineyard Way
Huntington, CA 95394

Date : 1/2/04
Preparer 1 Initial: MSB
Preparer 2 Initial: GLH

Customer/Description	Ref./Customer #	Invoice #	Amount
Bock Wines and Vines	0501	14944	$ 18,501.00
Glazer's Distributors of Ohio	3502	15163	12,365.40
Louis Carufel Wine Co	0503	15154	16,255.20
Bacchus Wine Wholesale Distribution	0902	15175	13,203.60
Prestige Wine Cellars	4301	15192	10,996.20
American Vineyards	3501	15129	12,533.40
Veritas Distributors Inc	2201	15189	14,125.80
Fine Wine Selection Company	0301	15170	11,164.20
Mountain Wine Distributing Company	0601	15121	13,581.60
World Vintage Imports Inc	2101	15153	8,950.80
Total			$ 131,677.20

Chateau Americana, Inc.
3003 Vineyard Way, Huntington, CA 95394
(707)368-8485

January 2, 2004

Bolliger, Inc.
88 Viaduct Road
Stamford, CT 06907

Ladies and Gentlemen:

In connection with an audit of the financial statements of Chateau Americana, Inc. as of December 31, 2003, and for the year then ended, our independent auditors wish to determine whether our records of your indebtedness to us agree with your records. According to our records, your indebtedness to us on December 31, 2003 included the following invoice(s):

Invoice Number	Invoice Date	Amount
15156	11/03/03	$ 23,532.00
15233	11/12/03	25,116.00
15308	11/21/03	29,407.20
15431	12/04/03	23,710.80
15542	12/17/03	30,110.40
15618	12/26/03	31,694.40
Total		$163,570.80

This is neither a request for payment, nor an indication of your total indebtedness to us.

Please confirm whether the information about your indebtedness to us presented above agrees with your records by completing and signing the information below and returning this letter directly to our independent auditors, Boston & Greer, LLP, 1000 Ridge Street, Sacramento, CA, 95814. An addressed envelope is enclosed for your convenience.

Sincerely,

Rob Breeden

Robert Breeden
Chief Financial Officer, Chateau Americana, Inc.

Dear Boston & Greer, LLP:

The above information regarding our indebtedness to Chateau Americana, Inc.

_X_ Agrees with our records.
____ Does not agree with our records as described below

Exception(s):

N/A

Name and Title (please print): Aroldo Tucci, Accounts Payable Manager

Signature: *Aroldo Tucci* Date: 1/13/04

Chateau Americana, Inc.
3003 Vineyard Way, Huntington, CA 95394
(707)368-8485

January 2, 2004

Pinnacle Wine Company
345 Underhill Blvd.
Syosset, New York 11791

Ladies and Gentlemen:

In connection with an audit of the financial statements of Chateau Americana, Inc. as of December 31, 2003, and for the year then ended, our independent auditors wish to determine whether our records of your indebtedness to us agree with your records. According to our records, your indebtedness to us on December 31, 2003 included the following invoice(s):

Invoice Number	Invoice Date	Amount
15047	10/21/03	$ 24,129.60
15132	10/31/03	24,502.80
15235	11/12/03	26,086.80
15312	11/21/03	29,254.80
15403	12/01/03	23,710.80
15525	12/15/03	26,086.80
15612	12/26/03	30,838.80
Total		$184,610.40

This is neither a request for payment, nor an indication of your total indebtedness to us.

Please confirm whether the information about your indebtedness to us presented above agrees with your records by completing and signing the information below and returning this letter directly to our independent auditors, Boston & Greer, LLP, 1000 Ridge Street, Sacramento, CA, 95814. An addressed envelope is enclosed for your convenience.

Sincerely,

Rob Breeden

Robert Breeden
Chief Financial Officer, Chateau Americana, Inc.

- -

Dear Boston & Greer, LLP:

The above information regarding our indebtedness to Chateau Americana, Inc.

_X_ Agrees with our records.
___ Does not agree with our records as described below

Exception(s):

Name and Title (please print): Maurice Vasser, Assistant Controller

Signature: *Maurice Vasser* Date: 1/14/2004

Chateau Americana, Inc.
3003 Vineyard Way, Huntington, CA 95394
(707)368-8485

January 2, 2004

Vintage Wine Company
2650 Commerce Way
Los Angeles, Ca 90040

Ladies and Gentlemen:

In connection with an audit of the financial statements of Chateau Americana, Inc. as of December 31, 2003, and for the year then ended, our independent auditors wish to determine whether our records of your indebtedness to us agree with your records. According to our records, your indebtedness to us on December 31, 2003 included the following invoice(s):

	Invoice Number	Invoice Date	Amount
	15038	10/20/03	$ 22,206.00
	15123	10/30/03	25,070.40
	15217	11/10/03	26,769.60
	15299	11/19/03	27,058.80
	15337	11/24/03	29,340.00
	15440	12/05/03	27,598.80
	15488	12/11/03	28,096.80
	15550	12/18/03	30,463.20
	15611	12/26/03	38,566.20
Total			$255,169.80

This is neither a request for payment, nor an indication of your total indebtedness to us.

Please confirm whether the information about your indebtedness to us presented above agrees with your records by completing and signing the information below and returning this letter directly to our independent auditors, Boston & Greer, LLP, 1000 Ridge Street, Sacramento, CA, 95814. An addressed envelope is enclosed for your convenience.

Sincerely,

Rob Breeden

Robert Breeden
Chief Financial Officer, Chateau Americana, Inc.

- -

Dear Boston & Greer, LLP:

The above information regarding our indebtedness to Chateau Americana, Inc.

_____ Agrees with our records.

__X__ Does not agree with our records as described below

Exception(s):

Invoice # 15611included an over shipment of 50 cases of Chardonnay (Product # W120080) at $84 a case. The 50 cases were shipped back to Chateau Americana on 12/29/03. Our records indicated that our indebtedness to Chateau American was $250,969.80 on December 31, 2003.

Name and Title (please print): Rachel Parks, Controller

Signature: *Rachel Parks* Date: *1/15/04*

Credit Memo

Chateau Americana, Inc.
3003 Vineyard Way
Huntington, CA 95394
Phone: (707)368-8485

Credit Memo: 2896	
Date: *1/5/04*	**Sales Person:** *WAB*
Customer Number: *0502*	**Customer PO No:** *287654*
Amount Net: *$4,200.00*	

Credit To: *Vintage Wine Company*

Comments:

Over-shipped customer 50 cases of Chardonnay

Item # / Description	Quantity	Price: Unit Price	Price: Amount
W120080 / Chardonnay	*600*	*$7.00*	*$4,200.00*

Customer Name: *Vintage Wine Company*

Credit Amount: *$4,200.00*

Chateau Americana
3003 Vineyard Way
Huntington, CA 95394
Phone: (707)368-8485

Credit Date: 1/5/04
Credit Memo #: **2896**
Customer Number: *0502*

Distribution: Copy 1 - Accounting; Copy 2 - Customer

Receiving Report

Date Received: *12/31/03*
Receiving Report #: **17263**

Received From: *Vintage Wine Company*

Purchase Order #: *Credit Sales Invoice # 15611*

Freight Carrier: *West Cost Shipping*

Received by: *BH*

Quantity	Item #	Size	Description
600	*W120080*	*0.750*	*50 Cases of Chardonnay*

Condition:

Excellent

Distribution: Copy 1 - Accounting; Copy 2 - Purchasing; Copy 3 - Receiving

COMPLETING THE AUDIT:
The Winery At Chateau Americana

LEARNING OBJECTIVES

After completing and discussing this case, you should be able to:

- Understand and identify audit procedures to detect contingent liabilities and commitments
- Understand and identify audit procedures to detect subsequent events
- Understand and evaluate information relevant to the assessment of the going concern assumption
- Evaluate and recognize potential limitations of responses to letters of inquiry sent to legal counsel
- Identify information that must be included in a management representation letter
- Understand and evaluate a summary of unadjusted differences schedule
- Prepare an audit report that is appropriate in light of client circumstances
- Understand the required communications with an audit committee

INTRODUCTION

Your firm's first audit of Chateau Americana is drawing to a close and your partner, Claire Helton, has just informed you that the next couple of days will be devoted to wrapping up the engagement. She plans to present the firm's audit report to the winery's chief financial officer next week; however, there are a number of audit procedures that remain open on this year's audit program and must be completed prior to next week's meeting.

Several client interviews were conducted by Elise Simpson, another senior auditor assigned to the engagement. You will find transcripts of these interviews and the accompanying documents useful in completing the open items.

INTERVIEW TRANSCRIPTS

Elise: Good morning Edward. I have several questions to ask you to help with completing our audit. Are you aware of any contingent liabilities that should be disclosed in the financial statements?

Edward: You've already received the letter from our attorney regarding the lawsuit filed by a former employee. We hope to resolve the suit in the very near future. I'm not aware of any other lawsuits or contingencies.

Elise: Have there been similar suits filed against your company in the past?

Edward: No, this is the first employee-initiated suit of this type. We've made every attempt to maintain excellent working conditions and relationships with our employees.

Elise: Does the company have any sales or purchase contracts?

Edward: We don't have any sales contracts, but we do have several purchase contracts that we use to secure our supply of grapes. We've maintained purchase agreements with the same growers for the past 12 years and we've never been disappointed by either the quality of their product or the contract terms. Under the terms of these agreements we are required to purchase a predetermined amount of grapes at prices based on existing market conditions, although some contracts establish minimum purchase prices.

Elise: I suppose such contracts can be beneficial or detrimental.

Edward: That's precisely why we're so methodical in establishing sales projections that we use to calculate our inventory requirements.

Elise: Does the company have any other commitments, such as equipment or building leases?

Edward: I personally own some of the production equipment that I lease to the company. I believe Rob provided a copy of the lease agreement to someone on the audit team. There are no other leases or commitments of any type.

Elise: My last question relates to subsequent events. Are you aware of any event that has occurred since the balance sheet date that requires either adjustment to or disclosure in the financial statements? For example, have there been any changes in the company's capital stock or long-term debt, or any unusual adjustments since the end of the year?

Edward: Rob and I met with representatives from the financial institutions that we have loans with several weeks ago to discuss the possibility of restructuring our long term debt. Given the recent downward trends in interest rates, we decided to attempt to secure a lower rate and shorter repayment terms for our debt. Although we're still negotiating, we expect to reach an agreement within the next week or two.

Otherwise, there have been no changes to our debt or capital structure and there have definitely been no unusual adjustments to our financial statements.

♦♦

After meeting with Edward, Elise met with Rob Breeden, CA's chief financial officer.

Elise: Hi Rob. Thanks for meeting with me this morning. I need to talk with you about several issues so that we can finalize our audit in time for your and Claire's meeting next week. First, are you aware of any contingent liabilities that should be disclosed in the financial statements?

Rob: No, our only current litigation relates to a lawsuit filed by a former employee. We're working very hard through our attorney to resolve the suit.

Elise: Are you likely to offer a settlement to the individual?

Rob: I can't say with any certainty what we'll do. Our attorney is still in the process of researching the case and formulating a position for us. We've never had a suit such as this brought against our company, so we're in new territory. I can tell you that Edward feels very strongly about resolving the case as quickly as possible and keeping it out of the press.

Elise: Could you tell me a little about the case?

Rob: William Simmons worked for the winery for six years prior to the accident. He was a dependable and competent employee according to his supervisor. As I understand it, William was injured while he was repairing one of our large storage tanks. The insurance report states that he fell when his safety harness broke. He sustained several broken ribs, a broken arm and a broken leg. He contends that the company was negligent in maintaining the equipment. We're not convinced that he was using it properly.

Elise: Do you have any idea of what the maximum settlement could be?

Rob: The suit seeks damages of $500,000, or almost 20 times the former employee's prior year's earnings.

Elise: Turning to a different subject now. Tell me about any sales or purchase contracts.

Rob: We don't enter into sales contracts. However, because we rely on outside growers for almost 75% of our grapes, we do contract with growers to ensure a flow of grapes. We've had agreements with a number of the same growers for many years. Based on my experience, the contract terms are relatively favorable. The greatest benefit to us is that we're assured a flow of inventory.

Elise: Do the agreements set minimum prices?

Rob: We obviously use these contracts to ensure a continuous source of grapes. While most of the contracts call for prices to be based on market conditions, several establish minimum purchase prices. However, we've been able to negotiate prices that we believe still provide a great deal of protection for us.

Elise: Edward mentioned that you are very careful in forecasting your grape needs. Who is responsible for the forecasting process?

Rob: I oversee the process. Our calculations are based on sales projections developed by our sales manager, Susan Platt. She has more years of experience in the wine industry than most of us and has always done a very competent job for us. After Susan finishes her calculations she and I meet with Taylor, the company's vice president of marketing, to go over the numbers.

Elise: What other commitments does the company have?

Rob: We lease certain production equipment from Edward. I think I may have mentioned that to you when were discussing related party transactions. Our total monthly lease payments are approximately $9,000. We have no other leases or commitments.

Elise: Have there been any subsequent events since the end of the year? Also, have there been changes in the company's capital stock or long-term debt, or any unusual adjustments since the end of the year?

Rob: You may be interested to know that Edward and I have had several meetings with our creditors in recent weeks to negotiate changes in our loan terms. I have been talking to Edward about our need to take advantage of the recent interest rates drops. Edward finally has agreed to pursue a shorter payback period in hopes of extinguishing our debt earlier than originally planned.

Elise: Have you reached an agreement with the financial institutions?

Rob: We're still in the process of working out the details. I'm hopeful that we'll agree on new terms within the next several weeks.

♦♦

The following documents are relevant to the completion of your firm's audit of Chateau Americana's financial statements and may be found on the following pages:

1. Draft of the current year's financial statements
2. Summary of Unadjusted Differences (prepared by the audit team)
3. Attorney's Response to Audit Inquiry Letter
4. Minutes from the company's Board of Directors meetings

The Winery at Chateau Americana, Inc.
Balance Sheets as of December 31, 2003 – 2001
(In Thousands)

Draft - for Internal Use Only

ASSETS

	2003	2002	2001
CURRENT ASSETS			
Cash	$ 3,005	$ 2,992	$ 3,281
Accounts receivable (net of allowance)	5,241	4,816	3,703
Investments	3,095	2,081	2,294
Production inventories	11,578	10,407	9,107
Finished goods inventories	4,015	3,902	3,567
Prepaid expenses	142	85	69
Total Current Assets	27,076	$ 24,283	$ 22,021
PROPERTY, PLANT & EQUIPMENT	30,230	28,135	27,612
Less accumulated depreciation	15,277	14,096	13,185
Net Property, Plant & Equipment	14,953	14,039	14,427
TOTAL ASSETS	$ 42,029	$ 38,322	$ 36,448

LIABILITIES AND SHAREHOLDERS' EQUITY

	2003	2002	2001
CURRENT LIABILITIES			
Accounts payable	$ 4,988	$ 3,683	$ 2,221
Accrued expenses	599	569	640
Notes payable	813	654	891
Current portion of long term debt	410	525	464
Payroll taxes withheld and payable	100	95	96
Federal income tax payable	172	157	134
Total Current Liabilities	7,082	5,683	4,446
LONG TERM DEBT	7,229	6,918	7,983
TOTAL LIABILITIES	14,311	12,601	12,429
SHAREHOLDERS' EQUITY			
Common stock (No par value, 5,000,000 shares authorized, 45,000 shares issued)	90	90	90
Additional paid-in capital	3,567	3,567	3,567
Retained earnings	24,061	22,064	20,362
Total Shareholders' Equity	27,718	25,721	24,019
TOTAL LIABILITIES AND SHAREHOLDERS' EQUITY	$ 42,029	$ 38,322	$ 36,448

Draft - for Internal Use Only

The Winery at Chateau Americana, Inc.
Statements of Income for Years Ended December 31, 2003 – 2001
(In Thousands)

Draft - for Internal Use Only

	2003	2002	2001
Sales	$ 21,945	$ 20,189	$ 18,170
Cost of goods sold	11,543	10,525	9,777
Gross profit	10,402	9,664	8,393
Selling, general and administrative expenses	7,017	6,824	6,218
Operating income	3,386	2,840	2,175
Interest expense	360	211	257
Provision for income taxes	1,028	927	483
Net income	$ 1,997	$ 1,702	$ 1,435

Draft - for Internal Use Only

Reference: *CA-4*
Prepared by: *WJ, 3-2-04*
Approved: ______

Summary of Unadjusted Differences

Client: The Winery at Chateau Americana, Inc.
Year ended: December 31, 2003

				Possible Misstatements Overstatements / (Understatements)			
Audit Schedule Reference	Description of Misstatement	Type of Misstatement	Total Amount	Current Assets	Noncurrent Assets	Current Liabilities	Income Before Taxes
R-210	*Write-off of customer account receivable*	*P*	*($13,488)*	*($13,488)*			
E-210	*Unrecorded accounts payable*	*P*	*61,917*	*(31,200)*	*($20,717)*	*($61,917)*	*10,000*
I-210	*Investment misstatements*	*P*	*$79,500*	*$79,500*			*$79,500*
I-210	*Unrecorded capital acquisitions*	*A*	*48,610*	*48,610*	*(48,610)*		
I-210	*Misstatement in depreciation expense*	*A*	*13,368*		*13,368*		*13,368*
				$	$	$	$

Conclusion:

	Possible Overstatement (Understatement)	Materiality
Current Assets	$	*$1,353,800*
Total Assets	$	*$210,145*
Income Before Taxes	$	*$199,700*

McKenna, Harmon, & Jacobs
First Union Square Place
1450 California Avenue
Napa, CA 41008

CA-201
PBC/AG
3/15/03

March 12, 2004

Boston & Greer, LLP
1000 Ridge Street
Sacramento, CA, 95814

Re: The Winery at Chateau Americana, Inc.

Dear Sirs:

By letter dated, March 1, 2004, Mr. Rob Breeden, Chief Financial Officer of The Winery at Chateau Americana, Inc., (the "Company") has requested us to furnish you with certain information in connection with your examination of the accounts of the Company as of December 31, 2003.

While this firm represents the Company on a regular basis, our engagement has been limited to specific matters as to which we were consulted by the Company.

Subject to the foregoing and to the last paragraph of this letter, we advise you that since January 1, 2003 we have not been engaged to give substantive attention to, or represent the Company in connection with, material loss contingencies coming within the scope of clause (a) of Paragraph 5 of the Statement of Policy referred to in the last paragraph of this letter, except as follows:

> On November 21, 2003, a suit was filed against The Winery at Chateau Americana, Inc. by a former employee who is seeking damages for injuries sustained while employed by the Company. The suit alleges that William Simmons (the "Employee") was injured as a result of the Company's negligent maintenance of workplace safety equipment as required by the Occupational Safety & Health Administration. In addition, the suit claims that Simmons was not instructed in the proper use of the safety equipment as required by applicable federal and state laws. According to the suit, Simmons was performing routine maintenance on one of the Company's wine storage tanks when a safety harness he was wearing failed. The fall resulted in a loss of work time, hospitalization, and significant physical therapy.
>
> In preparation of providing this letter to you, we have reviewed the merits of the claim against the Company. After careful consideration, we are unable to express an opinion as to the merits of the litigation at this time. The Company believes there is absolutely no merit to the litigation.

The information set forth herein is as of March 12, 2004, the date on which we commenced our internal review procedures for purposes of preparing this response, except as otherwise noted, and we disclaim any undertaking to advise you of changes which thereafter may be brought to our attention.

This response is limited by, and in general accordance with, the ABA Statement of Policy Regarding Lawyers' Responses to Auditors' Requests for Information (December 1975); without limiting the generality of the foregoing, the limitations set forth in such Statement on the scope and use of this response (Paragraphs 2 and 7) are specifically incorporated herein by reference, and any description herein of any "loss contingencies" is qualified in its entirety by Paragraph 5 of the Statement and the accompany Commentary (which is an integral part of the Statement). Consistent with the last sentence of Paragraph 6 of the ABA Statement of Policy and pursuant to the Company's request, this will confirm as correct the Company's understanding as set forth in its audit inquiry letter to us that whenever, in the course of performing legal services for the Company with respect to a matter recognized to involve an unasserted possible claim or assessment that may call for financial statement disclosure, we have formed a professional conclusion that the Company must disclose or consider disclosure concerning such possible claim or assessment, we, as a matter of professional responsibility to the Company, will so advise the Company and will consult with the Company concerning the question of such disclosure and the applicable requirements of Statement of Financial Accounting Standards No. 5.

Very truly yours,

McKenna, Harmon, & Jacobs

Napa, CA

The Winery at Chateau Americana, Inc.

CA-203
PBC/AG
3/05/04

Board of Directors Meeting
Minutes – March 3, 2004

The quarterly meeting of the Board of Directors of The Winery at Chateau Americana, Inc. was held at the Company's offices on Wednesday, March 3, 2004. Mr. Edward Summerfield, Chairman of the Board, called the meeting to order at 9:30 a.m. Eastern Standard Time.

Present at the meeting:

Mr. Edward Summerfield, Chairman of the Board
Ms. Taylor Summerfield, Vice President of Marketing and Member of the Board
Mrs. Charlotte Summerfield, Member of the Board
Mr. Rob Breeden, Chief Financial Officer and Member of the Board
Mr. Bill Jameson, Member of the Board
Ms. Susan Martinez, Member of the Board
Mr. Terrence Dillard, Member of the Board
Mr. Harry West, Outside Legal Counsel (Present only for discussion of pending litigation)

Action Items

1. **Approval of the Minutes**. On a motion duly made and seconded, the Board approved the minutes as distributed of the meeting of Wednesday, December 3, 2004.

2. **Creation of Committees**. As Chairman of the Board, Mr. Summerfield recommended that the Board establish an Audit Committee. Mr. Summerfield stated that the Company's audit firm had suggested that establishing such a committee would be beneficial to the Company in improving its corporate governance structure.

   On a motion duly made and seconded, the Board adopted the following resolution:

   Resolved, That the Board accepts the Chairman's recommendation to establish an Audit Committee effective as soon as such a committee can be formed.

3. **Nomination and Election of Committee Members**. Mr. Terrence Dillard nominated Ms. Susan Martinez to be the Chair of the Audit Committee and nominated Mr. Bill Jameson and Mrs. Charlotte Summerfield to be members of the Committee.

   On a motion duly made and seconded, the Board adopted the following resolutions:

Resolved, That the Board elects Ms. Susan Martinez as Chair of the Audit Committee and Mr. Bill Jameson and Mrs. Charlotte Summerfield as members of the Committee for a term of three years that shall begin immediately and that shall conclude at the close of the March 2007 quarterly Board meeting; and

Resolved Further, That the Board directs Ms. Martinez to adopt such practices as may be appropriate to assist the Committee in fulfilling its corporate governance responsibilities. The Committee shall meet no less than two times per year immediately preceding regularly scheduled quarterly Board meetings. Such requirement shall not be construed as limiting the Committee's prerogative to meet more frequently. Further, the Board understands the Committee will meet privately with the Company's auditor to discuss any matters it deems appropriate.

4. **Report on Pending Litigation – Confidential and Proprietary** – Executive Session. A confidential and proprietary supplemental issue paper was distributed at the meeting. Mr. Harry West, partner at McKenna, Harmon, & Jacobs, provided an update regarding the status of the lawsuit filed by William Simmons against the Company. Mr. West recommended that the matter be discussed in Executive Session because this item is about pending litigation matters that are subject to attorney-client privilege.

   On a motion duly made and seconded, the Board adopted the following resolution:

   Resolved, That the Board determines that discussion of an update on pending litigation to which the Company is a party shall be conducted in Executive Session.

Information Items

1. **Restructuring of Long-term Debt**. Mr. Rob Breeden reported that he and Mr. Summerfield have had several meetings with representatives of financial institutions from whom the Company has borrowed funds to discuss renegotiating the current terms of the Company's debt. Although no agreement has been reached, Mr. Breeden stated that he believes the Company will be able to successfully renegotiate debt terms with all related financial institutions.

2. **Update on New Accounting Firm**. Mr. Rob Breeden informed the Board that the Company has been very pleased with the service provided by the recently appointed firm of Boston & Greer, LLP. Mr. Breeden stated that he anticipates receiving the firm's audit report on the Company's financial statements in the coming week. Mr. Jameson inquired whether the firm had identified any significant accounting matters during the course of the audit. Mr. Breeden stated that no significant matters had been identified.

There being no further business, Mr. Summerfield adjourned the meeting at 11:25 a.m. Eastern Standard Time.

REQUIREMENTS

Completing an audit is a challenging process that requires auditors to make a number of critically important decisions. The following questions relate to some of these issues. You should answer these questions prior to completing the "open" audit procedures on the audit program.

1. SFAS No. 5, *Accounting for Contingences*, prescribes how companies must treat contingent liabilities in various circumstances. The likelihood that a contingency will arise in any given situation may be considered as probable, reasonably possible, or remote. If an auditor believes that an attorney's response is ambiguous as to the possible outcome of pending litigation, how may an auditor obtain evidence to assess the need for a possible accrual of a loss contingency or disclosure of the matter in the notes to the financial statements? You may wish to refer to SAS No. 12, *Inquiry of a Client's Lawyer Concerning Litigation, Claims, and Assessments*, for help in answering this question.

2. Describe three to five audit procedures that auditors commonly perform to search for contingencies.

3. SAS No. 59, *The Auditor's Consideration of an Entity's Ability to Continue as a Going Concern*, requires auditors to perform an evaluation of an entity's ability to continue as a going concern as part of each audit. Describe several audit procedures that may be used in the auditor's evaluation of going concern. What audit documentation is required if an auditor concludes there is substantial doubt about an entity's ability to continue as a going concern?

4. Generally accepted auditing standards require auditors to obtain written representations from management as part of each audit. To what extent should an auditor rely solely on a client's written representations? At what point in the audit should a representation letter be obtained and as of what date should the client make the representations? What are the implications of management's refusal to provide requested representations?

5. Claire Helton, the engagement partner has been very impressed with your work on Chateau Americana. As a consequence, she has asked you to identify the appropriate audit report for the company. Assuming that each of the following situations is independent from the others, determine the type of audit report which is most appropriate.

   a. Assume that subsequent to year-end, but before issuance of the audit report that one of Chateau Americana's customers filed bankruptcy. The customer's year-end account receivable was $50,750, an immaterial amount. Chateau Americana's CFO indicates that he neither wants to write-off the customer's account, nor record a specific reserve.
   b. Assume the litigation discussed in the case is settled subsequent to year-end for $200,000. The financial statements for the year ended 12/31/2003 did not include a loss accrual. The company does not want to include disclosure regarding the settlement in the financial statements.
   c. The company renegotiates certain terms associated with its long term debt subsequent to year-end. The new terms are more favorable than the previous

terms, but the principal amount of the outstanding debt did not change as a consequence of the renegotiation. No disclosure is being provided in the financial statements.

d. A flood destroys one-third of the company's vineyard shortly after year-end. The company is currently attempting to secure access to more grapes from the open market. While the company had some insurance on its vineyards, it appears likely that the company will not be indemnified for the full market value of its loss. The value of the lost inventory is material to the financial statements. Management does not intend to include a footnote in the financial statements.

6. Subsequent to year-end, Chateau Americana's board of directors passed a resolution to establish an audit committee. Does this action require any response by your audit team? Describe matters that your firm may discuss with such a committee in future years. Is your audit team required to have such discussions with Chateau Americana's audit committee?

The Winery at Chateau Americana
Partial Audit Program for Completing the Audit

For the Year Ended December 31, 2003

Reference:	CA-100
Prepared by:	AG
Date:	3/15/04
Reviewed by:	

Audit Procedures	Initial	Date	A/S Ref.
1. Request the client to send letters of inquiry to attorneys from whom the client has obtained legal services from during the year.	AG	3/15/04	CA-201
2. Review the response received from the client's attorney for information related to contingencies. Document issues related to ongoing or pending litigation.			CA-202
3. Obtain a copy of the minutes of all meetings of the board of directors subsequent to year end.	AG	3/05/04	CA-203
4. Review the minutes of the board of directors meeting for subsequent events affecting the current year financial statements. Note items for follow-up during next year's audit.			CA-204
5. Complete the Summary of Unadjusted Differences. Conclude whether the financial statements are fairly stated in all material respects.			CA-4
6. Prepare a memo to summarize your assessment of the validity of the going concern assumption for Chateau Americana.			CA-205
7. Prepare a draft of the management representation letter.			CA-206

The Winery at Chateau Americana
Review of Attorneys Letters
For the Year Ended December 31, 2003

Reference: CA-202
Prepared by: ______
Date: ______
Reviewed by: ______

Comments:

The Winery at Chateau Americana
Review of Minutes of the Board of Directors Meetings
For the Year Ended December 31, 2003

Reference: CA-204
Prepared by: ______
Date: ______
Reviewed by: ______

Notes regarding subsequent events affecting the current year financial statements:

Planning notes regarding next year's audit:

The Winery at Chateau Americana
Assessment of Going Concern Assumption
For the Year Ended December 31, 2003

Reference:	CA-205
Prepared by:	
Date:	
Reviewed by:	

Comments:

The Winery at Chateau Americana
Draft of Management Representation Letter
For the Year Ended December 31, 2003

Reference: CA-206
Prepared by:
Date:
Reviewed by:

Comments: